SQUEAK:
OBJECT-ORIENTED DESIGN WITH MULTIMEDIA APPLICATIONS

Mark Guzdial

GVU Center and EduTech Institute
College of Computing
Georgia Institute of Technology

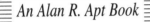
An Alan R. Apt Book

Prentice Hall
Upper Saddle River, NJ 07458

Library of Congress Cataloging-in-Publication Data

Guzdial, Mark.
  Squeak : object-oriented design with multimedia applications / Mark Guzdial.
    p. cm.
  "An Alan R. Apt book."
  ISBN 0-13-028028-3
    1. Object-oriented programming (Computer science). 2. Multimedia systems.
  3. Squeak. I. Title.
  QA76.64.G89 2000
  006.7′6 — dc21
                                                        00-046951

Vice President and Editorial Director, ECS: *Marcia Horton*
Publisher: *Alan R. Apt*
Associate Editor: *Toni D. Holm*
Editorial Assistant: *Amy K. Todd*
Vice President of Production and Manufacturing, ESM: *David W. Riccardi*
Executive Managing Editor: *Vince O'Brien*
Managing Editor: *David A. George*
Production Editor: *Lakshmi Balasubramanian*
Director of Creative Services: *Paul Belfanti*
Creative Director: *Carole Anson*
Art Director: *Heather Scott*
Cover Designer: *John Christiana*
Cover Art: *Robert Tinney*
Art Editor: *Adam Velthaus*
Manufacturing Manager: *Trudy Pisciotti*
Manufacturing Buyer: *Pat Brown*
Marketing Manager: *Jennie Burger*

© 2001 Prentice Hall
Prentice Hall, Inc.
Upper Saddle River, New Jersey 07458

Printed in the United States of America

10 9 8 7 6 5 4 3 2 1

ISBN 0-13-028028-3

Prentice-Hall International (UK) Limited, *London*
Prentice-Hall of Australia Pty. Limited, *Sydney*
Prentice-Hall Canada Inc., *Toronto*
Prentice-Hall Hispanoamericana, S.A., *Mexico*
Prentice-Hall of India Private Limited, *New Delhi*
Prentice-Hall of Japan, Inc., *Tokyo*
Pearson Education Asia Pte. Ltd., *Singapore*
Editora Prentice-Hall do Brasil, Ltda., *Rio de Janeiro*

To my parents, Gene and Nancy Guzdial

Contents

Foreword

Software:

Art, Engineering,

Mathematics, or Science?

by Alan C. Kay

A 500-foot-high Egyptian pyramid took hundreds of thousands of workers several decades to construct. They piled up material brick on brick and then finished the outside with a smooth layer of limestone. By contrast, the 1,000-foot-high Empire State Building was constructed from scratch in fewer than 11 months by fewer than 3,000 workers. Quite a bit of today's software and their construction processes resemble the Egyptian pyramid in the difficulty it took to build them; I would dare say that no one currently knows how to organize 3000 programmers to make a major piece of software from scratch in less than 11 months.

I interpret this to mean that "software engineering" is still an oxymoron (like "airline food," "university parking," or even "computer science"). Still, what we do today is rather like the design and construction of buildings before architecture— literally, the "tech-ing" of "arches"—in that we can occasionally make something that functions, even if it does resemble a jumble of materials. Software engineering is a kind of ancient engineering, an ad hoc cookbook of recipes that have somewhat worked in the past.

Today, science (a concern with what is real) is mixed with mathematics (a concern with what is true), which is mixed with engineering (a concern with how something can be made). Each worker in any of these fields also partly works in the other two. Each field has a different temperament associated with it: mathematicians tend to be idealists, scientists realists, and engineers pragmatists. And each field finds itself temporarily adopting a borrowed temperament when it uses the other areas to aid advances in its own.

Now, what is computing? It seems to be a kind of mathematics (in that the machine is a kind of inference engine that works out the consequences of relationships) coupled with a kind of engineering (in that rather large language representations usually have to be constructed in order to express anything really interesting).

But where is science in all this? In our normal use of the term, we think of being presented with a universe, which is not necessarily connected with any of our hopes or beliefs, science is a special way of getting at how this universe seems to work. In modern times, we especially like to express the way we think the universe works in terms of mathematical models that seem to have enough correspondences with reality to allow both discussion and prediction. We tend to think of science as being analytic.

By contrast, computering seems to be much more synthetic, in that we start with rules and compute a kind of "reality". In this light, can there be a "computer science"?

I think the answer is yes, and it lies in an analogy to the construction of the physical world. Historically it has not been possible to compute, from first principles involving fundamental particles, whether a large building or bridge would collapse or stay up. The approach has been to make large structures as sound as possible and to study them as though they were part of the universe given to us to understand. This has led to a new kind of scientific engineering that is not oxymoronic, and to a vastly improved set of techniques for building large, reliable structures.

I think that the following is what needs to be done to finally create software engineering: We need to do more building of important software structures, and we need to do it in a form that allows analysis, learning, and reformulating of the design and fabrication from what has just been learned.

There seems to be a bit of a chicken-and-egg problem here. If we don't really have an engineering discipline, then won't it be very difficult to make big constructions that are also understandable enough to learn from? And won't the mess we've made be too difficult to reformulate to give us a chance to understand whether our new findings really have value?

I believe that the secret weapon that can be used to make progress here is extreme late binding. But of what? Of as many things in our development system as possible.

One can make a good argument on the thesis that most of the advances in both hardware and software design have been facilitated through the introduction of new late-binding mechanisms. Going way back in hardware, we can think of index and relocation registers, memory-management units, etc. In software, we went from absolute instruction locations and formats to symbolic assemblers, to subroutines, to relocatable code, to hardware-independent data-structure formats, to garbage collection, to the many late-binding advantages of objects, including classes and instances, message sending, encapsulation, polymorphism, and metaprogramming.

In Squeak, you have in your hands one of the most late-bound, yet practical, programming systems ever created. It is also an artifact that is wide, broad, and deep enough to permit real scientific study and the creation of new theories, new mathematics, and new engineering constructions. In fact, Squeak is primed to be the engine of its own replacement. Since every mechanism that Squeak uses in its own construction is in plain view and is changeable by any programmer, it can be understood and played with to no end. "Extreme play" could very easily result in the creation of a system better than Squeak, very different from Squeak, or both.

We not only give permission for you to do this, we urge you to try! Why? Because our field is still a long way from a reasonable state, and we cannot allow bad de facto standards (mostly controlled by vendors) to hold back progress. You are used to learning a programming system as a language with certain features, with the goal of using the features to make things. Squeak is very good at this and has many features (too many actually!) with which one can build things. But the best way to approach the learning you are about to do is to consider Squeak a metalanguage that can build other languages. Besides learning how to make things with the existing features, try to learn how the features themselves were invented and made. All the code is visible, and much of it has explanations of how it works. Here, the system is the curriculum. Even the online version of this book will have a hard time keeping track of an ever-changing and improving system, so it is best to learn how to find out from the system itself what it does. Then try to add new deep features of your own. Eventually, you will form a point of view of your own about better ways to program. Squeak will allow you to add these, or even to replace all of its current features with new ones that you have invented. Some of these ideas will be good enough to advance the art and the engineering and the science and the math of programming.

Then you will have used Squeak in all the ways we intended. At some point, a much better system than Squeak will be created, and nothing could make us happier—especially if you can do it while we're still around to enjoy the new ideas!

Preface

The primary goal of this book is to help the reader create multimedia projects in Squeak. The book helps with other goals, too, but the reader-as-student is the primary audience here. "Student" will get swapped for "reader" in many places. The structure of this book is aimed at the undergraduate computer science student, though the content is more generally on multimedia projects in Squeak.

Whatever brings you to this book, the assumption is that you're trying to do *projects,* serious efforts requiring pages of code. This book provides the information needed to get going with objects, user interface, and multimedia in Squeak. The assumption is that you are using Squeak, and that you're actively trying to figure things out. This book gives you the tools to do that.

However, this book is not a reference to Squeak, in part because such a thing (on paper, at least) would be impossible, as suggested by Alan Kay in his foreword. Furthermore, the tools are in Squeak to serve as a form of dynamic reference (as seen in the *Tools and Strategies* sections of the book). But most importantly, making this book a reference would be a different task from the one I set out with: To create a tool for learning through Squeak projects.

Errata and additional information on the book will be available at http://guzdial.cc.gatech.edu/squeakbook/ or linked to my home page at http://www.cc.gatech.edu/~mark.guzdial.

This book was started in Squeak 2.5; at the time of this writing, Squeak Central was about to release Squeak 2.8. *Most* of the examples will work with all these versions of Squeak, but they are all *tested* against Squeak 2.7, and that's the version that is recommended for use with this book.

APPROACH OF THE BOOK

When many American universities were established in the late 1800s (e.g., Stanford, the University of Chicago, and others), they were designed to be a mixture of the English college, with its focus on undergraduate education, and the German university, with its focus on research. The goal was for the research to motivate, and even *inspire,* both students and faculty to be better learners and teachers. While this works in the best cases, it has most often led to a higher priority on research than on teaching. (For a fascinating analysis of this tension, see Larry Cuban's *How the Scholar Trumped the Teacher,* Columbia Teacher's Press, 1999.)

The approach of this book is to be the reverse—hopefully, closer to the aims of the original inventors of the American university system. The book aims to integrate the diverse areas of knowledge needed to create successful projects. The pedagogy of this book is based on research in the learning sciences, on how people learn. The content of this book is based on my research, and that of my students, in developing collaborative multimedia in Squeak. The case studies in the latter half of the book are real projects that we designed, implemented, and then evaluated with real users to test the usability and effectiveness of our software.

The structure and approach of the book may be uncomfortable to some. It may even seem intuitively wrong to some. Intuition can sometimes be a dangerous thing—science has shown that measurement sometimes leads to findings that are contrary to "common sense." Science has come up with many ideas that seemed intuitively wrong, like disease being caused by small things too small to be seen by the naked eye, and that all objects fall at the same rate. As the methods of science have been applied to learning, similar non-intuitive lessons have been learned.

I attempted to apply the lessons about learning to the design of this book. I recognize, though, that research's lessons are not obvious—they require interpretation. My interpretations may be controversial, and even outright *wrong.* The responsibility for these interpretations is my own, not the original researchers'.

Start from Where the Students Are

There is a school of thought that says that students should be taught the abstractions necessary for proper execution in a domain before they are taught the actual execution. The argument is that the students' minds are then prepared to learn the "right" way to do things. This argument has been used to push for theory ahead of practice, design before implementation, and learning algorithms and development methodologies before actually doing any programming.

One of the unfortunate realities of our cognitive system is that we're very bad at transferring knowledge from one domain to another, even when the two domains are tightly connected. We've known since the 1920s that students develop "brittle knowledge" (Alfred North Whitehead) that can be applied for a given exam or given course, but that seems to disappear outside of the original class. The formal study of "brittle knowledge" arguably began in mathematics education research, where students were found to become experts at one kind of equation, but were totally confused by the addition of a single extra term. The phenomenon was also noted in physics students, who could get A's with their tight explanations of acceleration and energy in a thrown ball, but who would explain outside of class that a ball falls because the atmosphere pushes on it. In my own research, I've been amazed to find that engineering students seem to forget almost all of their Calculus when they get to the junior and senior years.

If students do not see the connections between areas of knowledge, then they won't transfer the knowledge. If they do not understand what they're learning, they can't see the connections. But if students do understand material, if they can see lots of relations between what they're learning and what they've known before, the knowledge is more likely to transfer to other disciplines and to be retained longer.

Case-based reasoning, one theory for how our cognitive systems work, has an explanation for all of this. As information comes into a mind, it becomes indexed. When a new event appears, the mind uses its indices to figure out if it's ever seen anything like this before. If it has, then a connection is made. If our indices are developed well, we can match things as being similar. But if we learn things with indices that say "This is a fact for a specific course," as opposed to "This relates to design of programs," then we don't apply the information appropriately. It is possible to re-index things later, and it is possible to learn abstract things with appropriate indices, but it's easier to learn new things as variations of known things, and then extend the indexing schemes.

The goal of connecting to what students already know is to meet the students where they are. While a student can memorize and even learn to reason with abstract material, this is a sign of the intellectual capabilities of the student, not the usefulness of the material. The real test is whether the students can *use* the knowledge later. The odds of having usable knowledge are improved if the material is presented when it makes sense to students and can easily be related to knowledge that the students already have.

Academics, researchers, and other smart people often disbelieve this point. They reflect on their own learning and note that they often *prefer* to get the abstractions first. There are several responses to this kind of reaction. First, self-introspection is not necessarily the best way to come up with lessons about learning. People do fool themselves. (For example, people often believe that shortcut keys are faster than menus, but all explicit laboratory measurements show that mousing over menus is always faster—see Bruce Tognazzini's *Tog on Interface,* 1992, Addison-Wesley, for a review of this research.) But perhaps the more significant response is that smart people are already smart. They've picked up all kinds of concrete and abstract knowledge already. They're excellent learners who know how to figure out connections to new knowledge. As my advisor, Elliot Soloway, likes to say, "20% of the people will learn whatever you do to them. It's the other 80% that you have to worry about."

For these reasons, the order of events in this book is concrete and easily understandable first, and abstract and more general later:

- Squeak is first introduced as being like other languages that students might know, and then the new and original features are introduced.
- Two chapters on Squeak programming appear before the chapter on design of object-oriented programs.

- Technical details of building user interfaces are presented before interface design principles.

Learning involves Testing and Failure

Noted cognitive scientist Roger Schank has promoted the importance of "failure-based learning." If you're always successful, you don't learn much. But after you've failed, you're in the perfect position to learn a lot. Someone who has just failed is now interested in reading, in exploring theory, and in engaging in inquiry in order to understand the failure and how to avoid it next time. In order to fail, you must face a "test" of some kind. The test doesn't have to be of the paper-and-pencil type. It doesn't have to be formal at all. But if there isn't an event that tests your knowledge and provides the *opportunity* to fail, then the failing and the learning will never occur.

Computer scientists are well familiar with this process of testing, failing, and learning from the failure. We even have invented a nice word for it: *debugging*. Debugging is such an important part of computer science that computer scientist and educator Gerald Sussman has been quoted as saying, "Programming is debugging a blank sheet of paper."

But when it comes to user interfaces, computer scientists tend to shy away from a real test. The buttons get pushed, and the menus get dragged, and success is declared. However, the *design* of the user interface should be based on what the user wants, not whether the buttons can be pushed. To really test the *design,* one has to face the users. This is called *user-interface evaluation.*

Students cannot learn design without evaluation. Otherwise, it's almost impossible for the design to fail, and thus learning cannot occur. The evaluation does not have to be very sophisticated. The "discount usability methods" of Jakob Nielsen and others work because the real problems of user interface design tend to be right up front and pretty easy to see.

The chapter on user-interface design includes sections on evaluation. But more importantly, each of the case studies in the back of the book includes an evaluation with real users. Some of the evaluations are survey-based, others are observational with interviews, and still others use recordings of user events to figure out what happened. In every case, there is *some* testing of the design assumptions.

Generation and Inquiry, not Transmission

Even though people speak of "transmitting" or "delivering" material in a classroom, that isn't how learning works. Cognitive science has known for decades now that all real learning is *constructivist:* It's an active process of figuring things out and relating them to other knowledge. The goal of education is to motivate students to think about things, and thus learn.

The goal of a book, then, is not to deliver facts, but to provide methods of generating knowledge and fuel for students' inquiry. A list of phrases to be memorized doesn't lead to learning. But if a book explains *how* to do something, and then provides some interesting somethings to *do,* then the setting for learning is prepared.

There are sections of this book explicitly labeled *Tools and Strategies* that are meant to show how to dig into Squeak, how to study the exercises, and how to build your own things in Squeak. The rest of the book is meant to fuel inquiry, that is, students' exploration of things of interest. Inquiry can take lots of forms in lots of different directions. The goal of this book is to provide starting places for many of these: From a historical or technical perspective; from object-oriented design or user interface design; from building objects to building interfaces.

CONTENT OF THE BOOK

This is a book about using Squeak to build multimedia programs. It is not a general book about object-oriented design, interface design, or multimedia design. Rather, it's meant to be a book about using a particular programming language (that has a rich history and is particularly well suited for use in computer science education) to build projects that cross diverse areas of knowledge. In order to build multimedia programs in Squeak, students need to know the following things:

- How to program in Squeak, from both a language and an environment perspective;
- How to design programs for Squeak;
- How to build user interfaces in Squeak;
- How to design and evaluate user interfaces in Squeak;
- How to do multimedia in Squeak;
- Four detailed examples that describe how to do all of the above, with a particular emphasis on design and evaluation.

In short, that's the content of the book.

Readers who aren't interested in all six of these topics may want to take one of these other paths:

- *If you already know Smalltalk and want to learn Squeak:* Chapter 2 is an overview of Squeak, Chapter 5 (especially Sections 5.3 and 5.4) introduces user interfaces in Squeak, and Chapter 7 discusses multimedia. The case studies will also all be useful.
- *If you are focused on object-oriented design:* Chapter 3 is the transition from the focus on programming (in Chapter 2) to object-oriented design. Chapter 4 is the main chapter on object-oriented design issues, though the case studies also present object-oriented designs and evaluations of those designs.
- *If you are focused on HCI:* Chapter 5 tells how to build user interfaces in Squeak, and Chapter 6 centers on how to design them. The case studies provide HCI evaluation examples.

The book is particularly aimed at the early-to-intermediate undergraduate student. There is an assumption here that students already know *some* programming language, but little else. The goal is to quickly get students producing multimedia applications in Squeak. It serves as an excellent lead-in to more advanced classes in any of these subject areas.

At Georgia Tech, we have been teaching a course on material like this for over five years. It has met with success, in terms of student performance and satisfaction with the content. This book is based on the notes for that course. I hope that this book will be as successful in other classes, and for you, the reader, however you come to this book.

ACKNOWLEDGMENTS

This book builds on the efforts and contributions of many developers, reviewers, teachers, students, and colleagues. My listing their names here does not imply that the end product reflects their preferences, but they have been important influences for me in writing the book.

First of all, thanks to *Squeak Central:* Alan Kay, Dan Ingalls, Ted Kaehler, John Maloney, Andreas Raab, Scott Wallace, and Kim Rose (and Jeff Pierce, in his former intern role). The most obvious gratitude is for giving us Squeak, but I also owe them enormous thanks for the hours of help they have given me in answering questions, looking over sections of the book, helping me find resources, and so on. Thanks, especially, to Alan, for providing the thought-provoking foreword to the book.

Thanks to the Squeak community for answering questions and to many of them for explicitly reviewing and commenting on versions of these chapters. Special thanks to Stephane Ducasse (who gave an enormous amount of time and effort reviewing), Naala Brewer, Jennifer Brown, Piero Campanelli, Ward Cunningham, Marcus Denker, Andreas Dieberger, Steve Elkins, Dick Karpinski, Mayuresh Kathe, Patrick Milligan, Stefan Rieken, Mary Beth Rosson, Frank Sergeant, my colleague and coteacher Richard LeBlanc, and several anonymous reviewers. My thanks and admiration go to the teachers who first trialed this book in their classes and gave me some of the most valuable feedback I received: Rick Zaccone at Bucknell, Rik Smoody at Portland State University, and Cullen O'Neill at the University of Michigan.

Thanks to the many Squeak students at Georgia Institute of Technology's College of Computing who helped me learn how to teach Squeak and what difficulties people had in learning Squeak, especially to those students and teaching assistants in CS2340 who first trialed the book and gave me feedback on it. Some of the exercises here were based on labs invented by TAs Jennifer Brown, Anna Shleyfman, and Ivan Brusic. Special thanks to that special group of undergraduate and graduate students, the *Georgia Tech Squeakers* (housed in the Collaborative Software Lab, http://coweb.cc.gatech.edu/csl), who have been my closest colleagues in learning how to use and teach Squeak. At a risk of leaving out some of the Squeakers, I want to highlight the contributions of Ivan Brusic, Colleen Kehoe, Bolot Kerimbaev, Aibek Musaev, Bijan Parsia, Noel Rappin, Jochen Rich, Lex Spoon, Michael Terry, and Rodney Walker.

Alan Apt and Toni Holm of Prentice-Hall were amazingly patient and supportive of a first-time author, and I appreciate their help.

Thanks to Ivan Sutherland and Sun Microsystems for permission to use the picture of him running Sketchpad in Chapter 1.

Parts of the case studies (especially the Swiki or CoWeb) were developed with the support of the National Science Foundation as part of our work on collaborative learning environments.

Last, but not at all least, to my children Matthew, Katherine, and Jennifer and my ever-patient wife, Barbara, who gave me time to work at the book and had even more confidence than I that it would become finished one day. Thanks for your loving support!

PART 1
Foundations of Object-Oriented Programming and Squeak

The first part of the book introduces Squeak, its history, how to use it, and what to do with it. The goal is to provide enough background that the reader can do the following:

- Know the history of object-oriented programming and of Squeak.
- Appreciate that a goal of the computer is *personal dynamic media.*
- Understand how object-oriented approaches differ from more imperative approaches.
- Use the programming tools in Squeak.
- Be able to build useful programs in Squeak.
- Use Squeak's graphics and multimedia capabilities.
- Design reusable and maintainable object-oriented programs using CRC card analysis and UML class diagrams.
- Build user interfaces using frameworks provided in Squeak.
- Be aware of usability issues when designing interfaces.
- Be able to conduct a simple evaluation of your interfaces, to see if someone can use them.

1

Objects, Smalltalk, Dynabooks, and Squeak: Where the Objects Come From

1.1 OBJECT-ORIENTED PROGRAMMING

Object-oriented programming is a popular term these days. People who aren't even sure what programming is talk about "using that object stuff" as what they want in their programs. It has become a sign of our times that the promise of technology is so great that people know the words but don't really know where the words came from or what they mean.

Objects came to be, the way that we know them today, in the late 1960's and early 1970's. Think about what computer science was like then. Windows were made of glass, and mice were undesirable rodents. Microsoft didn't exist, and Bill Gates was still in school. Good programming in those days was "structured programming," and people talked about it in much the same way that people talk about objects today. Odds are good that even today, in your first programming classes (even if they were in an object-oriented programming language), you learned how to attack problems in a style that is like structured programming.

When you first learned to program a computer, you were probably taught to go about the process something like this:

- Define the tasks to be performed by your program.
- Break these tasks into smaller and smaller pieces (typically, functions) until you reach a level that you can implement.
- Define the data structures that these functions will manipulate.
- Design how the functions interact by defining what data each function will need to accept as input and what data should be output.
- Group these functions into components (such as "units" or even "classes").
- Write the code for the functions you have defined and the data structures that they will implement.

It's not important whether you tried to define abstract data types or not, or whether the order of the steps was a bit different. Generally speaking, this is not an *object-oriented process*. The key difference can be generalized in terms of the focus of the process. In the above process, you focused on what the program would *do:* the tasks and the functions. Data gets defined as something that the program acts upon. We might call this a *verb*-oriented process.

An object-oriented process starts out by defining the *nouns* in the part of the world that is relevant to the program that you are developing. You, as the *object-oriented designer,* identify the *objects* in the world of your program. You define what those objects know (that's their data), you define what they do (that's their behavior or operations), and you define how these objects interact. The definitions you develop are meant to *model* the world at large, or at least the world in which your program is meant to function. That portion of the world in which your program must function is called the *domain* of the program. If your goal is a student-registration program, your domain is the world of students and the registration system. The objects that you identify might include students, teachers, classes, pre-requisites, and other elements common in student registration.

An object-oriented approach is the structured approach sideways. Rather than starting with the program's task, you start with the world that the program will deal with. You still end up doing a kind of structured analysis when it comes to the structure of the behaviors of a given object. But that level of analysis is much later.

The process of object-oriented development goes something like this:

- *Object-oriented analysis:* The goal of object-oriented analysis is to define an object-based model of the domain in which the program will live. The analysis produces a list of objects with data and behaviors and the relationships between these objects. We say that the focus of object-oriented analysis is on the problem.
- *Object-oriented design:* The focus of object-oriented design is on the solution. You take what you have learned about the problem from the analysis, and you map it to an implementation in a language. The goal is a description of the final program in enough detail to actually implement it.
- *Object-oriented programming:* Here's where you actually build the program you designed previously.

A good way to come to understand object-oriented development is to understand where it came from, and how and why it developed in contrast to structured development. The rest of this chapter goes back to the beginning of objects, explains how object-oriented development came to be, and describes how Squeak fits into the whole story.

1.2 BIRTH OF OBJECTS

There were two pieces of software whose ideas most influenced the birth of object-oriented programming. The first wasn't a language at all, but a brilliant graphical editor called *Sketchpad* by Ivan Sutherland at MIT in 1963. (See Figure 1–1.) Sketch-

Figure 1–1:   Ivan Sutherland using Sketchpad

pad was the first object-oriented graphics editor, in the sense that we know it today. You didn't just put colored bits on a canvas with Sketchpad, where the bits all merge into a single canvas once placed. You created objects that could be manipulated as distinct from other objects. Even more significantly, Sketchpad allowed one to define a "master drawing" from which one could define a set of "instance drawings." Each of the instance drawings would be just like the master drawing, and if you changed the master, all the instances would change in the same way. The ideas in Sketchpad were the start of *inheritance,* where structure and behavior are passed on from some objects to others. In some ways, Sketchpad was better than even today's high-end drawing editors on their much faster computers. Sketchpad was amazingly fast and offered the user the ability to draw on a virtual canvas about one third of a mile square.

The second piece of software was a programming language designed to make simulations easier to implement. It was called *Simula,* was originally developed in Norway in the early 1960s, and was dramatically enhanced in Simula-67. Simula allowed one to define an *activity* from which any number of working versions of that, called *processes,* could be created. Essentially, this is very similar to the master and instance drawings of Sketchpad. Simula, however, was a general-purpose, procedural programming language that allowed users to create these objects as a way to model the world.

Each of Simula's processes was a distinct *object,* though that wasn't what it was called yet. A simulation had its own *class.* It had its own data and its own behavior, and no object could mess with the data and behavior of another object without permission. This is important in a language that is designed to build simulations. Real-world objects cannot mess with the internals of other objects. You cannot touch the insides of an animal, nor can you reach inside a room's wall and change the wiring. The concept that objects have their own data and behaviors, and that no other object can access the data without a given object's permission, is called *encapsulation.*

Each Simula object could act entirely on its own at the same time as the others. That is an important part of creating simulations. Two people in the same room can both talk and act at the same time. There is no universal time-share system that gives each person little segments of time to talk and act in. (One can almost imagine a *Universal Scheduler* announcing, "Okay, now you take a breath. Now you can say one syllable. Now you . . .") In the real world, things act all the time, simultaneously. Any system that supports simulation must support at least the illusion of multiple, simultaneous processes.

These two ideas met in 1966 with Alan Kay at the University of Utah. Kay was a graduate student in computer science who had just read about Sketchpad and was asked to get Simula running on the local computer. He saw how these two things were related, and that, in fact, they were the keys to creating large, complex, and robust systems. The best way to use a computer was as if it had thousands of little computers inside it—each independent, but interacting in clearly defined ways.

The metaphor of simulation was quite powerful. In a sense, all software simulates a piece of the world, and the job of the designer is to model the world in the software. Since programmers live in the real world and seem to understand it well enough to get around in it, a program that is explicit about modeling itself on the real world has a good chance of being understandable when it's maintained later. The real world becomes the common framework between the original programmer and the later ones.

One of Kay's undergraduate majors was biology. Nature really knows how to make complex things. Consider that a bacterium has about 120 megabytes of information in it, and it's 1/500th the size of a normal cell, and we have about 10 to the 13th power (10^{13}) of these bacteria in our bodies. Now think about *any* human-made, engineered item. How many of these scale up thousands or millions, let alone trillions, of times? If you take a simple doghouse, can you make a skyscraper by duplicating the doghouse a few million times and sticking all the doghouses together? Today, the Internet is perhaps the closest that any engineered artifact has come to this level of scaling; it has grown incredibly over many years, and still works. Kay wondered how we could make that kind of ability to handle growth and complexity the norm in software and not the exception.

Kay saw objects as the way to do it. Each object can be like a biological cell: independent and indivisible, but able to interact with its peers along standard mechanisms (such as absorbing food, expelling waste, etc.) By combining thousands or more of these cells, we can build very complex and robust systems that can grow and support reuse:

- The complexity is handled through each object's performing its own functions, without undue interference from others.
- The robustness comes from the fact that the loss of an object does not damage other objects, except those that rely on the services or roles of the lost object. The lost object can be quickly replaced through the creation of a new cell in an organism and a new instance in the computer system. We need to have a blueprint for how to build the cell or instance. We call that blueprint in an

object-oriented system a *class*. A class defines how to build new objects of the same kind.

- Supporting growth comes from using the same structuring and communication mechanism throughout. All biological systems are made of cells. If all software was made up of uniform objects, it might scale better than did software built via structured analysis. Further, objects could be combined, in the same way that organs are made up of cells. An object can contain other objects through *aggregation*.

- Finally, the reuse comes from each object's performing its own role, with only minimal connections to other objects. If the designer does a good job and makes the software objects model the real-world objects well, then those objects will probably have a future use. The same objects show up in lots of different forms in the real world: Pencils, paychecks, cars, customers. Model the objects well once, and you can use that model over and over again.

1.3 "A PERSONAL COMPUTER FOR CHILDREN OF ALL AGES"

The first attempt at an object-oriented programming system was FLEX, the focus of Alan Kay's dissertation. There were previous "object-oriented" systems—Sketchpad was an object-oriented drawing system, and Simula was a language that showed the start of object-oriented programming. The FLEX machine was a complete *personal* computer, based on objects and completely programmable. It wasn't the first personal computer, but the notion of a personal computer was still radical and even invited ridicule in some corners. In the late 1960s, computers were huge, room-filling machines that were tended to by a priesthood of administrators. The notion of one of these monstrous mechanisms being at the disposal of a single individual seemed to many like an enormous waste of resources. But Kay and others already knew that Gordon Moore's now-famous law of integrated chip density was proving true:[1] Computers were going to get much cheaper. Kay wanted his FLEX machine to serve the needs of an individual, and to serve Kay as a platform to explore what one *would* do with a personal computer.

It was already possible to list several things that one might want in a personal computer like FLEX. It was a given that it needed to be programmable, with a flexible and scalable language. Certainly both Sketchpad and Simula were on that list, though neither would fit in the 16K of 16-bit words available on the FLEX. As Figure 1–2 shows, the FLEX was designed to support freehand sketching. Douglas Engelbart's NLS (oNLine Systems) was another item on the wishlist.

Douglas Engelbart had a vision for computers as "augmentation of human intellect." He wanted computers to serve to help users perceive and manage their world differently. Engelbart demonstrated NLS in 1968 and blew the audience away with his use of a pointing device (i.e., Engelbart's invention of the mouse), multiple

---

[1] While Moore's Law refers strictly to the number of transistors on a chip at the same price, the impact of Moore's Law is that processing power at the same price roughly doubles every eighteen months.

Figure 1–2: Kay's drawing of Flex from *Early History of Smalltalk:* Flex's "Self-Portrait"

paned views, outline processing, and even interactive collaboration with live video connections!

While working on FLEX, Kay also learned of the pioneering work of Seymour Papert and his colleagues at MIT, who were having children program computers in a programming language called Logo. Again, in those days, this was just as radical a notion as personal computers. What would *children* ever want with the powerful and gargantuan computer? The Logo developers were having children explore issues of representation (graphical and symbolic) and knowledge by having them build programs. Children would program a graphical "turtle" that would draw sketches on the screen per their commands.

Kay saw that the role of the personal computer would be that of personal dynamic *media.* The computer can be something with which one could explore representations (Logo), draw (Sketchpad), and even simulate anything in the real world (Simula). Later, with Adele Goldberg, he described the personal computer as the first *meta-medium,* the first medium that could encompass all other media: Text, sound, graphics, animations, and others not yet invented. This was the vision of personal computing that Kay was exploring with FLEX.

FLEX didn't achieve all of the goals that Kay had for it, but it met several of them. It certainly served as a springboard to the ideas of what a *truly* personal computer *might* look like: small, even handheld; supporting keyboard or stylus for drawing, wireless networking, and so on. The name that Kay gave to this hypothetical device was *Dynabook* (Figure 1–3), and he talked about it as being a "personal computer for children of all ages" in his 1972 ACM Conference paper.

In 1970, Alan Kay joined Xerox's new Palo Alto Research Center to lead the Learning Research Group, in which Smalltalk was created. Smalltalk was the first object-oriented programming language, in the way that we think of object-oriented programming today (as opposed to the earlier Simula). Smalltalk eventually realized all of the pieces that we think about today when we think about personal computers—as well as included many of the features that were desired in the Dynabook. Smalltalk systems were the first to have bit-mapped displays, overlapping windows, menus, icons, and a mouse pointing device. Microsoft Windows, UNIX X-Windows,

Figure 1–3:   Cardboard model of Dynabook

and the Macintosh operating system all have their roots in Smalltalk. In a very real sense, modern user interfaces have evolved hand-in-hand with object-oriented programming.

Smalltalk evolved through several iterations. From Smalltalk-71 (which looked a good bit like Logo) and Smalltalk-72 (in which many of the media-oriented features were first implemented, from drawing to music programs and even iconic programming languages; see Figure 1–4), Smalltalk development led to Smalltalk-76, which was the first modern Smalltalk. Dan Ingalls was the main implementor of the Smalltalk implementations during this time, and the creator of Smalltalk-76. Ted Kaehler was another of the original Learning Research Group members, who built the music system for Smalltalk-72, the Logo "turtle" for Smalltalk, and Smalltalk's object-oriented memory structure.

Smalltalk-80 was released to a handful of computer companies (e.g., Hewlett-Packard, DEC, Apple, IBM, Tektronix) as a test of the *portability* of Smalltalk. Smalltalk-80 was implemented as a *bytecode compiler*. Smalltalk code was actually compiled, but it was not compiled into the machine language native to the computer it was running on. Instead, it was compiled into a machine language for a machine that did not exist in hardware, a *virtual machine*. It was easy to write a small program (an interpreter) in the native machine language that would execute the virtual machine *bytecode*. This interpreter would make it appear as if the native machine really *were* the virtual machine, and thus could run any program written for the virtual machine. The advantage of this scheme was that Smalltalk-80 was highly portable. Indeed, all of these companies were able to create versions of Smalltalk-80 on their systems easily. Bytecode compilers were not new, even then, and the scheme was later used by UCSD Pascal and is used nowadays by Sun with Java.

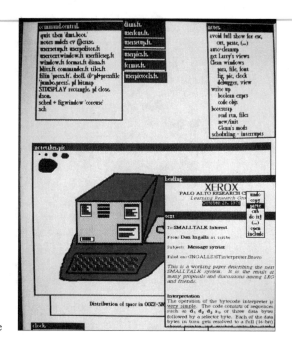

Figure 1–4: Smalltalk-72 User Interface

A basic Smalltalk-80 implementation consisted of four files:

- A virtual machine interpreter, executable on the native machine. This was the only non-portable part, the piece that each implementor had to get running on a new platform.
- An image file, which was a program in virtual machine object code that provided the Smalltalk compiler, the development environment, and associated tools.
- A sources file, which contained the Smalltalk source of all of the base objects in the image file.
- A changes file, which contained the Smalltalk source of all of the objects that the user had added to the image.

Smalltalk-80 has become the standard against which all current Smalltalks are measured. Xerox spun off Smalltalk into a separate company, called ParcPlace, which marketed various versions of Smalltalk as ObjectWorks and later Visual-Works. Adele Goldberg, of the original Learning Research Group, shepherded the new company and wrote the definitive books on Smalltalk-80. Other versions of Smalltalk were created by other companies, such as Digitalk's Smalltalk/V and Quasar's SmalltalkAgents. All have similar syntax and object structures, though the user interface code differs dramatically.

1.4 BACK TO THE FUTURE

In 1995, Alan Kay, Dan Ingalls, and Ted Kaehler all found themselves working at Apple Computer. Despite the intervening decades, they were still all interested in the vision of a Dynabook, "a development environment in which to build educational software that could be used—and even programmed—by non-technical people, and by children" (Ingalls, Kaehler, Maloney, Wallace, and Kay, 1997). While the user interface of Smalltalk had been copied and passed down through many other systems, the core ideas of the Dynabook as personal dynamic media had been lost. They considered developing with Java, but felt that it wasn't stable enough. Smalltalk would be great, but the commercial Smalltalks at the time didn't have the flexibility that they wanted for a real Dynabook. For example, sound had been removed since the commercial release of Smalltalk-80. They also wanted to build upon the strengths of open-source software, which had radically changed how people thought about software development.

The idea of open-source software is to let the source code be freely available on the Internet and to use the contributed code (bug fixes, enhancements, redesigns) to develop the code. Open-source software is best known as the development methodology of the Linux operating system, but many other pieces of software have been developed in the open-source model, including the Apache web server and the Python programming language. Open source has the advantage, over more traditional development methodologies, of using the enormous creativity distributed among the programmers on the Internet to advance software.

The group at Apple decided that if the right Smalltalk didn't exist, they'd have to build one. After all, they had done it before. And even better, they didn't have to start over—they still had the original port of Smalltalk-80 that Apple had made years before. This was the beginning of *Squeak*, the programming language used in this book.

The philosophy of Squeak was to write everything in Smalltalk. For Squeak to succeed as open source software, all of the source code to everything, including the virtual machine interpreter, had to be freely available. If some of the code were in C and other parts were in Smalltalk (for example), the system would be harder to understand and extend. But the virtual machine interpreter, as already mentioned, had to be written in the *native* machine language. The Squeak Team (Kay, Ingalls, and Kaehler, and also John Maloney and Scott Wallace) came up with a novel solution:

- They wrote the Smalltalk virtual machine in Smalltalk. This wasn't as hard as it sounds: Adele Goldberg's book on Smalltalk-80 had already described the virtual machine interpreter in Smalltalk. They only had to type in the code and get it running.
- They wrote a small Smalltalk-to-C translator. Now, even code that had to be executed as compiled C could be written originally as Smalltalk.

Once the Smalltalk virtual machine was written in Smalltalk, they could use the translator to convert it to C. They compiled the C code to create a native machine executable. They could then run the image from the new executable. From here on out, almost all of Squeak could be written in Squeak.

In September 1996, Squeak was released to the Internet. Within five weeks, it had been ported to several variants of UNIX, Windows 95, and Windows NT. It now runs on a huge range of computers, from handheld Windows CE devices, to some set-top boxes, to most major computing platforms. The Squeak Team is now (as of this writing) at Disney Imagineering Research and Development, but the Squeak license from Apple allows Squeak users to create anything they want with Squeak. Any enhancements to the base system, however, must be released back to the network, in the tradition of open-source software.

Since Squeak's original release, more and more of the desired Dynabook features have appeared in Squeak. Squeak has powerful 2-D and 3-D color graphics, multi-voice sampled and synthesized sounds, support for animations and even video, and tools for managing a wide variety of media formats, including MIDI, Flash, JPEG, and GIF.

One of the key advantages of Squeak as a language for learning computer science is that it continues to follow the philosophy of "Everything in Squeak." Consider the image shown in Figure 1–5.

The message **Line example** created this image. What you see here is a bunch of windows with a big fat line crossing all of them, breaking the title bars and even messing up the desktop. On all modern windowing systems, this is next to impossible. But Smalltalk-80 was the predecessor of these modern windowing systems. In Squeak, the window-drawing code is written in Smalltalk! The operation used to make that line is the same one used to make the lines of the windows, so neither one has precedence over the other.

For almost anything you would like to explore in computer science, from graphics to garbage collection, Squeak provides a wonderful workbench. You inherit all the great programming tools developed by the Smalltalk group, you have access to megabytes of source code that implements these features, and you can program as deep as you like while staying within Squeak. If you want to re-invent windows (or Windows), garbage collection, or even the virtual machine, all the tools are there to do it from within Squeak. Consider that the VM-in-Smalltalk is not just input to the translator for C output—it's also executable Smalltalk that you can use in debugging new variations on the virtual machine. Of course, running bytecodes on top of a bytecode interpreter that is itself interpreted on top of a bytecode interpreter is fairly slow, but it's a much nicer experimentation environment than dropping down into machine language debuggers. Dan Ingalls, in the OOPSLA paper that introduced Squeak, wrote that one of the goals for Squeak was to allow anyone to understand the whole system from a single language:

> Squeak stands alone as a practical Smalltalk in which a researcher, professor, or motivated student can examine source code for every part of the system, including graphics primitives and the virtual machine itself, and make changes immediately and without needing to see or deal with any language other than Smalltalk.

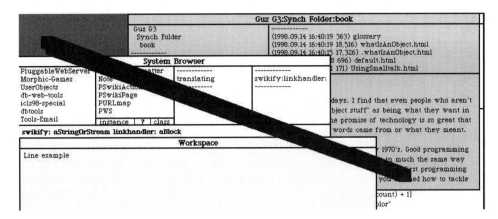

Figure 1–5:   A Line Example in Squeak

1.5 COMMON ANCESTRY OF OTHER OBJECT-ORIENTED LANGUAGES

Back in 1979, a separate thread of the object-oriented programming languages story was launched by Bjarne Stroustrup, who wanted to create a highly-efficient version of Simula. Bjarne worked at Bell Labs, where the programming language C had been invented. He created several versions of a programming language that was like C but had object-oriented extensions. In 1984, the language C++ was born.

C++ and Smalltalk both started from the ideas of Simula, but they are very different approaches. C++ is a compiled language that uses a traditional notion of functions and stack-based scoping, while Smalltalk is a dynamic language (feels more like an interpreter than a compiler) and has persistent objects that have nothing to do with what function is in scope. C++ is a strongly-typed programming language, in that all variables have a data type associated with them and only values of the right type can be stored in these variables. Smalltalk has no type declarations at all, every object is an instance of a class, and all storage is object storage that is managed automatically by the system using a process called *garbage collection.* You can't explicitly destroy any object in Smalltalk.

Java is a more recent programming language that starts merging these two threads of object-oriented programming. In 1991, Sun Microsystems began an internal project to produce a language that could run on intelligent consumer-electronic devices—everything from set-top boxes to toaster ovens. James Gosling created the programming language Oak through this project, as a highly portable, object-oriented programming language. When the Web came along, it was obvious that a highly-portable language could also be used to send around executable code over the Internet. The language, by then named *Java,* had a new focus. Java was announced to the world in May 1995. Java looks very much like C++, and is even more strongly typed. Yet Java also has features of an interpreter: It uses bytecode compilation and it offers automatic storage management.

EXERCISES

1. Given all of the preceding, what are the key features of an object-oriented system? Think about the various analogies that have been used: Objects as cells, software as simulation, objects as little computers. What do each of these analogies point out as key features?
2. What does inheritance buy you as a software designer? Do biological cells have inheritance? It is interesting to note that the earliest forms of Simula and Smalltalk did not have any form of inheritance.
3. Do biological cells have classes?
4. What is the most important aspect of object-oriented programming? Several have been identified here: Inheritance, encapsulation, aggregation. Which do you argue is most important?

REFERENCES

The discussion in this chapter merely touches on the influences and characters that led to object-oriented programming, Smalltalk, and Squeak. The references below provide much more detail.

For a great discussion of the history of Smalltalk, see

KAY, ALAN C. (1993). The early history of Smalltalk. *History of Programming Languages (HOPL-II)*. J. E. Sammet. New York, ACM: 69–95.

Bjarne Stroustrup's history of C++ appears in

STROUSTRUP, BJARNE (1993). A History of C++. *History of Programming Languages (HOPL-II)*. J. E. Sammet. New York, ACM: 699–769.

A nice on-line resource on Sketchpad is available from Sun Microsystems at http://www.sun.com/960710/feature3/sketchpad.html.

Alan Kay's Scientific American article where Joe the Box first appeared is in

KAY, ALAN C. (1977). "Microelectronics and the Personal Computer." *Scientific American* (September): 231–244.

My favorite paper that describes the Xerox PARC vision of the personal computer is

KAY, ALAN, & GOLDBERG, ADELE. (1977). Personal dynamic media. *IEEE Computer*, March, 31–41.

The classic paper on the design issues that influence Smalltalk is Dan Ingalls' paper from the August 1981 *Byte* magazine issue devoted to Smalltalk, *Design Principles Behind Smalltalk*. It's been made available (by Dwight Hughes) at http://users.ipa.net/~dwight/smalltalk/byte_aug81/design_principles_behind_smalltalk.html.

The Squeak *Back to the Future* OOPSLA paper is at ftp://st.cs.uiuc.edu/Smalltalk/Squeak/docs/OOPSLA.Squeak.html. The original reference is as follows:

DAN INGALLS, TED KAEHLER, JOHN MALONEY, SCOTT WALLACE, and ALAN KAY. (1997). Back to the Future: The Story of Squeak, A Practical Smalltalk Written in Itself, *OOPSLA'97 Conference Proceedings* (pp. 318–326). Atlanta, GA: ACM.

Probably the most influential paper in the open-source movement has been Eric Raymond's *The Cathedral and the Bazaar,* which is available at http://www.tuxedo.org /~esr/writings/cathedral-bazaar.

The main Squeak site is http://www.squeak.org. The main discussion site for Squeak is http://minnow.cc.gatech.edu/squeak.

2

A Tour of Squeak

2.1 BASIC RULES OF SMALLTALK

The basic rules of Smalltalk can be stated pretty simply:

- Everything is an object. (This is by far the most important rule in Smalltalk.)
- All computation is triggered through message-sends. You send a message to an object to make something happen.
- Almost all executable Smalltalk expressions are of the form **<receiverObject> <message>**.
- Messages trigger *methods,* in which the mapping of messages to methods is determined by the receiving object. Methods are the units of Smalltalk code. You can think of a method as being like a function or procedure in your favorite programming language.
- Every object is an *instance* of some *class.* 12 is an instance of the class **SmallInteger.** 'abc' is an instance of the class **String.** The class determines the data and behavior of its instances.
- All classes have a parent class, except for the class **Object.**[1] The parent class defines the data and behavior that are *inherited* by all of its children classes. The parent class is called a *superclass,* and the children classes are called *subclasses.*

Let's look at an example piece of Smalltalk code:

```
| anArray anIndex aValue |
aValue := 2.  "Set aValue to 2"
```

---

[1]Conceptually, **Object** is the root of the Smalltalk hierarchy. In reality, **Object** *does* have a parent class: **ProtoObject. ProtoObject** has no parent class.

```
anArray := Array new: 10. "anArray is an Array with 10 elements"
1 to: 10 do:"Store 2*index at each array element"
      [:index |
      anArray at: index
             put: (aValue * index)].
anIndex := 1.        "Walk the array again, printing out the values"
[anIndex <= anArray size]
      whileTrue:
      [Transcript show:
             'Value at: ',(anIndex printString),
             ' is ',
      (anArray at: anIndex) printString ; cr.
      anIndex := anIndex + 1.]
```

All of this prints onto the Transcript (more on that later):

```
Value at: 1 is 2
Value at: 2 is 4
Value at: 3 is 6
Value at: 4 is 8
Value at: 5 is 10
Value at: 6 is 12
Value at: 7 is 14
Value at: 8 is 16
Value at: 9 is 18
Value at: 10 is 20
```

This looks pretty similar to code that you might see in any programming language, and the result is also pretty much what you would expect. You see assignment statements, expressions, creation of an array object, a structure that looks like a **for** loop, and a structure that looks like a **while** loop. You may notice the lack of type declarations and some seemingly odd syntax. For the most part, your intuition about the meaning of these pieces will be correct. But the real semantics are different from what you may expect (and, in many ways, simpler and more consistent) because of the basic rules of Smalltalk:

- *Everything is an object.* This rule means that **aValue := 2** does not actually mean "Set the value of 'aValue' to integer 2" but instead means "Set the variable aValue to point to an **SmallInteger** object whose value is 2." (Be careful of the case of things here—Smalltalk *is* case sensitive, and **array** is not the same as **Array**.) There is no type associated with a variable. Variables merely point to objects, and everything is an object. If the next line had aValue being assigned to a string (e.g., **aValue := 'fred the string'**) or even a window, it would all be the same to Smalltalk. The variable aValue would still point to an object, and everything is an object.

- *All computation is triggered through message-sends.* This rule means that even the pieces above that look like special constructs, like **1 to: 10 do:** and **[anIndex < anArray size]** are just message-sends.

- *Almost all executable Smalltalk expressions are of the form* **<receiverObject>** **<message>**. This one can lead to some surprises when coming to Smalltalk from more traditional programming languages. **1 to: 10 do: [ ]** is a message-send to the object **1**. The message **to: do:** is a message understood by **Integers**. (Messages can be named with multiple words in Smalltalk, with colons appearing before each argument to the method.) 10 and the block of code (statements contained in square brackets) following **do:** are actually arguments in the message. Consider the expression **2 + 3**. In the semantics of Smalltalk, this is a message-send of **+** with the argument of **3** to the object **2**. While it may seem unusual, such adherence to a single-standard mechanism has proven to be amazingly powerful!

- *Messages trigger methods.* Each of the messages just mentioned (**to: do:**, **whileTrue:**, **+**) trigger *methods,* which are Smalltalk code units. You can view the implementation of control structures and operators—and even change them.[2]

It's important to note the difference between messages and methods. In many languages (e.g., C, Pascal, Fortran, Cobol), the function name defines the code to be executed. If you execute **foo(12)** in any of these languages, you know exactly what is going to be executed. Smalltalk is a kind of language that uses *late binding.* When you see the message **printString**, you actually do not know what is going to be executed until you know what object is being sent the message. **printString** always returns a string representation of the object receiving the message. **20 printString**, **32.456 printString**, and **FileDirectory default printString** actually have very different implementations, even though they are all responding to the same message. They also provide the same functionality—they return a printable string representation of the receiving object. If the receiver object is a variable, then it's not possible at compile time to figure out which method to invoke for the given message. The decision of which method will execute for the given message is made at runtime (hence, *late-binding*), when the receiver object is known.

Having the same message perform approximately the same functions on different data is called *polymorphism.* It's an important feature of object-oriented languages, as well as of other languages. Addition is polymorphic in most languages. Addition in the form **3 + 5** is actually a very different operation at the machine's level from **3.1 + 5.2**, but it's the same message or operation at the human's level. What's nice about most object-oriented languages is that you, the programmer, can define your own polymorphic messages.

The programmer is not specifying a piece of code when she sends the message **printString** to some object. Rather, she is specifying a *goal:* to get a printable, string representation of the object. Since this goal may be implemented differently depending on the kind of object, there will be multiple *methods* implementing the same *message.* Programming in terms of the goal shifts the focus to a higher level, out of the bits and into the objects:

---

[2]Some control structures are compiled in-line for efficiency, so it's not always possible to change every control structure.

```
Magnitude
        Character
        Date
        Number
                Float
                Fraction
                Integer
                        SmallInteger
        Time
```

Figure 2–1   The Hierarchy of Classes Below Magnitude

- *Every object is an instance of some class.* Since the class is where the definition of the instance's behavior resides, it's very important to find the class of the receiver object to figure out how a message will be interpreted.

- *All classes have a parent object.* Consider the code before **(aValue * index)**. **aValue** in this example is bound to a **SmallInteger**, and **SmallIntegers** know how to multiply (*****). But we might also ask **aValue** if it's positive (**aValue positive**), a test that returns true or false. **SmallInteger** instances do not know how to tell if they're positive, but **Numbers** do, and **SmallIntegers** are a kind of **Number**. (Strictly, **SmallInteger** is a subclass of **Integer**, which is a subclass of **Number**.) **aValue** can be asked whether it or another number is a maximum value (e.g., **aValue max: 12**). **max:** is a message understood by **Magnitude**, not by **SmallInteger** or **Number**—and **Number** is a subclass of **Magnitude**, and thus **aValue** inherits what **Magnitude** knows. **Date** and **Time** are two other subclasses of **Magnitude**, so it's possible to get the maximum between any two dates or any two time instances, but it may not be possible to do arithmetic on them. Figure 2–1 presents the hierarchy of classes below **Magnitude**. Indentation indicates subclassing. (This is a view that's easily generated in Squeak, as will be seen later in this chapter.)

2.2 DOING "NORMAL" THINGS IN SQUEAK

Much of your programming in Squeak involves the same kind of programming that you've done in any other language: Variables, control structures, and the manipulation of numbers, strings, and files. A good way to start with Squeak is to explain how you do these "normal" operations.

If you want to try out some pieces of this code (which you're encouraged to do!), you can try these expressions and code fragments in a workspace. Start up Squeak by opening the image with the executable. (In UNIX, you can type the name of the executable and then the name of the image file; on Windows or on a Mac, just drag the image file onto the executable.) Click the mouse button anywhere on the desktop and hold to bring up the Desktop or World Menu (Figure 2–2). Release the mouse with **Open...** highlighted. Choose **Workspace** (Figure 2–3).

Figure 2–2 The World Menu in Morphic, similar to the Desktop Menu in MVC

In a workspace, you can type code, select it, and then execute it and print the result. In Figure 2–3, the workspace contains **3 + 4**. On UNIX, you hit Control-P; on Windows, Alt-P; and on Macs, Apple/Command-P. This is referred to by Smalltalkers as a **PrintIt** operation. The result is that the expression is evaluated and the resultant object is printed.

2.2.1 Variables and Statements

A variable can be essentially any single word that starts with a letter. The assignment operator is := or can also be ← (which is typed as an underscore character in the basic Squeak font). The value of an assignment (what PrintIt displays) is the right-hand side of the assignment, as in the following code:

```
aVariable := 12.
aVariable ← 'Here is a String'.
```

Any Smalltalk expression can work as a statement. Statements are separated with periods. A perfectly valid sequence of Smalltalk statements is as follows:

```
1 < 2.
12 positive.
3 + 4.
```

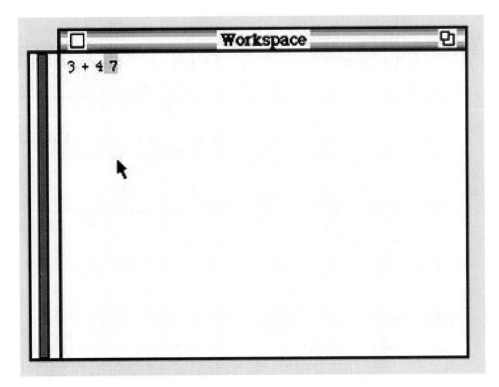

Figure 2-3 An example workspace

There is a *scope* associated with variables in Smalltalk. If you created **aVariable** in your workspace with the above example, your variable's scope would be that workspace. The variable would be accessible within the workspace, as long as the workspace was open, but nowhere else in the system. If you did a PrintIt on

myVariable := 34.5.

you would get 34.5. If you then did a PrintIt on

myVariable + 1

you would get 35.5. The variable exists within the workspace.

You can also create variables that are local only to the execution of a group of Smalltalk statements, as in this line from the example at the beginning of the chapter:

| anArray anIndex aValue |

The beginning of code segments can hold local-variable declarations. These variables will exist only for the duration of the code being executed.

As a matter of Smalltalk style, variables, method names, and other local names all begin with lowercase letters. Globals, a category that includes all class names,

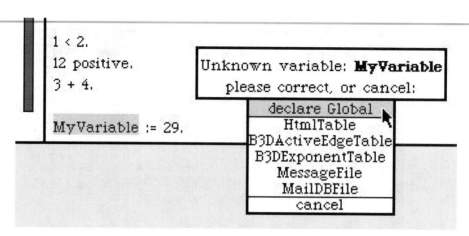

Figure 2–4   Dialog on Declaring a Global Variable

begin with an uppercase letter. This style rule is enforced at various places in the system. For example, if you PrintIt

MyVariable := 29.

you'll get a dialog box asking you if you really did want to declare a global variable (Figure 2–4). You can declare the variable to be global, but Smalltalk assumes that you were actually trying to reference an existing global variable, so it offers a selection of potential alternatives based on what you typed.

You've probably noticed that the variable declarations don't say anything about the *type* of the variables: integer, float, arrays, public or private, static or dynamic, etc. Smalltalk is essentially a *type-less* programming language. Everything in Smalltalk is simply an object. Any variable can reference any object. All *collection* objects (e.g., arrays, sets, bags, ordered collections, etc.) can contain any kind of object. There is no distinction between public and private, as there is in C++ or Java, for data or for methods.

You may be wondering what happens in Smalltalk when you try to evaluate something that depends on type, such as **3 + false** (adding the boolean false to the integer 3). The error that you get in this particular instance is "MessageNotUnderstood" (or something similar, the exact error message may depend on the version of Squeak that you're using). If you track down the debugging stack (which is explained later in this chapter), you find that what happened is that the boolean value "false" did not understand a message that numbers understand. The way types fail in Smalltalk is through an object's not understanding a message. But on the other hand, making **3 + false** actually work is simply a matter of teaching **Boolean** instances to respond to the appropriate messages. The flexibility of the system is enormous.

2.2.2 Control Structures

We've already seen basic Smalltalk expressions, which are obviously the simplest form of control: Just list one expression after another.

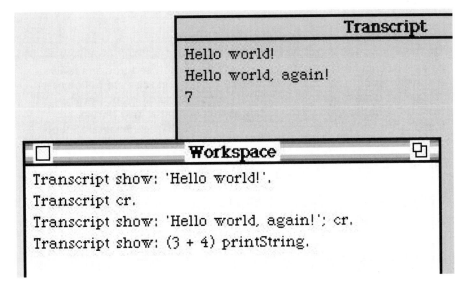

Figure 2–5   Transcript example

One of the "normal" things that programmers often want to do is print out results somewhere. Workspace code can't normally print back to the Workspace, but there is a window accessible via the global variable **Transcript** that can be printed to easily. To open a **Transcript**, choose **Open...** again from the Desktop Menu, and then select **Transcript**. You can display things to the **Transcript** by sending it the message **show:** with some string.

In the example in Figure 2–5, you see a string being printed to the Transcript. The **cr** message generates a carriage-return on the Transcript. The next **show:** will print on the line below. We also see a *message cascade*. A semicolon can separate a series of messages to the same receiver (**Transcript** in this case). We also see an integer being converted to a printable string and then printed to the Transcript.

All the control structures that you might expect in a "normal" language are present in Smalltalk, including the following:

```
"if...then"
a < 12 ifTrue: [Transcript show: 'True!'].
```

(Go ahead and PrintIt on the preceding example.) The first thing to notice is the comment in double quotes at the top of the example. Double quotes delimit comments in Smalltalk.

ifTrue: is a message sent to boolean values. **a < 12** will return either **true** or **false**. That object will then receive the message **ifTrue:** and a *block* of statements in square brackets.

The square brackets define a kind of object called a *block*. A block can be sent

---

CAUTIONARY NOTE

There are objects defined in Smalltalk as **true** and **false**. There are also objects **True** and **False**. True and False are the classes, and true and false are the instances of those classes (respectively). **True** and **False** are still *objects*—you can send messages to them. But they understand different messages from those understood by the instances **true** and **false**. **True ifTrue: [Smalltalk beep]** will generate only an error. **true ifTrue: [Smalltalk beep]** will beep.

---

messages or can even be assigned to variables. It's a first-class object, like any string or number, as in the following code:

```
"if...then...else"
((a < 12) and: [b > 13])
ifTrue: [Transcript show: 'True!']
ifFalse: [Transcript show: 'False!'].
```

The example above demonstrates an **ifTrue:ifFalse:** which would be an *if-then-else* in a more traditional programming language. The order doesn't matter: There is an **ifFalse:ifTrue:** message for boolean objects, too. You also see a logical *and* in this example. **and:** is a message understood by booleans. It takes a block that will be evaluated if the receiver object is true; that is, it creates a *short-circuit* where the second expression doesn't get evaluated and execution continues. There is also an **or:** message defined for booleans. There are also infix operators for **&** (and) and **|** (or), but these do not short-circuit—both terms are always evaluated.

The outer parentheses are necessary in this example. Without them, Smalltalk would interpret the message very differently. **(a < 12)** would be sent the message **and:ifTrue:ifFalse:**, which of course, is not defined. (See Figure 2–6; consider it a rule of thumb to put parentheses around a conditional test if it involves keyword messages.)

```
"A while loop"
a ← 1.
[a < 10] whileTrue:
        [a := a + 1. Transcript show: '9 times...'].
```

This example shows a traditional *while* loop. Both **whileTrue:** and **whileFalse:** are defined in Squeak. Note that the test is a block (enclosed in square brackets), and the body of the *while* loop is also a block. The multiple statements inside the body block are separated by periods.

```
"timesRepeat"
9 timesRepeat: [Transcript show: '9 times...'].
```

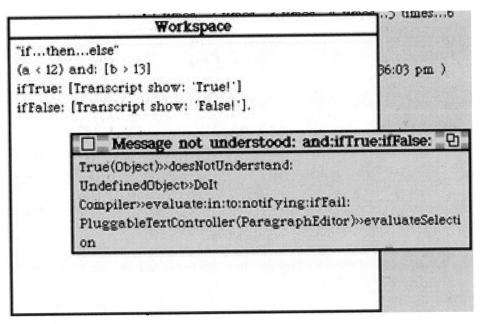

Figure 2–6 Error notifier resulting from removing the outer parentheses

A **timesRepeat**: isn't in most programming languages, but is pretty useful. Sometimes, you want something to happen a certain number of times, but you don't need the index variable of a *for* loop.

```
"for loop -- variable could be anything"
1 to: 9 do: [:index | Transcript show:
        (index printString),' times...'].
1 to: 9 do: [:i | Transcript show:
        (i printString),' times...'].
```

We refer to these two messages as **to:do:**. The arguments (the number and the block) are just interspersed amongst the pieces of the message (called the *selector*). Here we see two different **to:do:** loops (a *for* loop in other languages). The only difference between them is a change in the index-variable name. A vertical bar separates the definition of the index variable from the rest of the statements in the body of the loop.

2.2.3 Literals, Numbers, and Operations

What goes on the right side of an assignment is a very rich set of possibilities. Basically, any expression that returns a value (which is always an object) is valid on the right side of an assignment. Literals are certainly valid expressions.

Example	Meaning
12	An integer (in this example, because it's less than 30K, a **SmallInteger**).
34.56	A floating-point number (instance of **Float**).
$a	The **Character**, lowercase A.
'a'	The string with the single character of a lowercase A in it.
#(12 'a' $b)	A literal array with three elements in it: The integer 12, the string 'a', and the character lowercase B.
"a"	This actually means absolutely nothing to Smalltalk—anything inside of double quotes is considered a comment. You can intersperse comments anywhere in your code to help explain it to others or to yourself when you forget what your code means.

SIDE NOTE

As in any other programming language, Smalltalk arrays hold collections of the same kind of element. They are *homogeneous* collections. Smalltalk arrays hold only objects.

A whole set of infix numeric operations (called *binary messages* because they involve two objects) are also available for the creation of expressions.

Operation	Meaning
4 + 3	Addition
32.3 – 5	Subtraction
65 * 32	Multiplication
67 / 42	Division. The result here is the **Fraction** object **67/42**. Send the fraction the message **asFloat** to get a decimal value.
10 // 3	Quotient, truncating toward negative infinity. Result here is 3.
10 \\ 3	Remainder. Result here is 1.

Beyond literals and infix operations lies a vast collection of textual messages. Some of these are *unary,* which means that they take no arguments. Other messages are *keyword messages,* in which each *selector* ends with a colon ($:), which means that they take arguments. Here are a few examples:

Example	Meaning
(-4) abs	Absolute value. Returns integer 4.
90 sin	Sine of 90 radians. Returns 0.893996663600558
anArray at: 5	Returns whatever object is at position 5 in **anArray**.

$a asUppercase	Returns the character uppercase A
10 // 3	Quotient, truncating toward negative infinity. Result here is 3.
10 \\ 3	Remainder, truncating toward negative infinity. Result here is 1.

The order of precedence is as follows:

- Things in parentheses are evaluated first. For example, **3 * (4 + 2)** will result in 18. **3 * 4 + 2** will result in 14.
- Unary messages are next. For example, **3 * 8 sin** will multiply three by the sine of eight radians.
- Binary messages (infix operators) are next.
- Keyword messages (such as **at:**) are last.

2.2.4 Strings and Arrays

Strings and arrays, as in many languages, are similar to one another in Squeak. Strings and arrays respond to some similar messages, because they have a common ancestry in terms of the hierarchy of classes. They both inherit from the class **SequenceableCollection**. (See Figure 2–7.)

Strings can be created literally with single quotes, but you can also create them with a variety of commands. Here are three ways to create the exact same three-character string: We can create it literally; we can create it using the message **with:with:with:** (up to six **with:**'s are understood); or we can create a three-character **String** and then fill it with the appropriate characters, position by position.

The last statement in the next example is unusual. It's a return. Up-arrow says to return this value. If you select all of those lines, beginning with the **String new:** line, the return will make sure that the value of the whole collection is **aString** when you PrintIt. Without that last line, the value of the whole collection of lines is the last **at:put:**, and the value of an **at:put:** is the value being put, in this case, **$c**. The code is as follows:

```
        "A literal string"
'abc'
        "Using with:with:with:"
String with: $a with: $b with: $c
        "Creating a blank string then filling it."
aString := String new: 3.
aString at: 1 put: $a.
aString at: 2 put: $b.
aString at: 3 put: $c.
^aString
```

The latter example is not quite in traditional Smalltalk style. Typically, Smalltalkers don't create explicit sizes, preferring instead to let the system determine the size. Here's an alternative way do to the same thing. In the next example, we add

```
Collection
        SequenceableCollection
                ArrayedCollection
                        Array
                                        WeakArray
                        Array2D
                        ByteArray
                        FloatArray
                        IntegerArray
                                        PointArray
                        SoundBuffer
                        String
                                        Symbol
                        Text
                Interval
                LinkedList
                        Semaphore
                MappedCollection
                OrderedCollection
                        SortedCollection
        Set
                Dictionary
                        SystemDictionary
```

Figure 2–7   A Portion of the Collection class hierarchy

characters in two different ways. In the first, we use the concatenation operator, a comma (**$,**). The concatenation character takes an argument of a string, so the character must be converted to a string with **asString**. In the latter two, we put the new characters at the end of the string with **copyWith:**. We must reassign **aString** each time, because these operators create a new string. They don't modify the existing string. Following is the code:

```
"Creating a blank string then filling it."
aString := String new.
aString := aString , $a asString.
aString := aString copyWith: $b.
aString := aString copyWith: $c.
^aString
```

Strings do not expand their length in Squeak. If you want to replace a sequence in a string with a longer or shorter sequence, you need to make a copy of it as you do the replacement:

```
'squeak' copyReplaceAll: 'ea' with: 'awwww'
        "Returns: 'squawwwwk'"
```

Most of the preceding messages are not specific to Strings. Rather, they're defined higher in the Collections class hierarchy, so they're available to arrays as well. Here are the same four methods for creating an identical array.

```
    "A literal array"
#(12 'b' $c)
    "Using with:with:with:"
Array with: 12 with: 'b' with: $c
    "Creating a blank array then start filling it."
anArray := Array new: 3.
anArray at: 1 put: 12.
anArray at: 2 put: 'b'.
anArray at: 3 put: $c.
^anArray
    "Creating a blank array then start filling it."
anArray := Array new.
anArray := anArray , #(12).
anArray := anArray copyWith: 'b'.
anArray := anArray copyWith: $c.
^anArray
```

There are many operations that arrays and strings have in common. We can access components of each with **at:**; we can execute a block over each element of the array or string with **do:**; we can create a new string or array from evaluating a block to each element with **select:** They share these operations in common with all **Collection** subclasses. They also share operations from their superclasses **SequenceableCollection** and **ArrayedCollection**.

Example	Value
#(12 43 'abc' $g) at: 2 'squeak' at: 2	**at:** provides access to elements. Returns **43** and **$q**, respectively.
#(12 43 'abc' $g) do: [:element	Transcript show: element printString]. 'squeak' do: [:character	 Transcript show: character printString].	**do:** evaluates the block for each element of the array or string.
#(12 43 55 60) select: [:number	number even]' squeak' select: [:letter	letter isVowel]	**select:** evaluates the block for each element, and if the block returns true, will include the element in a new, returned string or array. Returns **(12 60)** and **'uea'**, respectively

There are many operations that **Collections**, such as arrays and strings share, besides the few examples above. You should look through the **Collections** class (and its subclasses) to find useful messages, using the tools described in Section 2.3. There are four general categories of messages that Collections understand:

- Messages for adding elements, such as **add:** (to add an element) and **addAll:** (to add all of the elements from one **Collection** instance into another).
- Messages for removing elements, such as **remove:** and **removeAll:**
- Messages for testing, such as **isEmpty** (to test if a Collection instance is empty), **includes:** (to test for the existence of a given element), and **occurrencesOf:** (to count the number of a given element in a collection.)
- Messages for enumerating elements, such as **do:** and **select:**, as well as **reject:** (to collect only the elements that do *not* match a given block), **detect:** (to find the first element that matches a block), and **collect:** (to apply a block to each element of an array and return a collection of the *values* from applying the block).

2.2.5 Files

Files are manipulated in Squeak via the **FileStream** class. A instance of **FileStream** is opened on a given file, and then access to that file is permitted as a **Stream**.

A **Stream** is a powerful kind of object. It allows access or creation of a large data structure, one element at a time. It reduces memory demands by not requiring the large data structure to be resident in memory all at one time.

Create a **FileStream** by opening it on a file with **fileNamed:**. The default, if you don't specify a complete path, is to create a file in the same directory as the current image:

```
aFile ← FileStream fileNamed: 'fred'.
aFile nextPutAll: 'This is a test.'.
aFile close.
```

You can read the file by, again, opening a FileStream on it. There are two ways of manipulating files. The first is just to read the whole thing in as a String, which can be useful for novices who know strings but not streams. **contentsOfEntireFile** will return a string with the file's contents, and will then close the file:

```
aFile ← FileStream fileNamed: 'fred'.
^aFile contentsOfEntireFile Does close for us.
```

Finally, you can also read a file element by element, by sending **next:** to the stream. For a text file, each element is a character:

```
aFile ← FileStream fileNamed: 'fred'.
[aFile atEnd] whileFalse:
    [Transcript show: aFile next printString].
Needed because can't open file twice.
```

This prints: **This$ is$ a test$**

Streams are actually general objects that do not have to be connected to files. A **ReadStream**, a **WriteStream**, and a **ReadWriteStream** (among others) are available when a fast and space-efficient data structure is needed for manipulating strings an element at a time. These understand the same **next** and **nextPutAll:** messages described earlier.

2.3 DOING "OBJECT" THINGS IN SQUEAK

If Squeak were yet another C or Pascal with an unusually consistent syntax, it would hardly be interesting. Squeak is much more than that, in several different ways. Some of the ways in which Squeak is different are simply due to Squeak's being interpretive in nature. The compiler is always available to you, e.g., **Compiler evaluate: '3 + 4'** returns 7 from a PrintIt.

Squeak's strength is deeper than its interpretive nature. This section introduces some of the powerful *language* features that were touched upon only briefly in the previous sections. In the sections to come, the *environment* of Squeak is introduced, as well as how you use that environment to learn Squeak.

2.3.1 Blocks

Unlike many other programming languages, blocks in Squeak are not just syntactic sugar that are gobbled up by the compiler. Blocks are really objects. (Again, *everything* is an object in Smalltalk.) They can be held in variables, and they can be passed as arguments. You can write code that will create and return blocks.

You can assign a block to a variable just as you would assign any other object to a variable. If you PrintIt on this statement, you will assign a block to the variable aBlock, but what will print won't look like much that makes sense to you (the printout will look pretty strange—you can just ignore it for now):

```
aBlock ← [Smalltalk beep].
```

Now, if you ask this block for its **value**, you will hear the beep. Do a PrintIt on this statement.

```
aBlock value.
```

We have also seen blocks that take an argument. Remember the blocks in the **to:do:** and **select:** messages? Those messages don't require a special syntax—they use ordinary blocks that accept arguments. We can create blocks that take arguments and store them in variables, too:

```
anArgumentBlock ← [:x | x + 1].
anArgumentBlock value: 5.
```

If you PrintIt on the above, you'll get **6** printed. We can create blocks that take many arguments. Besides **value** and **value:**, blocks also understand messages **value:value:** and **value:value:value:**.

Let's consider an example statement from the beginning of the chapter:

```
1 to: 10 do:
    [:index |
    anArray at: index
        put: (aValue * index)].
```

This statement is primarily a keyword message **to:do:** to the receiver object, integer 1. The message takes two arguments, the number 10 and the block of code, delimited by square brackets. The block of code is evaluated within the method **to:do:**, with an argument passed in. The input argument is bound to the *local variable* **index** (it could be named any valid variable name) in this block. The rest of the block is then executed. In this case, there is only a single statement, which fills each element of **anArray** with twice the value of its index (since **aValue** is set to 2 at the beginning of the example).

We can actually look at the implementation of **to:do:**. It's defined in the class **Number**, which is a *superclass* of **Integer**. The *method* that follows is the actual implementation of the control structure **to:do:**. **stop** and **aBlock** are the arguments to the method. You see that the method creates a local variable, **nextValue**. **nextValue** is originally set to **self**, which is a special variable that is bound to the receiver object. In the previous example, **self** is integer 1. Then there is a **whileTrue:** loop which says that while **nextValue** isn't at the stop value, the block takes its value with the **nextValue**. **nextValue** then increments. The code is as follows:

```
to: stop do: aBlock
        "Evaluate aBlock for each element of the interval (self to: stop by: 1)."
        | nextValue |
        nextValue := self.
        [nextValue <= stop]
            whileTrue:
                [aBlock value: nextValue.
                nextValue := nextValue + 1]
```

2.3.2. Variables and Memory

Variables in Smalltalk are different from those in many other languages. Variables are not objects *per se*. They are also not just memory locations. Variables *always* point to objects. An uninitialized variable is said to point to **nil**. Any reference to a variable is always a reference to the underlying object. Unlike C or other languages in which pointers can be manipulated, the variable itself can never be manipulated in Smalltalk.

The pointer-to-objects nature of Smalltalk variables also means that you can easily, even accidentally, have more than one variable point to the same object. PrintIt on the following:

```
a ← #(1 2 3).
b ← a.
a at: 2 put: 75.
^b
```

The result is **#(1 75 3)**. (Actually, the PrintIt shows just **(1 75 3)**, but it's actually an array.) In this example, **a** points to a literal array, **#(1 2 3)**. **b** is then set to **a**, which means it points to the same object. When **a**'s second element is changed, **b**'s second element is changed. If we wanted **b** to have a duplicate of **a**'s array, we could say **b ← a copy**. (If **a** was a complex object with internal instance variables that you *also* wanted to copy, you would use **deepCopy**.)

This raises the question of how one would find out if two variables point to the same object or just have the same values. If **a** has the same value as **b**, a=b will return true. But only if **a** and **b** are *actually* the same object will a==b return true. One = tests for equality, but == tests for *equivalence*.

For the most part, all memory management is automatic in Smalltalk. You cannot explicitly release memory. Instead, memory is allocated as needed, and is released when there are no further references to the memory. The process of reclaiming unused memory is called *garbage collection*, and it occurs in the *background* while other processing is going on. The programmer doesn't see memory allocation nor reclamation, nor does even the user see a pause for garbage collection while moving the mouse or clicking on buttons. The programmer just creates objects as needed. The programmer never sees an empty pointer reference nor a memory fault, which is the real benefit of Smalltalk garbage collection.

Garbage collection occurs when an object has nothing else pointing at it. If you have a workspace in which you have created several variables, all those variables point to objects that cannot be reclaimed by garbage collection. When you close the workspace, the workspace will be reclaimed, as will all the objects to which those variables pointed. Garbage collection doesn't happen immediately, though. Rather, it happens when an object is being allocated and not enough memory is available.

2.3.3 Creating Classes, Instances, and Methods

By the way, Squeak is an object-oriented programming language, as is Smalltalk, which Squeak is based on. You can create classes in it, as well as instances of those classes. You can define data that are possesed by all instances of the class. You can define methods in that class that all instances of that class will understand.

As one of our basic rules, all computation in Smalltalk proceeds from messages. It shouldn't be surprising that creating classes, instances, and methods is all done through messages, too.

The basic format of the message to create classes looks like this:

```
Object subclass: #NameOfClass
        instanceVariableNames: 'instVarName1 instVarName2'
        classVariableNames: 'ClassVarName1 ClassVarName2'
```

```
poolDictionaries: "
category: 'Collections-Abstract'
```

The message is sent to the superclass. In this case, it's already set up to be **Object**. Replace the **NameOfClass** with the name of the class that you want to create, but leave the # there. It's a necessary part of the syntax. Replace **instVarName1 instVarName2** with the names of any data variables that you want all instances of the new class to have. You very rarely need class variables, so you can just delete **ClassVarName1 ClassVarName2** — but leave the quotes! (Remember, this is a message, and a string must be passed in as an argument, even if it's an empty string.) Ignore pool dictionaries, too. Finally, you can structure your classes into groups by defining their category.

CAUTIONARY NOTE

Smalltalk *is* case sensitive. **Person** is not the same as **person**. Standard style in Smalltalk is that all classes and global variables are capitalized. All instance and local variables begin with a lowercase letter. Multiple words are combined in Smalltalk using the mixed-case notation, such as **NameOfClass** above.

Here is a filled-out message that creates a class called **Person**, in which instances of **Person** know their **name** and **address**:

```
Object subclass: #Person
        instanceVariableNames: 'name address'
        classVariableNames: "
        poolDictionaries: "
        category: 'People-Project'
```

If you select the above and PrintIt, you will create a new class in your image called Person. (The first time that you do something to create a new class or method in your image, you'll be prompted for your initials. It's okay—go ahead and enter them in. They're used to label your code when you work in groups.) To create a new **Person**, just send the message **new** to the class. **fred ← Person new** will create a new **Person** instance and put it in the variable **fred**.

Methods always have the same format:

```
messageForThisMethod
        Smalltalk-statements-to-executed-for-this-message
```

We can define a new method with a message to the class. Because the **compile:** message takes a string, we have to embed quotes in our string if we want them. We do that by duplicating the quotes. The classification string allows us to create groups of methods that have similar functionality. In this case, we'll call this a kind of **Greeting** method:

```
Person compile:
    'greeting
        Transcript show: "Hello world!";cr.'
        classified: 'Greeting'.
```

If we now PrintIt **fred greeting**, we'll get a **Hello world!** in our Transcript from **fred**.

The rule "Everything is an object" is still true with respect to classes. Classes *are* objects. Unlike object-oriented programming languages like Java and C++, classes in Smalltalk can understand messages that the instances of the class do *not* understand. For example, *new* is understood by classes in Smalltalk, but not by instances of those same classes.

It is also still true that "Everything is an instance of some class." Classes are instances of other classes called *metaclasses,* which, in turn, are subclasses of the class **Metaclass**. But metaclass programming can get pretty complicated, and we won't be getting into it in this book.

All of this said, nobody programs Squeak this way. Squeak provides wonderful tools for programming that don't require anyone to memorize the syntax of messages like these. In the following sections, the environment of Squeak becomes the focus.

CAUTIONARY NOTE

Somewhere in this process, when creating new classes and methods, Squeak will ask for your initials. Go ahead and enter them, then press Accept. Squeak labels new code in the changes file with your initials, so that when you share code, it's possible to see who wrote what.

2.3.4 The Squeak Model of Execution

Squeak doesn't work the way that you may think about programming languages working. In languages like C or Pascal, the mental model of how the language works is simpler. Simple statements (like assignments and if-thens) are executed serially. Control structures like while and for loops are well defined, with reserved functionality: Programmers cannot invent new control structures. There are function calls that can be mapped to either library-based functions or programmer-provided functions.

But a statement like **12 printString** cannot be explained by this kind of model. **printString** is not predefined in the language, and its meaning can be rewritten by the programmer. The mapping from the word **printString** to a piece of code that actually executes is not direct.

Here is a way to think about how Squeak executes statements:

- Arguments are evaluated first, following precedence rules.
- The message and its arguments are sent to the receiving object.
- The class for the receiving object is checked to see if it has an instance method for the given message. If so, the method is executed—following this same model of execution.
- If not, the parent class is checked, and then the parent's parent class, all the way up to the class **Object**.
- If a method is not found for the message, a **doesNotUnderstand**: message (with the original message, an instance of the class **Message**, as an argument) is sent to the original object. Interesting behavior can be created by *overriding* the default behavior of **doesNotUnderstand**:; the default behavior (in the method in **Object**) is to open an error notifier.
- If execution arrives at a *primitive*, the primitive is executed. Think of the primitive as a subroutine written in the native code of the processor. Primitives are less flexible than is Smalltalk code (e.g., you can't see their implementation or change it easily), but they're faster and they can do things that raw Smalltalk code cannot (e.g., manipulation of hardware devices).

As complex as this process seems, it's actually quick and quite flexible. It predefines very little and allows the programmer maximum flexibility. Even on relatively slow computers (e.g., Pentium I class), Squeak executes millions of bytecodes (machine-language operations of the virtual machine) per second and hundreds of thousands of message sends per second.

EXERCISES: ON SQUEAK THE LANGUAGE

1. Can you find the implementing method for **whileTrue**:? For integer addition?
2. Almost all statements in Smalltalk are of the form **recieverObject message**. We have seen two syntactic forms in Smalltalk that break that rule. What are they?
3. Write a piece of workspace code, using the language elements of the previous sections to do the following:
   (a) Replace all vowels in the string 'Squeak' with dashes.
   (b) Compute the average of a set of integers in an array.

2.4 USING SQUEAK

The first thing you need to do is get Squeak itself for your platform. You can get it from the CD included with this book, or from the Squeak website at http://www .squeak.org. Squeak is available for most desktop platforms (and a few palmtop and set-top-box platforms). You are going to need four files:

- A *sources* file. This is where all the source code for Squeak is stored. Theoretically, if you could compile all of the sources, you'd have an *image* file.
- An *image* file. This is the binary (bytecode) of the sources that you will execute.
- A *changes* file. This is where your code that you add to Squeak will go. It's kept separate from the sources file to separate the distribution from what individuals add. The most important thing about the changes file is that it saves *everything* that you write, as soon as you do it. It's automatic backup. If anything goes wrong (and yes, you can crash Squeak), none of your code is ever lost. It's stored, as text, in the changes file.
- An executable *virtual machine* (VM). This is machine-dependent and allows your machine to understand the Squeak bytecodes (the machine language of Squeak).

Don't be worried about having *extra* pieces, like a ReadMe file or additional files like *Squeak3D*. These aren't absolutely necessary to run Squeak, but they do provide useful features, like the 3-D graphics and text-to-speech facilities of Squeak.

Smalltalk has a different model of programming from what you might be used to, in comparison with more traditionally compiled languages such as C or Pascal. There are not separate code files lying around. (Actually, you can create code files for sharing with others, but they're only useful when you *file them in* for use in your image file.) Instead, you write your programs while executing in Squeak! Squeak is both a language and a complete development environment with editors, debuggers, inspectors, and other tools. As you work, your code gets stored to the changes file, and your binary object code gets added to the image in memory (which you need to save to disk in order to be able to reuse it later.)

Everything that you do goes into the changes file as soon as you do it: Every DoIt, every new class, every new method. This means that if you crash Squeak, your work isn't lost. It's probably in the changes file. The changes file is just a text file—you can copy out anything that you need in order to recover from a crash. From the Desktop Menu, you also have access to several changes utilities that let you look over your changes file and recover lost things. For example, select *Changes,* then *recent change log,* see all the changes from every quit or save that you've executed.

The sources file and the executable remain virtually unchanged when you use Smalltalk. (It is possible to save your changes into the sources file, but you rarely really need to.) *The image and the changes file, however, always need to be manipulated in pairs.* You can create yourself a new image (by doing *Save As* from the Desktop Menu), you will also create a changes file of the same name at the same time. It makes sense that these two files have to be kept in synch. The image file is the binary executable of the virtual machine. The changes file (with the sources) is the source for that executable.

You start the VM with the image file in whatever way works for your platform. On Macs and Windows, you can probably just double-click the image file, or else drag it onto the VM file. On UNIX boxes, you'll type a command like **squeak squeak .image**. Soon, you'll see something like the screen shown in Figure 2–8.

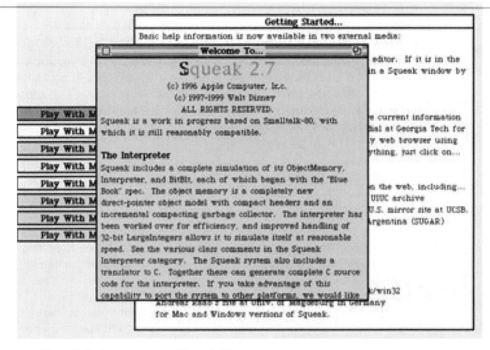

Figure 2–8   Start-up screen of Squeak 2.7

CAUTIONARY NOTE

Always keep a "fresh" image available on your disk. Save your image as a new name, and use the new image. That way, if you crash your image, you can always recover the "fresh" image. When you know that (a) all your text is always saved and (b) you can quickly start over in a new image, you feel much freer to experiment. Later chapters will explain how to recover source code from a "broken" image.

This is Squeak. Some of the windows look obviously like windows. Others are collapsed windows showing just the title bars. Click the boxes in the right corner of the title bar to toggle expansion of the window. The windows in the initial Squeak display contain interesting demos, information about Squeak, and other neat things. Do play with them at some point.

Click anywhere on the desktop where there is no window, and you will get a menu that looks like Figure 2–2 at the beginning of this chapter. This is where you create new windows and start activities in Squeak.

A brief tour of the menu items from the Desktop Menu:

- *Keep this menu up* creates a window with the same items, so that they're always available.

- The project items let you jump between projects. Projects have their own set of menus, and they remember in a special way all the code entered into them, so you can save out all the code from a single project regardless of how many different classes you worked on.

- If the display becomes messed up due to experimentation, *restore display* will fix it.

- *Open...* allows you to open a variety of tools and projects.

- *Windows...* provides tools for managing windows, collapsing windows, and re-opening them.

- *Help...* has a grab bag of tools and options. *Update code from server* under the Help menu downloads the latest updates for your version of Squeak (and even lets you upgrade to a new version) from a central server. *Command key help* provides a list of all the special keys available when you're text-editing, including font selection and options for creating clickable active text. *Preferences* lets you set options like always showing scrollbars (instead of the default pop-up scrollbars).

- *Appearance...* lets you predefine things like the color of the windows in Squeak.

- *Do...* provides a set of easily accessible commands to execute. This set of commands is easily user-definable, so you can create your own "menu items" under this menu.

- *Save* saves the current state of your image into your current image file. *SaveAs* prompts you for a name (e.g., *mySqueak*) under which to save an image and changes file. *Save and Quit* saves and then quits. *Quit* just ends your session.

2.4.1 Starting a New Project

You should start working in a new project, without all of these windows cluttering things up, but without having to close any of them and thus lose their contents. Choose *Open...* and a menu item, and then *Project (MVC)*. A small window appears on your desktop. Click and hold in that window, and you'll get an option to *Enter* the project. Do so.

All the windows go away! Actually, they're back in your parent project. Here in this project, you can set up windows to your liking without disturbing the others. You can have as many projects as your memory will allow, and nest them however you like (e.g., all off on the toplevel project, one inside another, whatever). You can always get back out by choosing *Previous Project* from the Desktop Menu (or World Menu, if you're in Morphic). Go ahead and do that. Name your project by clicking on the current name of the window, typing a new name, then hitting return. Re-enter your project.

You do your programming in Squeak in a set of windows that serve as *browsers* and other facilities. We've already seen Transcripts and Workspaces. Let's open a

---

SIDE NOTE

You could use *Project (Morphic)*, and all would work well for most readers.
MVC is an older interface infrastructure. It works better on older and slower
computers. Morphic is the newer interface infrastructure, and it's where
the future of Squeak lies. The differences between MVC and Morphic are
described more in Chapter 5.

Transcript for displaying text in. Choose *Open...* then *Transcript* (Figure 2–5). You can
drag around the lower right-hand corner of the window to resize it to your liking.

It's easy to write some code that will put something in the Transcript. Choose
Open... again and open a *Workspace*. The workspace is basically a blank text editor.
Type into your workspace:

```
Transcript show: 'Hello, World!'.
Transcript cr.
```

Select those lines of text after you type them. We have been using only the
PrintIt option to execute code, but there are several ways of getting the lines to be
executed:

- On a Macintosh, type Command-D for "DoIt." On a Windows-based computer, type Alt-D.
- If you have a two- or three-button mouse, press and hold the second (middle,
  if you have three buttons) button on your mouse inside the workspace. You'll get
  a text-editing menu with options to "find" text and such. One of these options
  is "Do It". Select: above that. If you have a Macintosh with a one-button
  mouse, press the Option key as you click your mouse button.

You should see the text **Hello, World!** appear in the Transcript.

You will want to save the state of your session with Smalltalk occasionally, so
that you don't lose things in case of a crash. If you go back to the desktop menu, you
will see options to **Save** (saves your current image so that all windows and everything
else will be just as they are now when you restart the image), **Save As** (save the image
to a new name), and **Save and Quit** (saves the image, and then quits Squeak). If you
ever have a crash *before* you save your image, don't worry! Everything you do is always
stored in text form to the changes file. From the desktop menu, you can choose
changes, and you will find a variety of methods for looking through the changes file
and recovering things that were lost, because the system crashed or because you for-
got to save, or for whatever reason.

The changes file has been an absolute necessity for Smalltalk programmers
over the years. Everything in Smalltalk is written in Smalltalk, including things like
the definitions of windows, integers, and other basic building blocks of the system. A
programmer can easily do something that makes the image absolutely unusable (say,

---

CAUTIONARY NOTE:

If you trash your image, you can grab the text of your work out of the old changes file and file it into the new image. A good old-fashioned text editor works fine—simply select the code you want to recover (include the !'s as delimiters), copy it into a new file, then fileIn the new file from the FileList. You can also *browse code* or *browse changes* from the FileList when a *.changes* file is selected—beware, though, that it takes a long time to process a large changes file for browsing.

If you're looking at code in your image and you see "t1, t2, t3" variables instead of your variable names, your changes file has been damaged. Somehow, the connection between the image and the changes file has been broken (e.g., perhaps you were using Squeak across a network and there was a network glitch). FileOut your code (or recover it from the changes file, where the variable names still exist) and move to your backup image.

---

delete the Integer class). The changes file is what makes sure that work isn't lost even if the image is now trashed.

2.4.2 Extended Example: Muppets in Squeak

Let's create some classes and a small example as a way into Squeak programming. You will do most of your programming in Squeak within a System Browser (Figure 2–9). A browser lets you inspect the code that is currently executing within your image. Choose *Open...* and *Browser* from your desktop menu.

- *Class categories* do not mean anything in terms of the Squeak language. They are just shelves for grouping classes.
- *Classes* are important to Squeak. These are the objects that create instances for you and which serve as the template for your objects. Think of a class as an *object factory*. A class creates objects of a particular kind, with particular factory settings:
- *Method categories* (also called *protocols*) group methods into types: For printing, for accessing data in the object, for iterating, and so on.
- Finally, *methods* are the units used for executable Smalltalk code.
- Classes actually serve as the entry points for two different kinds of methods. There are methods that the class itself understands. **new** is a good example of a method that the class itself understands. There are methods that instances of the class understand, such as **greeting** and **do:** The instance/class buttons in the browser allow you to switch between the sets of methods associated with a class. *Almost always* you will want to have the instance button selected.

You usually start a new programming task in Squeak with a new class category. With your mouse over the class-category pane, press your middle mouse button (the

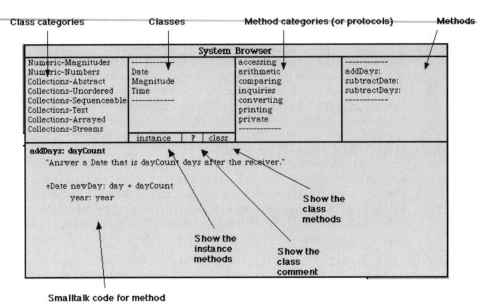

Figure 2–9   Annotated System Browser

CAUTIONARY NOTE

A very common bug in early Squeak programming is to create a class category (say, **Person**) and find that Squeak complains when you try to execute **Person new**. A class category is *not* a class.

---

right button on a two-button mouse, or option-click on a one-button Macintosh mouse). Over the class-category pane, you get the option to create a new class category. Name it something like *Muppet Classes.* (See Figure 2–10.)

The original Smalltalkers also got confused talking about which mouse button was which, so they came up with a set of position-independent terms for the mouse button. The pointing mouse button is called the "*red*" button, the middle mouse button is called the "*yellow*" button, and the rightmost mouse button is called the "*blue*" button. The red button is always used for pointing, and the yellow button brings up a context-sensitive menu that is dependent on where you're pointing. The blue button typically brings up the menu for manipulating the window in MVC and is used for selecting graphical objects in Morphic.

Operating System	Red Button	Yellow Button	Blue Button
Macintosh	Mouse click	Option-click	Command-click
Windows	Left-click	Right-click	Alt-left-click
UNIX	Left button	Middle button	Right button

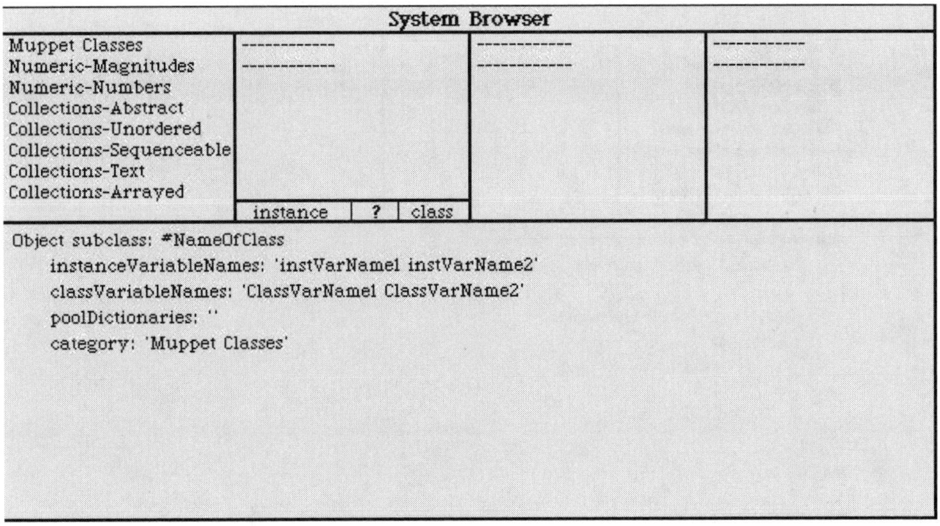

```
                        System Browser
 Muppet Classes       ----------    ----------    ----------
 Numeric-Magnitudes   ----------    ----------
 Numeric-Numbers
 Collections-Abstract
 Collections-Unordered
 Collections-Sequenceable
 Collections-Text
 Collections-Arrayed
                      instance  ?  class
 Object subclass: #NameOfClass
     instanceVariableNames: 'instVarName1 instVarName2'
     classVariableNames: 'ClassVarName1 ClassVarName2'
     poolDictionaries: ''
     category: 'Muppet Classes'
```

Figure 2–10　A Browser ready to create a new class

When you select the Muppet Classes category, the browser displays a template for creating a new class (Figure 2–10). This template is the same message from back in Section 3.3, *Creating Classes, Instances, and Methods.* You don't ever have to type the message. Simply select a class category, and the template is provided for you to fill in.

As we saw earlier, you literally just fill in the obvious spots on this template to define the class you want. Leave **Object** as the first word—that's the *superclass.* Object is a very frequent superclass. (As in the basic rules, *every class is a subclass in Smalltalk.*) Change the **NameOfClass** to be **Muppet.** You don't need any class-variable names (**classvariablesNames:** in the template), so *delete* everything inside those quotes, but leave the quotes themselves. The *instance variables* are the names for the data that all objects of this type will have. Select everything inside the single quotes on the line **instanceVariableNames:** and type simply **name.** This will let every new Muppet have a name.

To get Squeak to compile the definition you have created, simply choose "Accept" from the text pane where you typed your definition (or type Alt-S/Apple-S to accept or *save*). You will now have a **Muppet** class appear in the class list.

Before we do anything else, we can create Muppet instances, and they know how to do things. Type into your workspace:

```
kermit := Muppet new.
Transcript show: kermit printString
```

Select this and DoIt. The Transcript will now read **a Muppet,** because the default way to print an object is simply to give its class name. Kermit knew how to respond to **printString** because Kermit is an instance of **Muppet,** and **Muppet** is a subclass of **Object.** Everything that **Objects** know, **Muppets** know. **Object** provides a method for **printString,** so Kermit knows how to **printString.**

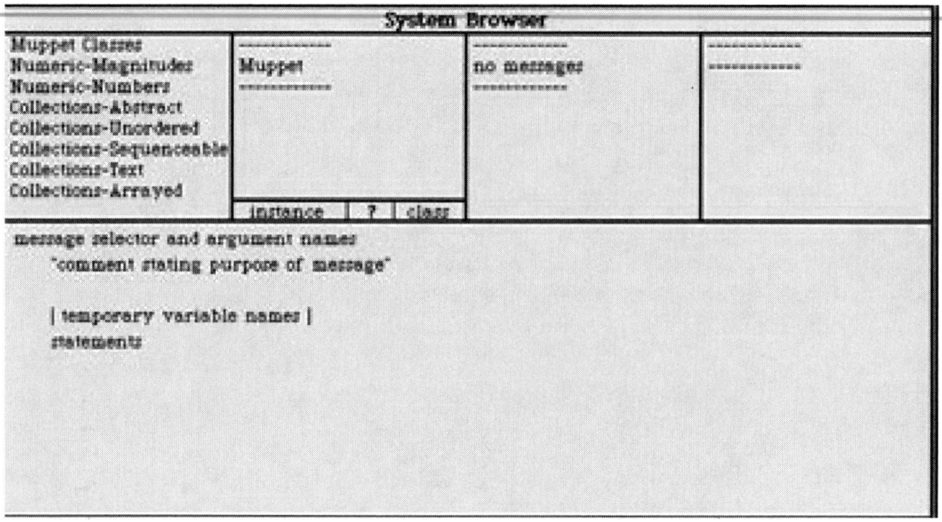

Figure 2–11 Browser with method template

Now let's actually teach Muppets to do something. Select the default message category **no messages**; a method template will appear in the text pane. (See Figure 2–11.)

Now you edit the template to create a method. You edit just as you would any other text in any word processor: Select text you want to change and start typing. We are creating a method to have the **Muppet** greet us in the Transcript. The first method we'll create is to return a general greeting. Don't worry about trying to get the boldface "greeting." Squeak will boldface that for you when you save. The code is as follows:

greeting
      "Return a predefined greeting"
      ^'Hello there!'

To get Squeak to compile this method, as well as store the object code into the image and store the source code into the changes file, all you do is *accept* the method. Use the context-sensitive menu (remember that it's attached to the *yellow* button) to choose *Accept*. (On a Mac, command-S will also accept. On Windows, alt-S will accept.) You will see the method name **greeting** appear in the rightmost pane of the System Browser.

The first line of the method is just the message selector, **greeting**. The second line is a comment explaining the method. The third line is the one and only statement in this method. It says to return to whoever sent this message with the **String** object **'Hello there!'**.

Next we want to define a method to use the greeting. You can either select the method category again, to bring up a new method template, or simply select the greeting method, and type this in instead:

greet
> "Have the Muppet greet us to the Transcript."
> Transcript show: self greeting; cr.

Accept this one, too. You now have two methods for **Muppets**. **greet** is the method that will call the greeting method and actually display things to the Transcript. **self** is a special reference in Smalltalk. It always refers to the object that received the original message that led to this method's being executed.

self won't always be an instance of **Muppet**. Let's say that you create a subclass of **Muppet** called **FrogMuppet**. An instance of **FrogMuppet** might have a different greeting from that of a **Muppet**. By sending the message **self greeting**, we ask the instance to give us its greeting. In this way, the subclass's (**FrogMuppet's**) method would *override* the one in the superclass (**Muppet**).

We can now use these methods. Try typing this in the workspace and DoIt.

kermit := Muppet new.
kermit greet.

You'll see the greeting appear in the Transcript. Here is exactly what happened in those two lines that were just executed:

1. **Muppet** was asked to create a new instance. It doesn't know how (it has no class methods right now, let alone one for **new**), so it passes the request up to its superclass. **Object** does know how to **new**, so by inheritance, **Muppet** does, too. A new instance of **Muppet** is returned.
2. **kermit** is a variable that is bound to a new instance of **Muppet**.
3. The new instance of **Muppet** is asked to **greet**.
4. The **greet** method will send out to the Transcript whatever **self greeting** returns.
5. The message **greeting** is sent to **self**, and it returns '**Hello there!**'.
6. The **cr** message puts a carriage return to the Transcript

We need some ability to set the name of the Muppet, if we ever want to use the Muppet's name. No internal data of an object can be manipulated directly. If we want any method external to Muppet or piece of code in a workspace to set the name of a Muppet, we must have a method to do it, Select all that text again, and type this one:

name: aString
> "Set the name of the Muppet"
> name := aString.

We could also define a method to allow an external object query, the value of an object's name. That method would look like this:

name
> "Get the name of the Muppet"
> ^name

Smalltalk has no problem distinguishing between **name:** (which takes an argument) and **name** (which does not). A colon is a significant character in the name of the method. It indicates where arguments appear in the message: A colon appears at the end of each keyword that precedes an argument.

Now, let's redefine **greet** so that it presents the name, too. Reselect the greet method so that it's showing in the Browser, enter the following code (just add the last line), and then reaccept. A new definition of **greet** will then be entered into the system:

greet
```
    "Have the Muppet greet us to the Transcript."
    Transcript show: self greeting; cr.
    Transcript show: 'My name is ', name; cr.
```

Accept this last one. Now you have enough for a fully functioning Muppet! In a workspace, type this:

```
| someMuppet |
someMuppet := Muppet new.
someMuppet name: 'Elmo'.
someMuppet greet.
```

If you don't have a Transcript open, open a new one. Then select all the code in your workspace and choose DoIt from the yellow button menu (or type Command-D on a Mac, or Alt-D on Windows). You should see Elmo introduce himself and greet you in the Transcript. (You could have also used PrintIt, but we don't care about the return value from this workspace code.)

There are several ways to save your work in Smalltalk:

- You should frequently save your image from the Desktop Menu. That writes out a new images file.
- You can also fileOut your code. A fileOut is a text-only representation of your code. It can be filed back in from the **File List**, which can be opened from the *Open...* menu (use the yellow button menu on a filename). Wander through the System Browser to try the yellow button menu over various panes. You'll find that you can fileOut a whole class category, just a class, just a single-method category of a class, or even a single method. The best reason for doing your work inside of a project is that you can fileOut all the changes made within a project, in any class or category—take a look at a *Simple Change Sorter* or *Dual Change Sorter* from the *Changes...* menu.

EXERCISE: ON MUPPETS

4. If Kermit was actually an instance of **FriendlyMuppet** (a subclass of **Muppet**) whose greeting returned 'Well, Howdy!', how would the above chain of events change? Create

---

HISTORICAL NOTE

It's quite appropriate for this first example of using Squeak to involve the Muppets. The Xerox PARC *Alto* was developed to be the "interim Dynabook"—a place to explore Dynabook ideas until the hardware could catch up. The very first test of the Alto was to move the image of Cookie Monster across the cool new bitmap display.

FriendlyMuppet as a subclass of **Muppet**, create a new greeting method, and try the above example with Kermit as a **FriendlyMuppet**.

5. Not all Muppets greet you with "Hello there!" Kermit, being an especially friendly Muppet, would say "Hey-Ho!" Oscar, being an especially grouchy Muppet, would say "Go Away!" Create the subclasses **FriendlyMuppet** and **GrouchyMuppet** with Muppet as the superclass. By adding a **greeting** method in each (thus *overriding* the one in Muppet), we can specialize the greeting for each kind of Muppet.

6. Our method category name has been turned into "As Yet Unclassified" instead of "No messages," which is not a very useful name. You can select the name and change it using the context-sensitive menus. There may not be a single name that classifies all three of these methods. Both **greet** and **greeting** are about "Greeting," but **name:** is about "Accessing" (data). If you create new categories, you can reorganize methods to make sense. Use the yellow-button menus in the message-protocols pane to add new categories. Create at least the Accessing method category. Use the *Reorganize* menu item to change the destination of the messages. When you do, you get a list of methods and categories in the code pane. Copy paste until the method names are in the desired method categories:

```
('accessing')
('as yet unclassified' greet greeting name:)
```

7. We didn't implement the message **new** for **Muppet**. Can you find the method that is processing it?

8. Squeak has a case statement (**caseOf:**), but we can also create one ourselves. Build one that can be used like this:

```
#(    ('a' [Transcript show: 'An a was input'])
      ('b' [Transcript show: 'A b was input']))
      switchOn: 'a'
```

In this example, if the input is 'a', the first block is executed. If it's 'b', the second block is executed. Note that the parentheses inside the #( ) will define subarrays.

2.5 TOOLS AND STRATEGIES: FINDING MORE IN SQUEAK

That's your whole introduction to using Squeak! There are lots of external resources to help you in learning to Squeak, like the Squeak Swiki at http://minnow.cc.gatech.edu/squeak.1 and the Squeak Documentation website at http://minnow.cc.gatech.edu/squeakDoc.1.

But there is also a great deal of internal support within Squeak. There aren't big books of API (Application Programmer Interface) calls for Squeak. First, they would do little good because you change them all the time—there's nothing hidden or unmodifiable in Squeak. But more importantly, it's pretty easy to find anything you want to find in Squeak.

Here is a collection of sample questions or situations that Squeak can help you with. These are useful in demonstrating several of Squeak's tools for helping programmers find things.

2.5.1 Finding Classes: There has got to be a Window or a TextField class around here somewhere. Where is it?

There are several ways of trying to find classes like that:

- If you know the name of the class, type it anywhere (say, in a Workspace window), double-click on it to select it, then choose *Browse* from the yellow-button menu (Command-B for Macs, Alt-B for Windows). A System Browser will open with the correct class selected.
- If you have a System Browser open, you can do a *Find Class* from the yellow-button menu over the class categories list. Type the name of the class (or even a portion of a name, like "window"), and you'll get a list of names to choose from.

But what if you have no idea what the name of the class is? There are two strategies you can use to find it. First, walk down all the categories in the class-category list. There aren't that many, so it won't take you too long, but it will give you a sense of the kinds of classes located under each kind of category.

The second strategy is to find an instance of the kind of thing you want and to *inspect* it. Every object understands the message **inspect**. If you can write a Smalltalk expression that is the kind of thing that you want, then you can inspect it. Try typing **Transcript** in any window, selecting it, and then choosing *Inspect* from the yellow-button menu (also Command-I on Macs, Alt-I on Windows). Equivalently, you might also DoIt on **Transcript inspect**.

You get an inspector window displaying the class name of the instance (**Transcripts** are an instance of **TranscriptStream**) and displaying all the instance variables of the instance. (See Figure 2–12.) You can click on each of the instance variables to see its value. You can also ask to inspect any one of these using the yellow-button menu. You may also choose *browse class* to see the class of the data in the instance variable. (Remember, *everything* is an object, so even data in instance variables are objects, so they have classes, too.)

If you did this example and are now inspecting Transcript, you can choose **self**

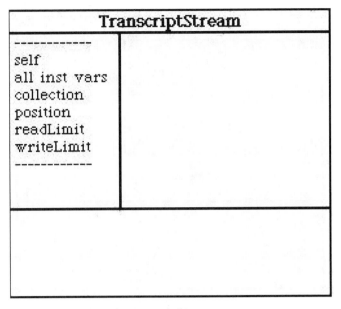

Figure 2–12   An inspector window

and choose *browse class* from the yellow-button menu. You'll get a different kind of browser from the System Browser seen earlier. The class browser works the same way as the System Browser: For example, you can add new methods from here. From there, you can see how Transcript is implemented and dig further.

Inspectors are *amazingly* powerful tools for debugging (Figure 2–13). Play with some of the yellow-button menus in the inspector. As an example of a powerful tool, you can find all references to the object you're inspecting, which can be very useful when trying to figure out why an object hasn't been garbage-collected yet. Also, the bottom pane of the inspector is actually a workspace where **self** means the object being inspected! You can send messages to the object while debugging, like **self printString**, by typing them into the bottom pane and doing PrintIt.

2.5.2 Exploring Objects: I'm exploring a complicated object, and now I've got a bazillion inspectors all over the screen. Is there some other way to explore an object?

A new kind of inspector available in Morphic is the Object Explorer (by Bob Arning, one of the Open Source contributors to Squeak.) Instead of **inspect**, send the message **explore** to any object. The Object Explorer provides an outline view on any new object.

For example, if you wanted to explore how a literal-array object is parsed, you might DoIt:

#(123 'a' (a b c) 34.5) explore

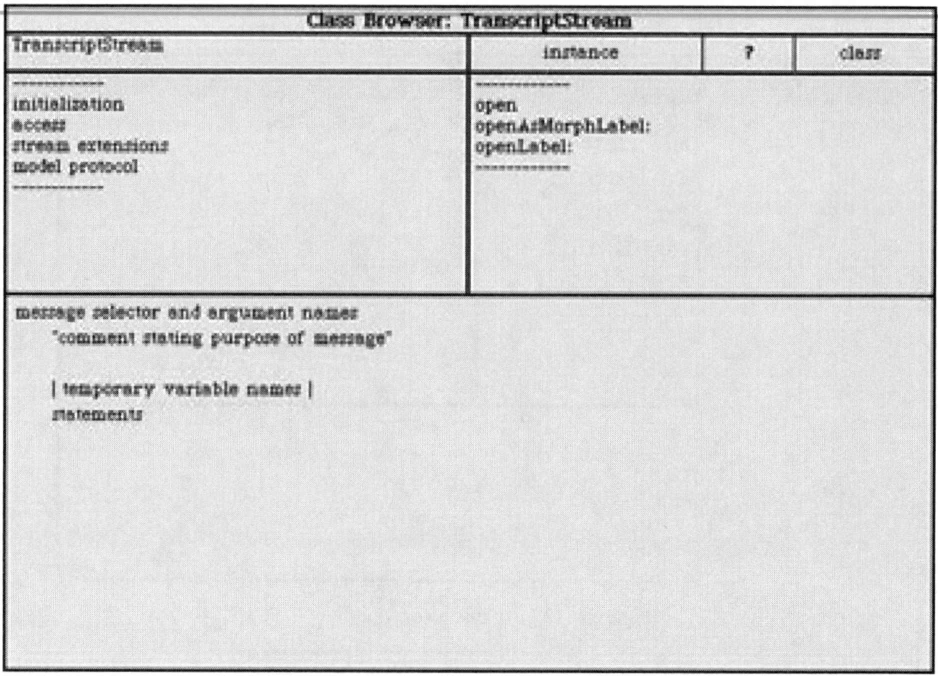

Figure 2–13   A Class Browser on Transcript's Class

The result (seen in Figure 2–14) is an outline on the original object. Selecting (clicking) any object allows the user to bring up a yellow-button menu that allows the user to open a traditional inspector or a new explorer on the selected item. A traditional inspector allows you to (as seen earlier) find the class of the object and browse that class.

2.5.3 Finding Methods: I remember there's a way of getting an element, 'at'-something, but I can't find it.

Squeak contains a very powerful tool for finding methods in the system. It's called a *Method Finder*. You can open one from the *Open...* menu on the main Desktop Menu. The bottom pane gives the instructions for its use. (See Figure 2–15.)

If you remember part of a method's name, but not the whole thing, just type the part you remember in the upper pane, then choose accept (Command-S on Macs, Alt-S for Windows). The list on the left shows all method names (also called *selectors*) that contain the accepted name. Selecting one of those shows all the specific classes that implement that selector (on the right). Choose one of the items in the right list to open up a browser on that method.

Even more powerful is the find-by-example aspect of the Method Finder. If you know that a method must exist for a set of inputs and an output, you can use the Method Finder to find the method. You simply type the inputs and the output,

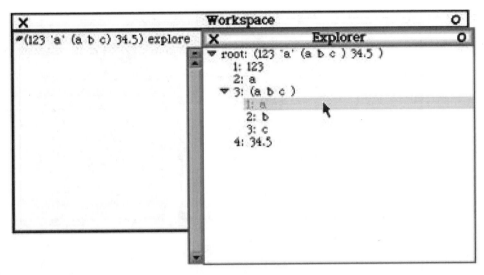

Figure 2–14   Object Explorer on a Literal Array

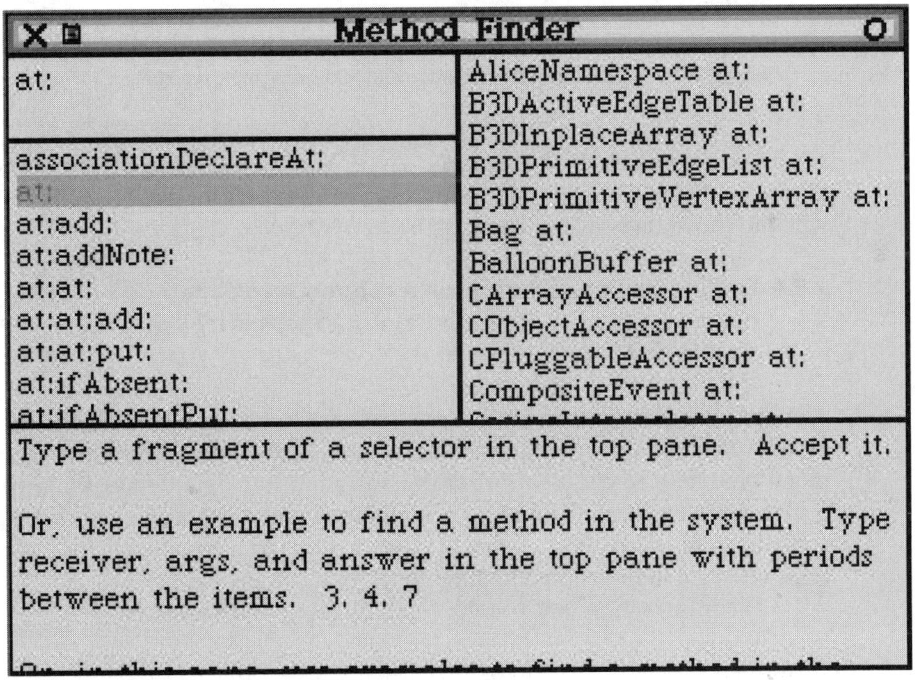

Figure 2–15   Using the Method Finder with Part of a Message

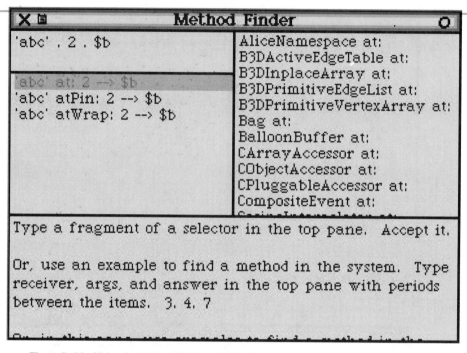

Figure 2–16 Using the Method Finder with find-by-example searching

separated by periods, in the top pane. Accept, and the selector list will show all those messages that will actually do the operation you describe! **'abc' . 2 . $b** as the input will find the **at:** message (Figure 2–16).

2.5.4 Finding Implementors: I see a reference to a method named findTokens: (or whatever). Where is it? What does it do?

The easiest way to figure out what anything is, from methods to class names to globals to even constructs like $c, is to select it and choose *explain* from the yellow-button menu (you have to choose *more* at the bottom of the first menu.) What you will get is a text description of the thing you selected and a piece of executable Smalltalk code that you can DoIt to open a browser for more information. The text is inserted right after the item you had highlighted.

The information that you get for explaining **findTokens:** is

```
"findTokens: is a message selector which is defined in these classes (String )."
Smalltalk browseAllImplementorsOf: #findTokens:
```

The *explain* option leaves the text highlighted; you can just hit Delete to get rid of the text, or DoIt to execute the command that opens a browser.

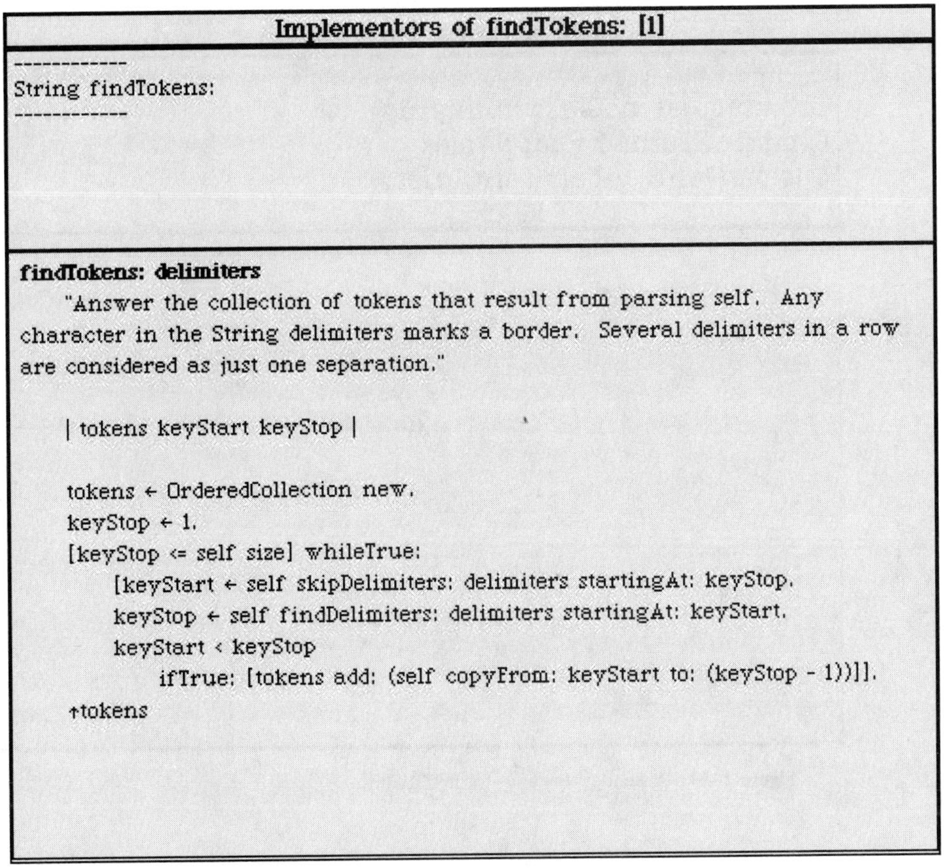

```
Implementors of findTokens: [1]

-----------
String findTokens:
-----------




findTokens: delimiters
    "Answer the collection of tokens that result from parsing self. Any
character in the String delimiters marks a border. Several delimiters in a row
are considered as just one separation."

    | tokens keyStart keyStop |

    tokens ← OrderedCollection new.
    keyStop ← 1.
    [keyStop <= self size] whileTrue:
        [keyStart ← self skipDelimiters: delimiters startingAt: keyStop.
        keyStop ← self findDelimiters: delimiters startingAt: keyStart.
        keyStart < keyStop
            ifTrue: [tokens add: (self copyFrom: keyStart to: (keyStop - 1))]].
    ↑tokens
```

Figure 2–17 An Implementors browser for findTokens:

The next-easiest way is to simply select the method and choose *Implementors...* from the yellow-button menu (Command-M on Macs, Alt-M on Windows).

We can see in Figure 2–17 that there is only one class that implements a method for the message **findTokens:**, and that is **String**. We can see the comment for the code, and the actual code, here.

It should be noted that anywhere you can see a method, you can edit a method. If you wanted to change **findTokens:**, you could simply edit it from this window and accept. All browsers work as well as any browser.

2.5.5 Finding Senders: That's what findTokens: does. Who uses it?

Select the selector message anywhere it appears, and use the yellow-button menu *Senders...* (Command-N on Macs, Alt-N on Windows). It turns out that **findTokens:** is a very popular method that is used frequently to break strings into arrays of tokens (Figure 2–18).

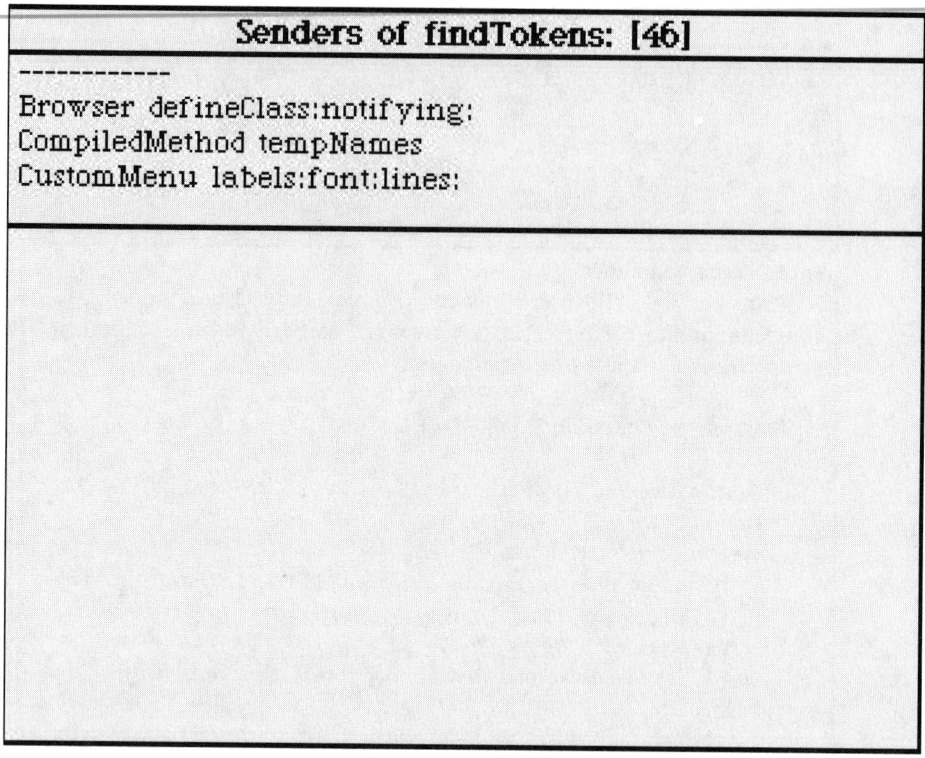

```
         Senders of findTokens: [46]
------------
Browser defineClass:notifying:
CompiledMethod tempNames
CustomMenu labels:font:lines:
```

Figure 2–18 A Senders browser for findTokens:

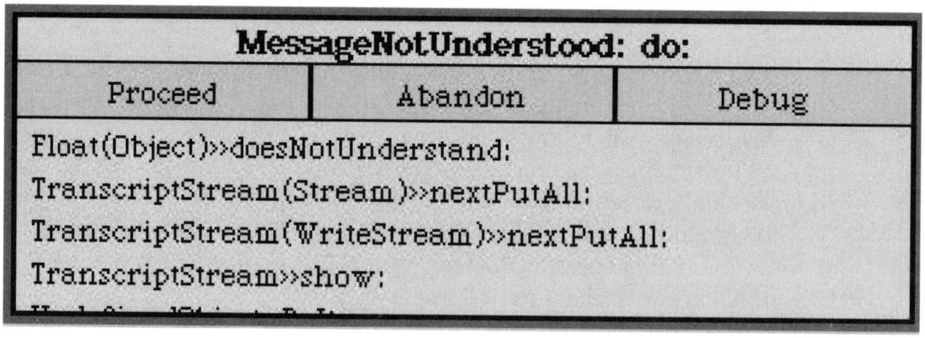

```
         MessageNotUnderstood: do:
    Proceed    |    Abandon    |    Debug
Float(Object)>>doesNotUnderstand:
TranscriptStream(Stream)>>nextPutAll:
TranscriptStream(WriteStream)>>nextPutAll:
TranscriptStream>>show:
```

Figure 2–19 An Error Notifier in Squeak 2.7

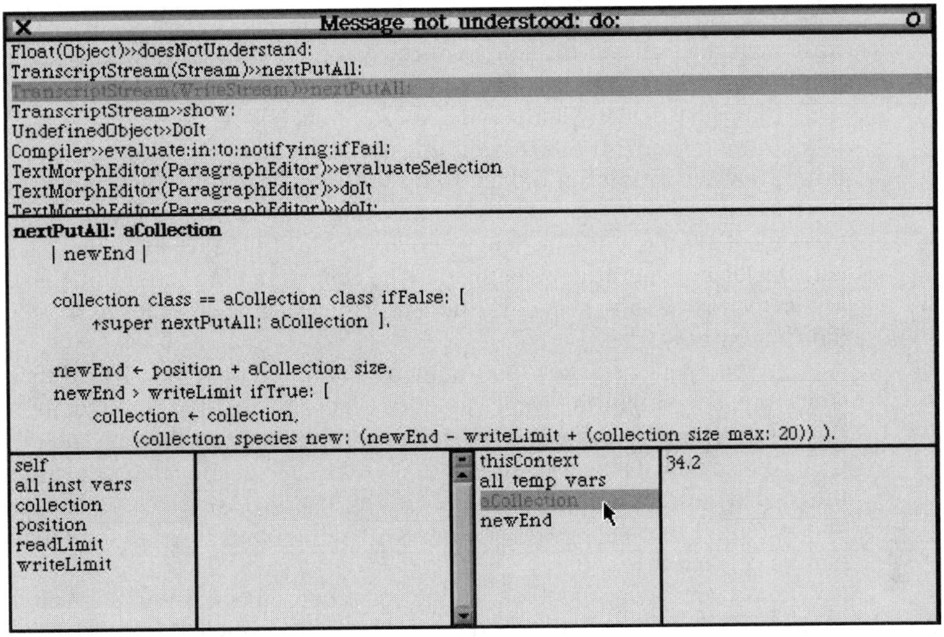

```
✕                    Message not understood: do:                          ○
Float(Object)»doesNotUnderstand:
TranscriptStream(Stream)»nextPutAll:
TranscriptStream(WriteStream)»nextPutAll:
TranscriptStream»show:
UndefinedObject»DoIt
Compiler»evaluate:in:to:notifying:ifFail:
TextMorphEditor(ParagraphEditor)»evaluateSelection
TextMorphEditor(ParagraphEditor)»doIt
TextMorphEditor(ParagraphEditor)»doIt:
nextPutAll: aCollection
    | newEnd |

    collection class == aCollection class ifFalse: [
        ↑super nextPutAll: aCollection ].

    newEnd ← position + aCollection size.
    newEnd > writeLimit ifTrue: [
        collection ← collection,
            (collection species new: (newEnd - writeLimit + (collection size max: 20)) ).
self                            │ thisContext          │34.2
all inst vars                   │ all temp vars        │
collection                      │ aCollection          │
position                        │ newEnd           ▶   │
readLimit                       │                      │
writeLimit                      │                      │
```

Figure 2–20   Squeak's Debugger

2.5.6 Debugging: I can't figure out what my code is doing! I've got an error, but it makes no sense to me.

Squeak errors are often hard to figure out because the error message expects that you understand the basic notions of Squeak. Fortunately, the debugging tools in Squeak are excellent.

Let's say that you executed something like **Transcript show: 34.2**. You will get a notifier like the one shown in Figure 2–19.

This can be a confusing message because you don't see that you sent the message **do:** anywhere. But remember that your basic message-send, **show:**, led to many other message-sends. (See Section 2.3.4.) It makes sense if you dig deeper. **show:** is meant only to take strings, and you handed it a floating-point number.

We can see this directly. Choose *debug* from the notifier's title bar, or use the yellow-button menu from within the notifier to choose proceed. A screen like that in Figure 2–20 will appear.

The top list pane is showing you the backtrace of all methods currently in execution when the error occurred. If you select one of those, you will actually see the method in the middle pane, with the currently executing message selected. The bottom sets of panes are actually inspectors. The left two lower panes are showing the inspector on the object receiving the message. The right two lower panes are showing the inspector on the context of the method, i.e., the local variables and the arguments to the method.

The top message in the list is actually the message that generated the debugger window, so that's never the source of the error. Instead, that's where this debugger window was generated. (Recall, all of Squeak is written in Squeak.)

In this particular example, we can see what happened pretty easily. Five messages down is the DoIt that started this whole process. We can see (fourth message down) that the Transcript did try to do the **show:** message. But take a look at the third message down, the **nextPutAll:**. Selecting that shows the problem. **nextPutAll:** expects a **Collection, aCollection**, as an argument. In the lower right panes, we can actually look at the variables defined in the context of this method. **aCollection** is the argument passed in to **show:**. It's not surprising that when **34.2** was asked to **do:**, it didn't know how.

If you open the yellow-button menu in the top pane, you'll find that you can **step** (next line within the same method, *whichever* method is currently selected), **send** (following a call into a lower message), **proceed** (go through the code at full speed outside the debugger), and other options for executing the code slowly. Again, the code in the middle pane is like code in any browser: You can actually change code and recompile during debugging, then continue stepping through the code after you make a correction.

If you are having trouble tracking your code, you can insert **self halt** anywhere in your code to force an error notifier and thus allow you into the debugger. Once in the debugger, you can step through your code, using the inspectors to check the values of things as you go.

2.5.7 Learning to Use a Class:
What-all does `String` or do other classes understand?

There are a couple of ways to look at what a class knows how to do. From a System Browser with String selected, open the yellow button menu over the class list pane. You'll see an option to *spawn protocol*. This menu item opens up a browser that shows all the messages that String understands from all of its inherited classes. (See Figure 2–21.)

For classes that have lots of parents and lots of methods, the protocol list can be long and intimidating. But it is probably the best browser for seeing *everything* that a class understands. Another useful option from the basic system browser is to choose *spawn hierarchy*.

The hierarchy browser shows you only the classes that are parent (and children, if any) classes of the selected class. You can wander up and down the hierarchy to look at all the methods that the selected class understands (Figure 2–22).

2.5.8 There seem to be a huge number of command keys.
Is there a listing somewhere of all of them?

Yes—under the *Help* menu from the Desktop Menu, there is an item called *Command-Key Help*. That lists all of them. You should definitely look at the list—there are a lot of powerful ones that you may not expect (like W for deleting the preceding word, and Y for swapping characters). A brief summary of the most often used ones follows:

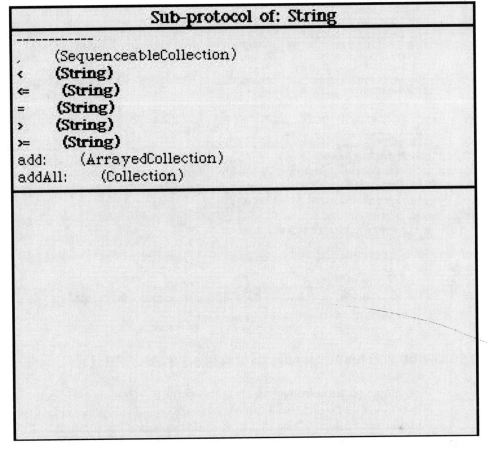

Figure 2–21 A Protocol Browser on String

Command Key	Meaning
a	Select all
b	Browse it (selection is a class name)
c	Copy
d	Do it (selection is a valid expression)
f	Find
g	Find again
i	Inspect it (selection is a valid expression)
k	Set font
m	Implementors of it (selection is a message selector)
n	Senders of it (selection is a message selector)
p	Print it (selection is a valid expression)
s	Save (i.e. accept)
v	Paste
w	Delete preceding word
x	Cut
z	Undo

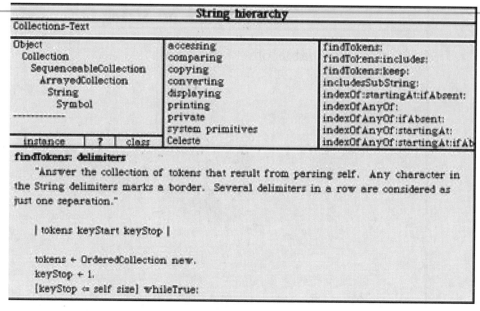

Figure 2–22   A Hierarchy Browser on String

2.6 HOW DO YOU MAKE AN APPLICATION IN SQUEAK?

A common question from students at this point is, "How do I make applications in Squeak? In other languages, I can create an executable file and hand it to them. How do I do that in Squeak?" There are several answers to this question.

It's possible to create something like a standard, standalone application in Squeak. Essentially, you can hand someone a stripped-down image with only necessary classes in it. Of course, you always have to give people the virtual machine (VM)—that's the only part that's really executable on a native platform. You can get Squeak to do without the sources and changes files. (Hint: Check out *Preferences* under the *Help* menu.) You don't really need sources and changes if the user is not going to be compiling anything. If you set up your image with just your windows available, and you strip out everything else, you essentially have an "executable" with a VM "runtime". There is even work in the Squeak community on building the image and the VM into a single file so that it truly is a one-file application.

There's a second answer that's more powerful, though. Squeak is based on a version of Smalltalk that is nearly preapplications. It came before our current software market was established. Of course, people bought and sold applications software then, but what didn't exist was Word, WordPerfect, AutoCAD, and the thousands of individual programs that you buy and sell and lose on your hard disk and have trouble uninstalling.

In Smalltalk, there is an idea of a "Goodie." A Goodie was a piece of code that you would *fileIn* (which we will see in the next chapter) that would give you new capabilities—maybe a new image editor, or a spreadsheet. These had many of the characteristics of applications, yet were different. When you loaded in the new image editor, all those new classes and methods were also available for other application goodies. Sometimes goodies conflicted. There were tools for figuring that out, and there was always the solution of having multiple image-and-changes sets on your disk. But the interesting thing about goodies that was different from applications was that a "Goodie" was just Smalltalk code. You could look at it and change it. You could use all the powerful features of Smalltalk with it (such as multiprocessing, which we see in a future chapter). The notion of an "integrated suite" was completely transparent—how much more integrated can you get than to have everything as an object in the same image?

The third answer is that a current trend in computing is toward *embedded applications*—software that is built into hardware devices. The notion of "application" is very different when it comes to embedded devices: You don't talk about buying a new application for your cell phone, car, or refrigerator. Squeak is well situated for embedded computing and has already been used in several embedded computing applications. Because the image can be stripped down very small, and the VM is small already, Squeak applications can be run in less than 1 Mb of RAM. That's appealing in small devices that have very little memory space available.

Having early Smalltalk running on modern machines with modern extensions allows us to rethink some of the accepted notions of computing that have become entrenched in the last twenty-plus years. Applications and windows used to be software that anyone could change and that could naturally interact. It's an important lesson to consider what strengths that model had and how we might gain those strengths today.

EXERCISES: USING SQUEAK

9. Build a binary tree representation in Squeak such that you can create and manipulate tree elements, and do traversals. Implement **inorder**, **preorder**, and **postorder** traversals.

```
root := Tree new."Make a new tree"
root left: (Tree new). "Make a left tree"
root info: 'This is the root info'.
root left info: 'The is the left subtree info'.
root left left: Tree new.
root left right: Tree new.
root left left info: 'Left sub-subtree.'.
root left right info: 'Right side of Left sub-subtree.'.
root right: (Tree new). "Make a right tree."
root right info: 'I am the right tree.'.
root inorder "Return the inorder traversal."
OrderedCollection ('Left sub-subtree.' 'The is the left subtree info' 'Right side of Left sub-subtree.' 'This is the root info' 'I am the right tree.')
```

10. A great way to get to know Squeak is to modify some existing piece of the system. Here's an example. There is a **ScorePlayerMorph** (presented in Chapter 7) that knows how to play MIDI (a sound format). You can find some MIDI files on the CD or on the Web (e.g., http://www.midi.com). You can open a **ScorePlayerMorph** by choosing to play a MIDI file (yellow-button menu) from the FileList, or by executing

|r|

```
r := ScorePlayerMorph new.
r initialize.
r openInWorld.
```

ScorePlayerMorphs don't have a "close" button. Add one.

11. A good way to get to know the tools of Squeak is through a "Treasure Hunt." Try to find the answers to the following questions in Squeak:

- What class implements **fork**?
- Find a method that pops up a dialog box to ask the user a question and then returns the user's answer.
- Find a method that will take a filename as an argument and return the image from that filename. (Hint: images in Squeak are **Form**s).

REFERENCES

There is a wonderful quick reference to Squeak by Andrew Greenberg at http://www .mucow.com/squeak-qref.html.

The book *Smalltalk-80: The Language,* by Adele Goldberg and Dave Robson, is clearly the best definition of the language that underlies Squeak.

3

Your First Program:

Joe the Box

3.1 ADELE GOLDBERG'S JOE THE BOX

Joe the Box was one of the very first activities invented for teaching Smalltalk. It was originally developed by Adele Goldberg for Smalltalk-72. Most recently, she has created a version of it for her LearningWorks Smalltalk-based environment for learning about systems. Alan C. Kay used Joe the Box in his 1977 *Scientific American* article.

Joe the Box works as an introduction to object-oriented programming at two levels. At the first level, it's a *microworld* for exploring objects. There are a couple of different kinds of boxes, several basic operations that you can do with them, and many ways of combining the operations to do something interesting. "Microworlds" were invented by the MIT Logo Group as a programmable space for exploring and learning.

At the second level, Joe the Box is an interesting small program to build. It's an interesting exploration of user input, computer graphics, and creating an interface for programmers.

Working through the second level with the book is easy: Start with a bare Squeak image, type things in, and try them! However, this is in some conflict with the first objective, which is to play with the space first. What you might do is to load up the Boxes microworld to play with it, and then delete it before exploring how it's implemented.

We'll start out by talking about filing things in, which is an important skill in its own right. The Smalltalk community has always been one whose members share what they do. You use things that others have shared by filing them in.

3.2 TOOLS AND STRATEGIES: FILING IN NEW CODE

The process of gathering someone else's code into your image (and compiling it) is called *filing in.* You usually do it from the file list. You typically file in a thing whose file suffix is *.st* (for SmallTalk code) or *.cs* (for Change Set, which we'll talk about more in a later chapter.)

You load up the Boxes microworld by *filing in* the source code from the disk. To file in a piece of code is to (a) load the class and method definitions into your image (i.e., compile them) and (b) execute commands to set up objects and do initializations. The source-code file for Boxes is named *Boxes.st.* It's provided on the CD and on the Web.

It's easy to create source files by *filing out* sections of code. FileOut files are just plain text files with exclamation points "!" in them to delimit sections. The easiest way to create one is to use the yellow-button menu over any pane in the System Browser and choose *File Out.* You can file out a whole category of classes, or any class, or any protocol of methods, or any single method. In the next chapter, we talk about more advanced mechanisms for managing any code that appears in different categories and classes.

You find files and file them in with the File List (Figure 3–1). Choose *Open...* from the Desktop Menu, then *File List.* You navigate into a directory by clicking on its name on the right pane. You move up by clicking on the directory in the left pane. You can limit the filenames that appear by changing the filename pattern and then choosing Accept (yellow-button menu) on the new pattern. * matches everything, ***.st** only matches things that end in ".st", and so on. When the file that you want

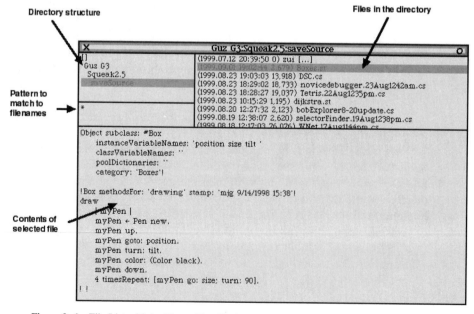

Figure 3–1   File List with its Pieces Identified

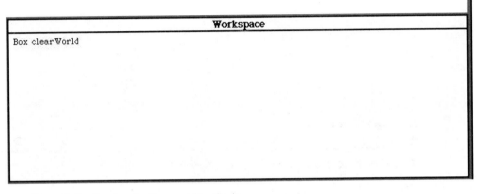

| Workspace |
| Box clearWorld |

Figure 3–2   Creating the Box world to play in

appears, use the yellow-button menu above the file name and choose *File in*. After a moment (barring syntax errors), the code is loaded into your image for you to use.

To remove the Boxes microworld, find the Boxes category in the System Browser. Use the yellow-button menu in the category pane to remove it. It's okay *not* to remove it, too. Later sections of the chapter show how to extend the existing code to do interesting things.

3.3 PLAYING WITH BOXES

First, we'll create a Box world. Create a workspace and drag it to the left of your screen, about halfway down the display. Type **Box clearWorld** and DoIt (Figure 3–2).

The word **Box** refers to an object. It's an object that defines other objects, like the master documents in Sketchpad or like a factory for creating objects. Box is a kind of object called a *class*. We can create a box named Joe by asking **Box** to give us a new object. (See Figure 3–3.)

joe is an object. **joe** is an *instance* of the class **Box**. **joe** knows that he is an instance of Box. If we ask him his class, he will print it for us. Do a PrintIt on **joe class printString** (Figure 3–4).

Joe (we'll anthropormophize the object here) understands several *messages*. He knows how to turn himself a certain number of degrees. (See Figure 3–5.)

He knows how to move himself a given number of pixels. In the message shown in Figure 3–6, Joe is asked move 30 pixels horizontally (to the right) and 30 pixels

Workspace
joe ← Box new

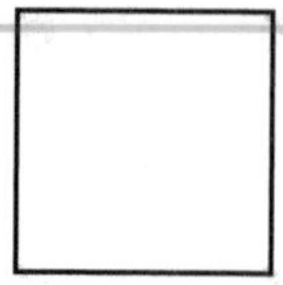

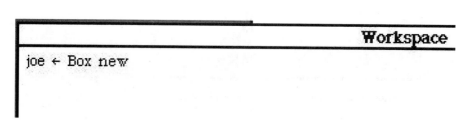

Figure 3–3 Creating the Box Joe

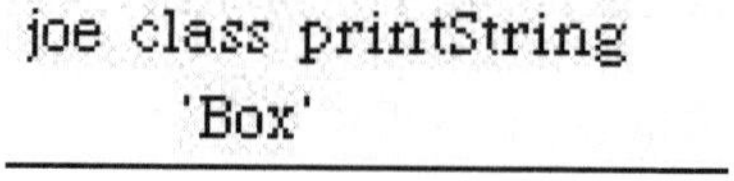

joe class printString
'Box'

Figure 3–4 Joe knows his Class

vertically (down). By saying **30 @ 30**, you define a **Point** object, which is added to Joe's current location.

He also knows how to make himself grow larger or smaller by a certain number of pixels. (See Figure 3–7.)

Joe also knows how to go to a given point. This message can be combined with messages understood by **Sensor** (the object that represents the hardware mouse on the device) to create an interactive Joe:

```
[Sensor anyButtonPressed] whileFalse:
    [joe moveTo: (Sensor mousePoint)].
```

When this code is executed, Joe moves to whatever point the **Sensor** says the mouse is pointing at. It keeps doing this until a mouse button is pressed. What you see when this code is executing is that Joe follows the mouse pointer wherever it is dragged on the screen.

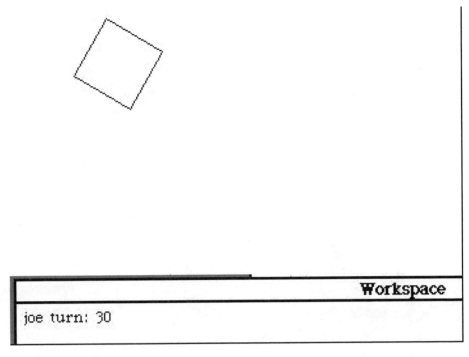

Figure 3–5   Joe can turn

Let's create another Box, named Jill (Figure 3–8).

Jill understands the same messages that Joe does (Figure 3–9). But Jill and Joe are completely separate objects. Joe and Jill are at separate positions on the screen, and they can have different turn angles. They cannot *directly* influence one another. Joe cannot change any aspect of Jill, nor can Jill change any aspect of Joe. All that they, or any two objects, can do is send messages to one another. For example, if Joe and Jill were "dancing," one object might tell the other to turn or move forward— but the "partner" object might decide to actually do the turn or movement in a slightly different way, depending on the dance. Objects provide services (like turning and moving) that other objects can use, but the implementation of these services is known only to the service provider.

3.3.1 Joe and Jill as Example Objects

But Jill and Joe are *instances* of the same *class*. They are both instances of **Box**. Classes perform several important roles which were presented in earlier chapters. The Box world makes the roles more concrete:

- Classes group definitions of *attributes* (the data that objects carry with them) and *services* (the behavior that objects perform in response to messages). Without classes, each object would have to be taught its own attributes and services.

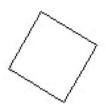

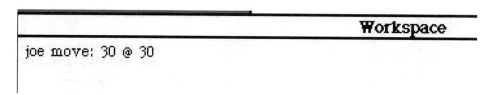

Figure 3–6   Joe can move

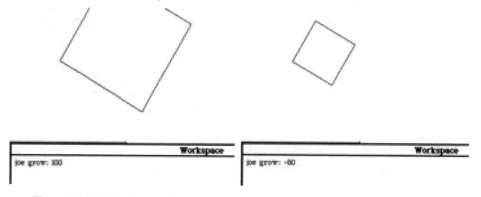

Figure 3–7   Making Joe grow larger and smaller

Instead, Joe and Jill have the same attributes (e.g., an angle of rotation, a size) and the same services (e.g., **grow:**, **move:**)

- Classes provide pieces to reuse. Whole classes can be reused (e.g., maybe you want to use Boxes in another project), or you can *inherit* the attributes and services of one class into another. By creating a *subclass,* you create something that is just like the class (we say it's a *specialization* of the *generalization,* or the subclass *IsA* superclass), but that can add its own special attributes and services, too.

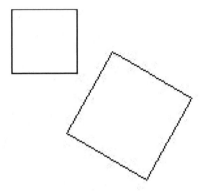

jill ← Box new.

Figure 3–8   Creating a second Box

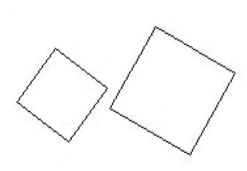

jill turn: 127

Figure 3–9   Jill understands Joe's messages

- Classes act as *factories.* They produce new instances of themselves. They can also reprogram instances already created. If the definition of a given service (that is, a *method*) is changed in the class, all instances will now use the new definition of the given service. Later in the chapter, we redefine a method in Boxes, and Joe and Jill will then respond differently to that method.

We've seen that the class **Box** understands a couple of different messages:

Class message	Meaning
new	Creates a new **Box** and has it display itself.
clearWorld	Clears a portion of the screen for Boxes.

Box *instances* understand *different* messages. **joe new** would generate an error. Instances of **Box** know the *instance* methods defined in **Box**.

Joe and Jill respond to several other messages. The following table lists the messages that **Box** provides for Joe and Jill:

Instance message	Meaning
draw	Draws the **Box** instance.
undraw	Erases the **Box** instance from the display (but it still exists).
move:	Moves a given increment, where the increment is expressed as a **Point** object.
moveTo:	Moves the instance to a specific point.
grow:	Expands or shrinks the instance to the size specified.
turn:	Tilts the box a certain amount.

If the definition of what it means to **draw**, for example, were changed in **Box**, it would be changed for both Joe and Jill. The definition of how to behave in response to a message resides in the class. That means that all instances of the same class behave the same in response to the same messages. But the data in each object is its own—it has its own copy.

3.3.2 Adding a New Kind of Box

There is another *kind* of **Box**, called a **NamedBox**. Instances of **NamedBox** are **Box**es, but they have some changed features. We say that **NamedBox** is a *subclass* of **Box**. Instances of **NamedBox** know everything and can do anything that a **Box** can do, but they may know other things or respond to messages slightly differently. This is an example of *inheritance.*

We create a **NamedBox** somewhat differently, for reasons we'll see shortly.

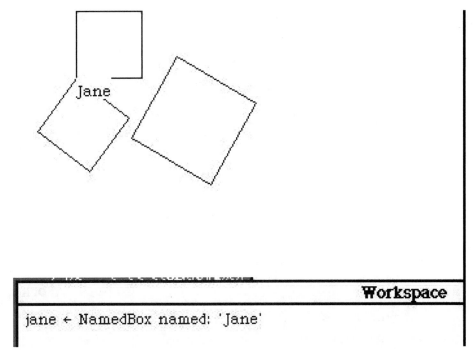

Figure 3–10　Creating a NamedBox

Rather than asking **NamedBox** for a **new** box, we tell **NamedBox** that we'd like a new box **named:** something. **jane := NamedBox named: 'jane'** gives us a new box named "Jane." (See Figure 3–10.)

Notice that Jane draws herself differently on the screen. Jane knows that she's a kind of **Box**:

jane isKindOf: Box "PrintIt to see true"

And Jane knows how to do the kinds of things that Joe and Jill do (Figure 3–11).

Jane, as an instance of **NamedBox**, really understands two messages differently from Box, and adds the definition of one new message. The redefinition is called *overriding* the definition in the superclass. Overriding is necessary when a subclass wants to perform its own special behavior in response to a common message.

NamedBox instance messages	Meaning
draw	A NamedBox draws itself with its name.
drawNameColor:	A NamedBox knows how to draw itself in a given color (black for display, white to erase).
undraw	When a NamedBox erases itself, it also erases its name.

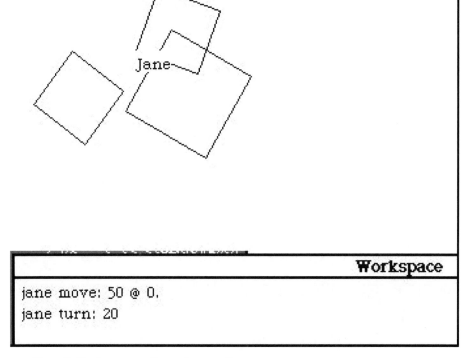

Figure 3–11   Jane responding to the same Box messages

The rest of what an instance of **NamedBox** knows how to do is *inherited* from **Box**. The class object **NamedBox** itself knows a message that the **Box** object does not.

NamedBox class message	Meaning
named:	Creates an instance with the given name.

3.4 CREATING THE BOX CLASS AND BOX INSTANCES

The definition of the class **Box** says that instances know three things about themselves: Their position, their size, and their tilt. Every object of class Box (and any of its subclasses, such as **NamedBox**) will have these attributes, that is, these same *instance variables*. We can create the definition of Box the same way that we created **Muppet** in the previous chapter. We fill out the template and accept. If you already have the Boxes microworld loaded, you can just select the **Box** class to see the following definition:

```
Object subclass: #Box
        instanceVariableNames: 'position size tilt '
        classVariableNames: "
        poolDictionaries: "
        category: 'Boxes'
```

Boxes get created through the sending of **new** to the class. There is a class method **new** defined in Boxes. You can find (or create) this method by clicking on the class button in the browser with the class **Box** selected. The code is

new

        ^super new initialize

This is the method that gets executed when you execute **Box new**. It says that it returns (using ^) whatever the superclass (**super**) of **Box** returns when sent **new**, after that new object has been initialized. The superclass of **Box**, according to the class definition (seen earlier), is **Object**. The following method is equivalent:

new

        | temporaryNewObject |
        temporaryNewObject ← super new. "Create the new object"
        temporaryNewObject initialize."Initialize it"
        ^temporaryNewObject"Return it"

An interesting puzzle is why the new object returned by **new** is actually an instance of the class **Box**. We know that it is, because we asked Joe what his class was. Why isn't the new object an instance of Object?

What happens is that the method that actually creates new objects creates them as instances of **self**, that is, the object that received the original message. **Box new** is a message to the class **Box**, so it's **self**, and so an instance of **Box** will be created. So, whatever object is originally sent the message **new** will be the class from which the new instance will be created.

The **initialize** message is one that instances of Box understand. There is no method **initialize** for the class **Box**. Here is the instance method that actually gets executed when a new **Box** instance is created:

initialize

        position := 50@50.
        size := 50.
        tilt := 0.
        self draw.

The purpose for an initialize method in any class is to set the instance variables to the correct initial values for an object of this type. The **initialize** method for Boxes sets a default position for a new box, a default size, and a default tilt. It then asks the new **Box** to draw itself for the first time.

Before we see the **draw** method for **Box** instances, let's see what the instances are going to be drawing on. If you recall, the first statement that we executed when working with Joe the Box wasn't **joe := Box new**, but **Box clearWorld**. **clearWorld** is another *class* message that **Box** understands:

clearWorld
    (Form extent: 600@200) fillWhite display

This method creates the white rectangle on which the boxes appear. Let's dissect that single line of code a bit:

- A **Form** is the Squeak object that represents a bitmap graphic. Smalltalk has always supported interesting operations on a **Form**, and Squeak also provides support for multiple resolutions, graphics formats, and new color transformations.
- **Form extent: 600@200** creates a blank rectangular bitmap that is 600 pixels across and 200 pixels high.
- **fillWhite** makes the new **Form** instance completely white.
- **display** puts the new **Form** instance onto the computer display. The display itself is a kind of **Form** that can be accessed via the global variable **Display**. There are many options for displaying forms. **display** simply puts the form at the upper left corner of the **Display (0@0)**. **displayAt:** displays the form at a given point, and there are many others (under the class **DisplayObject**) that can display under various transformations.

clearWorld basically paints some white on the screen as a nice backdrop to our boxes. Note that this backdrop is not a window. If you chose *restore display* from the Desktop Menu, the white form (and all our boxes) would disappear, because these forms aren't on the list of objects to refresh when the screen is repainted. Nonetheless, this works as a simple place for displaying boxes.

3.5 BASICS OF DRAWING

Forms are very important in Squeak, so it's worthwhile to take a short side trip to talk about some of the things Squeak can do with forms.

3.5.1 Creating Forms

There are many ways to create a **Form**:

- The easiest way to create a **Form** is simply to grab one from the screen. **Form fromUser** will let you drag a rectangle over a section of the current display and return it as a **Form** instance. Try **Form fromUser display** as a simple test for selecting a chunk of the display and putting it up in the upper left corner of the display. You can also assign a **Form** to a variable to keep it around for a while.

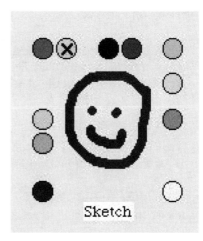

Figure 3–12   Colored halos on a sketch

- The second easiest is to use one of the several editors built into Squeak. Try this in MVC (but not in Morphic!):

```
| f |
f := Form fromUser.
f edit.
```

- Morphic has a wonderful editor built into it. Morphic is the alternative user-interface world in Squeak that was mentioned in the previous chapter. From the Desktop Menu, choose *Open...*, then *New project (morphic)*. Enter the Morphic project by clicking into it.

  Click anywhere to get the World menu, then choose *new morph...* and then *make new drawing*. Draw using the various tools, and then choose the button *keep*. The new sketch (actually an instance of the class **SketchMorph**) can now be dragged around or captured from the screen. You can open up an inspector on the object to do things with it. Morphic objects are manipulated via a set of colored halos (Figure 3–12). To bring up the menus, select the object (using command-click on a Mac and alt-click on Windows). Hold your mouse over each halo for a moment to get help on what the halo does. Once you bring up an inspector on the sketch (via the *Debug* menu, on the white halo), the message **form** to a **SketchMorph** returns its form. (To do something interesting, try something like **self form display** or even **GlobalVariable := self form display**.)

- If you have a file somewhere in GIF, JPEG, or BMP format, you can read it into a **Form**. **Form fromFileNamed: 'my.gif'** will read in any of the above formats and will return the Form for you to manipulate. (For example, in a workspace, do **myForm := Form fromFileNamed: 'my.gif'** and then **myForm display**.)

- You can also grab images straight from the Web. Take a look at the class methods for **HTTPSocket**. You can grab a GIF image from, for example, Georgia Tech's College of Computing website:

HTTPSocket httpGif: 'www.cc.gatech.edu/gvu/images/headers/titles/gvu-center.gif'

Once you have the form, you can do amazing things with it. Squeak has a wide variety of graphics primitives available. For example, any **Form** can be shrunk by program. Try this (which is the class method **exampleShrink** in **Form**):

```
| f s |
f := Form fromUser.      "Let the user define a rectangle"
s := f shrink: f boundingBox by: 2 @ 5. "Shrink it"
s displayOn: Display at: Sensor waitButton"Display it"
```

This code will let you select a section of the screen, and then will wait for you to click somewhere. It will then shrink the selection and display it. (Note: In Morphic, try clicking on the workspace itself to drop the image. If you try dropping the image on the desktop, the World Menu will be brought up and will overdraw your image.) Try the same example with **s := f magnify: f boundingBox by: 5 @ 5.** and you'll magnify instead of shrink.

In addition to shrinking and magnifying, you can rotate. All forms understand the message **rotateBy: someDegrees**. Here's an example that's built into Squeak:

```
| a f |
f := Form fromDisplay: (0@0 extent: 200@200). "Save the screen"
a := 0. "Rotation value"
[Sensor anyButtonPressed] whileFalse:"Rotate until mousebutton"
      "Grab screen from mousepoint, rotate, and display"
      [((Form fromDisplay:
            (Sensor cursorPoint extent: 130@66))
            rotateBy: (a := a+5)) "Increment by 5, then use it"
      display].
f display "Put the original corner of the screen back"
```

Until you press a mouse button, this will capture a chunk 130 pixels by 66 pixels from wherever your cursor is and will rotate it in the space 200 × 200 pixels in the upper left corner of the display. The use of **a := a + 5** is an example of doing an assignment while taking the value of the assignment (the new value of **a**) as an argument in a message. The effect is to rotate the form around and around in five-degree increments.

The lower level code that enables all of these form capabilities is **BitBlt**, the Bit Block Transfer. Basically, graphics manipulations such as these are carefully constructed memory moves: blocks of bits that are transferred in specialized ways. **BitBlt** (which is actually a class in Smalltalk) also allows you to do things like create transparent sections of images, merge sections of images, and crop images, in addition to the translations and rotations we've seen here. Squeak includes a new kind of **BitBlt** called **WarpBlt**, which can do very powerful color manipulations. Investigate the example methods in the **WarpBlt** class to see some demonstrations.

3.5.2 Teaching Boxes to Draw

Now, let's see how Box instances draw themselves:

draw
```
    | myPen |
    myPen := Pen new.          "Create a new Pen for drawing"
    myPen up.        "Don't draw while setting it up"
            "Set up the Pen with the Boxes' characteristics"
    myPen goto: position.
    myPen turn: tilt.
    myPen color: (Color black).
            "Now put the Pen down and draw the box."
    myPen down.
    4 timesRepeat: [myPen go: size; turn: 90].
```

Boxes draw themselves using a **Pen** class. **Pen** instances, by default, draw directly on the display, but you can get them to draw on a given **Form** by creating them with the **newOnForm:** class method.

Pens are a form of Logo turtles, a Logo turtle being a computational object (in our sense of the word "object") that can be used to draw. Think of a Pen as a turtle that is carrying an ink pen. It starts out facing straight up (**north**) and has the pen pressed to the surface of the paper (in our case, the display screen). You can then make drawings by sending messages to the **Pen** instance.

Pen instance message	Meaning
up	Picks the pen up, so that the turtle/pen moves without drawing
down	Puts the pen back down again for drawing
go:	Move the pen forward along its current heading so many steps (pixels on the display)
turn:	Turn the pen a given degree angle
color:	Sets the color of the pen
north	Sets the turtle's heading toward the top of the display

The **draw** method for a **Box** merely creates the **Pen**, moves it to the position of the **Box**, sets the tilt appropriately, and draws the box. **4 timesRepeat: [myPen go: size; turn: 90].** is the classic way of drawing a Box with a **Pen** or turtle.

Note that the **Box** draws itself in black. (**Color** is a class, and the class knows several messages for creating colors of various kinds.) To erase itself, **undraw**, the Box redraws itself in white:

undraw
```
    | myPen |
    myPen := Pen new.          "Create a new Pen for drawing"
```

```
myPen up.
        "Set it up for drawing the Box"
myPen goto: position.
myPen turn: tilt.
        "Now draw it with the background color"
myPen color: (Color white).
myPen down.
4 timesRepeat: [myPen go: size; turn: 90].
```

draw and **undraw** are really the heart of the **Box** class. Once we have these, all of the other messages are just

- Undrawing the current Box representation,
- Changing one of the Box instance variables, and
- Drawing the new Box representation.

Given that basic template, here are all of the other **Box** drawing methods:

```
grow: increment
        self undraw.
        size := size + increment.
        self draw.
move: pointIncrement
        self undraw.
        position := position + pointIncrement.
        self draw.
moveTo: aPoint
        self undraw.
        position := aPoint.
        self draw.
turn: degrees
        self undraw.
        tilt := tilt + degrees.
        self draw.
```

3.5.3 Getting Input from the User

When we were first playing with Joe the Box earlier in this chapter (page 64), Joe followed the mouse through a small example in the workspace:

```
[Sensor anyButtonPressed] whileFalse:
        [joe moveTo: (Sensor mousePoint)]
```

Sensor is actually a global variable that references an instance of **InputSensor**. The **Sensor** is the access point for the mouse and keyboard in Squeak. You can use `Sensor` to get low-level user input.

Sensor messages for accessing the keyboard	Meaning
keyboard	Returns the next character that the user types.
keyboardPeek	Looks at the next character that the user types and returns it, but leaves it available to be retrieved with **keyboard**.
keyboardPressed	Just returns *whether* any key has been pressed since the last time it was checked.
shiftPressed, commandKeyPressed, controlKeyPressed, macOptionKeyPressed	Indicates whether the specified modifier key is currently pressed.

Sensor messages for accessing the mouse	Meaning
mousePoint, cursorPoint	Points where the mouse/cursor currently is.
anyButtonPressed, noButtonPressed, redButtonPressed, yellowButtonPressed, blueButtonPressed	Returns true if any button is pressed (**anyButtonPressed**), if no button is pressed, or if the specified button is pressed.
waitButton, waitClickButton, waitNoButton	Pauses execution until some mouse button is pressed, or until it's both pressed and released (a *click*), or until all buttons are released.

3.6 EXTENDING BOX TO CREATE NAMEDBOX

The **NamedBox** is a subclass of **Box**, which means that it *inherits* all of the attributes (instance variable definitions) and services (methods) that **Box** already has. But the **NamedBox** can specialize and extend those definitions:

```
Box subclass: #NamedBox
        instanceVariableNames: 'name '
        classVariableNames: "
        poolDictionaries: "
        category: 'Boxes'
```

In the definition of **NamedBox**, we see that one new instance variable has been added, **name**. So, **NamedBox** instances have the same **position**, **tilt**, and **size** instance variables as **Box** instances, but **NamedBox** instances also have a **name**. None of the existing **Box** methods manipulate the name instance variables, so we need to create *accessors* if we want to be able to access the name from the outside of this object:

Figure 3–13   An unnamed NamedBox
named Jane

name
      ^name
name: aName
      name := aName

Smalltalk can differentiate between **name** and **name:**. We could have named these **getName** and **setName:**, for getting and setting the value of the name instance variable. Get/set methods are the style in Java. In Smalltalk style, the instance variable name without the colon is typically the getter, and the instance variable name with the colon is the setter.

We might now try to create a **NamedBox** instance with code like this:

```
jane := NamedBox new.
jane name: 'Jane'.
jane draw.
```

But the results are not what you might expect (Figure 3–13). We know that **NamedBox**'s **draw** is going to have to draw the name of the box. **NamedBox** will try to draw Jane as soon as she's created, but her name will still be **nil** (the default value of all new variables). There is code that enables this to work, but the default name is "Unnamed." When the box is then named Jane, it becomes the mishmash of Figure 3–13. A new way to created **NamedBox** instances should provide a name immediately. A new class method **named:** will create a new instance, and will also set its name from the input argument:

```
named: aName
    | newBox |
    newBox := super new.        "Do the normal Box draw"
    newBox undraw.        "Erase it – using NamedBox erase"
    newBox name: aName.        "Set the name"
    newBox draw.        "Draw it with the name"
    ^newBox
```

For the most part, this method is not too surprising. It looks like the same pattern used in **move**, **grow**, **moveTo**, and other methods. The object "undraws" itself, sets its name, and then redraws itself. There are two interesting pieces to note:

- The first line, **newBox := super new.**, accesses **super**. **Super** is a predefined special variable that accesses the superclass of the method. In this example,

super will be **Box**, since **Box** is **NamedBox**'s superclass. This is an explicit call to **Box new** that does not use the name **Box**. (Note: **newBox** here is a **NamedBox**, not a **Box**.)

- This doesn't really get around the problem of drawing an unspecified name! **undraw** is going to have to erase the name even if it is not yet defined.

All that's left to define of **NamedBox** now is the new definition of how to **draw** and **undraw NamedBox** instances:

```
draw
        super draw.        "Draw myself as a Box"
        self drawNameColor: (Color black).      "Draw my name in black"
undraw
        super undraw.      "Undraw myself as a Box"
        self drawNameColor: (Color white).      "Erase my name in white"
drawNameColor: aColor
        | displayName |
        (name isNil) ifTrue: [name := 'Unnamed'].      "If no name, fake one"
        displayName := name asDisplayText.      "Make the string a kind of Form"
        displayName      "Set its color"
                foregroundColor: aColor
                backgroundColor: (Color white).
        displayName displayAt: position.      "Display it"
```

Both **draw** and **undraw** ask **Box** to perform its version of these methods (via the reference to super), then draw the name—in black for drawing, in white for undrawing. The interesting part of these methods is **drawNameColor:**:

- The first line of **drawNameColor:** saves the day if the name isn't provided. It explicitly checks whether the name exists, and if it doesn't, sets it to **'Unnamed'**. That explains the funny look of Figure 3–13. But why don't we ever see 'Unnamed' when using the new **named:** method for creating objects? Because in **named:**, the default name is only drawn in white on a white background, via **undraw**, before the name is set and **draw** is called.
- We can convert the name from a **String** into a displayable object via **asDisplayText**. We store that new object in the local variable **displayName**.
- **DisplayText** instances can set their foreground and background colors, so we set it up for our white background, with the foreground whatever the argument color is.
- The name is then displayed as **displayName** at the **Box** instances' position.

EXERCISES: EXPLORING CLASSES AND BOXES

1. Let's say that **NamedBox**, a subclass of **Box,** also defined a class method **new** as **^super new initialize**. Will this work? Why or why not? What's the downside? (Hint: Print something to the Transcript inside of **initialize**. How many times does it print?)

2. What would happen if the **new** method started with **self new** instead of **super new**?

3. Smalltalk's iteration can be applied to Joe. **10 timesRepeat: [joe move: 10 @ 0]** will move Joe horizontally a total of 100 pixels, in 10-pixel increments. What would you write to get Joe spinning? To get Joe and Jill spinning at the same time? At different rates?

4. Even though **super** just looks up the message starting at the superclass, we cannot simply replace **super** with the name of the superclass and have everything work okay. **super new** in **NamedBox** is not the same as **Box new**. **super draw** is not the same as **Box draw**. Why not?

5. **Pen**s already know how to display text. Modify **NamedBox** so that it uses the Pen's method for drawing text, rather than using **DisplayText**.

6. Should **initialize** *not* draw the **Box**? Why or why not? If not, rewrite the **Box** microworld without it.

3.7 TOOLS AND STRATEGIES: HOW TO GO FROM "SAMPLE CODE" TO "REUSE"

There are several neat techniques in the Box microworld, as well as in the other examples we're going to be exploring. You will probably want to use them in your own code. But it's not always obvious how to go from a sample piece of code to something that you can control. Fortunately, Squeak provides lots of tools to help with this process.

Let's say that you want to create an interesting effect on the screen. You want to print your name in a bunch of colors, maybe even random colors. You saw this piece of code in the earlier example, so you know that it should be possible:

```
displayName := name asDisplayText.
displayName
        foregroundColor: aColor
        backgroundColor: (Color white).
displayName displayAt: position.
```

Let's start out by finding the original method that does the color drawing. If you type into a workspace **foregroundColor:backgroundColor:**, you can type Alt-M (Apple-M) to get the *implementors* of this method. There is only one, so you can click on it to see what's going on. Nothing much, really. Now, click on the list and choose (yellow-button menu) *Senders* (or just type Alt/Apple-N). Now we can see how the code gets used in a variety of situations. There's even an example, a class method in **DisplayText** (Figure 3–14). You can try it by DoIt on the comment (the line at the bottom in double quotes) **DisplayText example**. It generates an interesting pattern with text.[1]

The example shown (**DisplayText example**) and the other senders give us a bunch of examples of drawing text with color. We can even see from the implemen-

---

[1] In Squeak 2.7, the comment on this method is wrong. The example ends with a mouse click, not a keypress. It's fixed in 2.8.

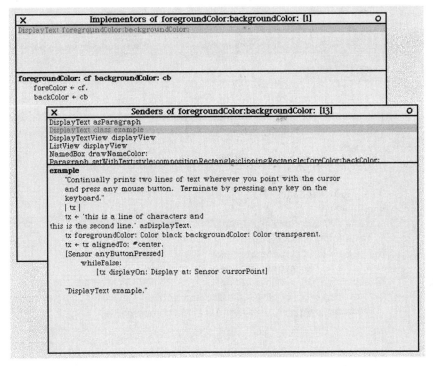

Figure 3–14   Implementers and Senders of foregroundColor:backgroundColor:

tation of the example that there is a transparent color for a background. However, these examples don't help us generate different colors.

We know that there is a class named **Color**, both from the original sample code and from the example. We can browse the class **Color**. The easy way to get there is to select the word "Color" somewhere and type Alt-B/Apple-B. Choose the class methods of Color, since that's what all the colors we've seen have been. We can see that there are a lot of named colors (click on the method category "named colors"), as well as many ways to generate colors ("instance creation"). One of them, **r:g:b:** just takes three numbers between 0 and 1 to generate a color. That sounds useful for generating random colors.

How do we get random things? A good strategy is to look for a class that does what you want. If you choose "Find Class" from the first pane of a Browser, and type Random, you'll find that there is a class named **Random**. That seems to be getting closer, but it isn't clear how to use it.

When facing a new class, the first thing to do is to check the class comment. Click on the "?" button on the browser. In this case, the class comment on **Random** tells you about how the class is implemented, but not how it's used.

The second thing to try is to look for class methods. There are often examples in class methods that explain how to use classes. In this case, **Random** does have an example method with lots of examples. One of the things it says is:

The correct way to use class Random is to store one in
an instance or class variable:

```
        myGenerator ← Random new.
```

Then use it every time you need another number between 0.0 and 1.0

```
        myGenerator next
```

That sounds useful, since the range is the same as the range expected by **r:g:b:**. Also, there is a way of generating random integers by sending **atRandom** to the highest possible integer. That can be useful to generate random points where to display names.

Here's a piece of workspace code based on all of this:

```
myGenerator ← Random new.
30 timesRepeat: [
        name ← 'Mark Guzdial' asDisplayText.
        name foregroundColor:
                (Color r: myGenerator next
                       g: myGenerator next
                       b: myGenerator next)
                backgroundColor: (Color transparent).
        name displayAt: (100 atRandom) @ (100 atRandom).]
```

SIDE NOTE:

You may be wondering why we assign **name** inside the loop. Why don't we create **name** as a **DisplayText** before the loop starts, then just reuse it? It's a loop invariant, isn't it? Try it! You'll find that all the names are the exact same color. **asDisplayText** creates a new **DisplayText** object each time it's called. With only one instance, created *outside* the loop, we end up with all the same color.

This does what we wanted (Figure 3–15). Through hunting up implementors and senders, and looking through examples and comments in the classes, it becomes pretty easy to build what you want from a good sample piece of code.

3.8 IMPROVING BOXES:
EFFICIENCY, ANIMATION, AND DESIGN

The real advantage of an object-oriented structure is the ease with which changes can be made. We can show that feature most easily by actually making some changes to **Box** and **NamedBox**. In this section, we make them more efficient and more amenable to animation. Then we begin introducing a design perspective on Boxes.

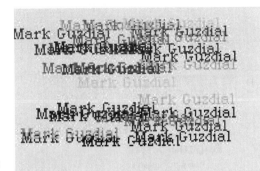

Figure 3–15   Result of the Random Name Code

3.8.1 Drawing Boxes Better

The previously described **Box** and **NamedBox** are ineffecent and poorly designed. There are two obvious places where the system is flawed:

- **Box**es have a **tilt** and a **position**, and they use **Pen**s for drawing. **Pen**s already have a heading and a location. Why not just create one **Pen** per **Box** instance so that we no longer need the tilt and position variables inside Box?
- **draw** and **undraw** are almost identical pieces of code, which is a bad design. Any changes to the way **Box** instances are drawn requires changes to both methods.

Implementing these two fixes requires changing fairly little code. First, we have to redefine the **Box** class so that we have new instance variables. We'll need a **pen** instance variable to hold the **Box**'s **Pen** instance. We'll still need a **size**, but **tilt** and **position** will get passed on to the **Pen**. The new code is as follows:

```
Object subclass: #Box
        instanceVariableNames: 'size pen '
        classVariableNames: ''
        poolDictionaries: ''
        category: 'Boxes'
```

The way that **Box** instances get initialized also has to change in order to use the **Pen**:

```
initialize
        pen ← Pen new. "Put a pen in an instance variable."
        pen place: 50@50.
        size ← 50.
        self draw.
```

The various accessor methods also need to change, since some of them now access the **Pen** instance instead of the **Box** instance variables. This activity of asking another object to perform a service for the original object receiving the message is called *delegation*. The **Box** instance is delegating some of its services down to the **Pen** instance. Following is the code:

```
grow: increment
        self undraw.
        size ← size + increment. "This stays the same"
        self draw.
moveTo: aPoint
        self undraw.
        pen place: aPoint.
        self draw.
move: pointIncrement
        self undraw.
        pen place: (pen location) + pointIncrement.
        self draw.
turn: degrees
        self undraw.
        pen turn: degrees.
        self draw.
```

Drawing and undrawing also have to change in order to utilize the **new** pen variable. The code becomes much smaller, since a **Pen** instance doesn't have to be created and loaded up with the right values. But while we're at it, it seems like the right time to remove the code duplicated between **draw** and **undraw**. The right thing to do is to create a **drawColor:** method that draws whatever color is needed. This makes **draw** and **undraw** very simple. The code is as follows:

```
draw
        self drawColor: (Color black).
undraw
        self drawColor: (Color white).
drawColor: color
        pen color: color.
        4 timesRepeat: [pen go: size; turn: 90].
```

All of the things that we were asking Joe and Jill to do previously now work just fine. Jane the **NamedBox** won't work quite yet. If we try it, we'll find that the **drawNameColor:** method needs the position of the **Box** instance. We can solve that by delegating to the **Pen**, as in the following code:

```
drawNameColor: aColor
        | displayName |
        (name isNil) ifTrue: [name ← 'Unnamed'].
        displayName ← name asDisplayText.
        displayName foregroundColor: aColor
                backgroundColor: (Color white).
        displayName displayAt: (pen location).
```

Now, all of the previous examples work just fine. From the user-programmer's perspective, nothing has changed in the Box world at all. Yet from the microworld-programmer's perspective, we know that the world has changed considerably.

3.8.2 Animating Boxes

This next change will impact how the user of the Box microworld sees the system. One of the original uses of the Box microworld was to explore animation. **Box**es were moved and spun on the screen, and one of the activities was to invent a "dance" for the **Box** instances. However, animation requires slightly *slower* performance than modern computers give.

Modern computers move so fast that the Squeak boxes do many operations before the eye can see them. We need to slow them down so that the eye can register their positions before they move again. The delay doesn't have to be much. Motion pictures show 30 frames per second, which means that our eye can register a static image in at least 1/30 of a second. Let's use that number as a reasonable guess.

Creating a delay is really easy. There is a class in Squeak called **Delay** that can create delay objects. We can create them for a certain amount of time. When the object gets the message **wait**, it pauses the processor for the correct amount of time.

Where should we have the Box slow down? The first guess might be in **draw-Color:** so that every drawn object would be slowed down. But this turns out to produce really jerky animations. (Please do go ahead and try it.) The reason is that we now use **drawColor:** for erasures, too. We don't need to wait for undraws, just for draws.

If we add a **Delay** creation and wait in draw, the result is very nice:

```
draw
        self drawColor: (Color black).
        (Delay forSeconds: (1/30)) wait.
```

Try something like this workspace code to see the effect:

```
joe ← Box new
jane ← Box new

30 timesRepeat: [jane turn: 12. joe turn: 10.
        jane move: 3@4. joe move: 2@3].
```

3.8.3 Designing Boxes

What we did in Section 3.8.1 isn't that complicated. We simply moved variables from one object to another. But that may not be obvious to anyone. We could show them the code, but it would be nice if there was a way of describing the objects that we manipulated and how we did it.

One way of describing the two sets of relationships is with *UML* (*Unified Modeling Language*). Figure 3–16 is one way of looking at the original class structure that was in the Box microworld. **NamedBox** is a subclass of **Box**, and **Box** provided **posi-**

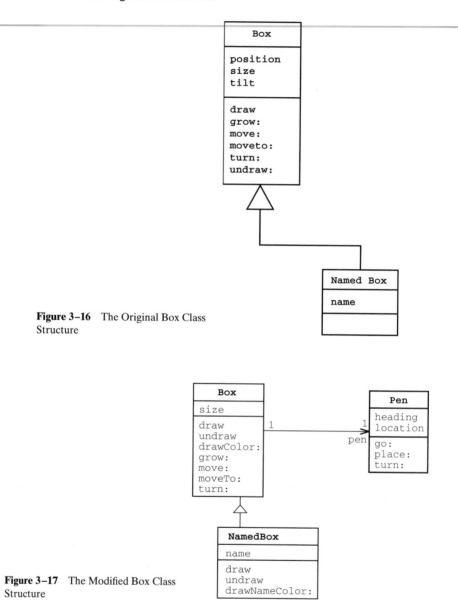

Figure 3–16   The Original Box Class
Structure

Figure 3–17   The Modified Box Class
Structure

tion, **size**, and **tilt** attributes. We can also see that **NamedBox** inherits a bunch of services from **Box**.

Figure 3–17 is a UML depiction of how the Box microworld was modified. A
Pen was included as part of the **Box**. We removed two of the attributes of the **Box**
because we were able to delegate them to the **Pen**. We added one attribute to **Box** to
keep track of the new **Pen** instance.

The next chapter starts from here: How do we think about designing in objects,
and how do we use things like UML to facilitate the designing?

EXERCISES: MORE WITH BOXES AND GRAPHICS

7. Try to create a "dance" with the Box microworld. Create two boxes that move around the screen and respond to each other's motions, e.g., move Jill to the left and Joe to the right, then back together, and move in parallel, and. . . .

8. Write the workspace code to assemble a pyramid of boxes.

9. Extend and improve the **Box** microworld. Imagine that you want boxes that can have thick lines, and that play different tunes when they move and when they turn (see the later chapter on Multimedia for how to play these tunes). How would you change the **Box** design? Try implementing one or two additional **Box** subclasses and see what difficulties you encounter.

10. Create a tiny painting program. Simply follow the Sensor and move a Pen to follow it. As an extra challenge, put up a couple of graphic images that the user might click to change colors or to quit drawing. (There is a hierarchy of **Button** objects that might be useful here.)

REFERENCES

Joe the Box appeared in

KAY, ALAN C. (1977). Microelectronics and the Personal Computer. *Scientific American* (September), 231–244.

Turtle graphics (the way that Pens work) is an amazingly powerful way of looking at mathematics. For a formal and deep treatment, see

ABELSON, HAL and ANDREA A. DISESSA (1986). *Turtle Geometry: The Computer as a Medium for Exploring Mathematics.* Cambridge, MA, MIT Press.

BitBlt is covered in great detail in the original Smalltalk-80 book:

GOLDBERG, ADELE and DAVE ROBSON (1983). *Smalltalk-80: The Language.* Reading, MA, Addison-Wesley.

4

Designing Object Systems

It's easy to think about object-oriented programming as no big thing. It's got objects, classes, and inheritance, but a fast machine, a good hacker, and a few cases of Jolt can make any programming language usable, right? To a certain extent, that's certainly true: You can just sit down and start hacking Squeak like any other programming language.

The problem comes later. Can you still maintain your code? Can you or anybody else reuse your classes in another application? Can you make good use of others' code?

Simply building with objects doesn't insure that you get reusable, maintainable code. Object-oriented programming makes it *easier* to write reusable and maintainable code, but there are definitely good and bad object programs. Consider a large program that has only one class and creates only one instance. How is that any easier to maintain than the equivalent program in an imperative programming language?

There is a process to follow that can result in a good object-oriented program, that is, one that *is* reusable and maintainable. No process or methodology can *guarantee* a good result. In the end, it really comes down to whether the programmer thinks through the problem and the program. What a good process or methodology can offer is a set of activities that has worked well for others.

The focus of this chapter is how to do object-oriented analysis and design. A single chapter can provide only an introduction. *Many* books have been written on the subject of object-oriented analysis and design. The approach of this chapter is to provide a *minimal* process. It's compatible with most of the methodologies and processes out there. It's complete enough that it does actually provide something useful. After the presentation of the basic process, several examples are presented that apply the process.

4.1 THE OBJECT-ORIENTED DESIGN PROCESS

There are a variety of definitions of a good object-oriented design process. The basic stages of the one that we'll use are as follows:

- **Object-oriented analysis:** In the analysis stage, your goal is to *understand the domain.* What are the objects in this domain? What are the services and attributes of each? In other words, what does each object *do* and what does each object *know?* How do the objects interact with one another? Analysis is completely programming language independent. The real world is not written in *any* programming language! You don't *need* a programming language here, and trying to remain language-independent at this stage will allow you to switch languages easily later.
- **Object-oriented design:** In the design stage, your goal is to *figure out the solution.* You get down to the nitty-gritty at this point. What instance variables do you need? What methods do you need? There is some contention in the field as to whether object-oriented design can be language independent or not. Try to remain as independent as possible, but at some point, the detailed design involves issues of how existing classes are provided and structured. At that point, your design becomes language dependent.
- **Object-oriented programming:** Finally, you build the code. That's what we've been talking about thus far in the book, and now we step back and get to the earlier parts of the process.

A very important lesson is that *this is not a linear process.* You are expected to go back and forth between analysis and design, between design and programming, or even between domain (in the analysis stage) and programming. There are software engineers who argue that it is simply not possible to define all of the specifications before implementation. You can't know all the analysis details before designing, and you can't know all of the designing details before programming. You will go back and forth. That's not a bad thing—it's the way that even experts do it. Iterating on the design is actually one of the signs of an expert designer.

4.1.1 Object-Oriented Analysis Stage

Throughout all of the analysis, what you're really *doing* is figuring out what you're *doing.* You may have a problem statement that you're starting from in any project, but that problem statement is *always* ill-defined and incomplete. You have to fill in the blanks even on the problem itself. What is it that you really want to do? What is really the domain in which you're working?

4.1.1.1 Brainstorming candidate classes

We will use two kinds of activities in our object-oriented analyses. The first one is simply *brainstorming.* Try to write down all the objects you can think of that relate to the domain in which you are working. The only rule is that everything you write down should be a *noun,* since your focus is on the objects, not the tasks at this point.

A good object should have *attributes* and *services.* If two potential objects differ only in their value for the attribute, then they will be reflected as one *kind* of object (that is, a *class,* when we go to implement the objects). If Fred and George are going to be represented in our system, but they only differ because of values of attributes like *name* and *address,* then they should be reflected as one kind of object. If, however, Fred is a fireman and George is a policeman, and you're building a model of an emergency-response system, then Fred and George do reflect different services and perhaps different attributes, so they should be different candidate objects. (But you should probably be thinking fireman and policeman objects, not Fred and George.)

After you have brainstormed all the possible objects, start filtering and sorting them:

- Filter out those objects that have to do with the human interface from those that have to do with the problem domain. In most cases, the interface objects are not part of understanding the domain. Most objects in the real world don't have an extrinsic interface. Pencils and soda cans are held the way that they are because of their shape—no special buttons or handles are necessary. The interface is their physical structure. Other objects have interfaces that are important but don't relate to the basic services of the object. Refrigerators need to have a handle on the door for the door to open, but the handle isn't involved in keeping things cold. A radio does have a volume knob, but the radio still has to tune a station and play regardless of what the volume is currently set to. Focus on the core capabilities, not how some future user will interact with those capabilities.

- Are some of the candidate objects really attributes of other candidate objects? For example, a Name is rarely an object itself, though it's often an attribute of a class like Person.

- Are some of the candidate objects really subclasses of some other candidate objects? This does not mean that you throw any of the candidate objects out. But it does mean that you can start thinking about structuring your hierarchy of potential objects early on.

- Are some of the candidate objects really instances of some other object? Think about general objects here, even if there will only be one instance of the given object when you finally design the sytem.

The final filter of your brainstormed candidate objects gets back to what is it that you really want to do. Which of these objects are *really* ones that you want to be dealing with? Some of your candidate objects really belong to some other domain. Some of your candidate objects may be related to your domain, but adding them in at the beginning is going to be hard. Be realistic. For example, designing a cash register system can easily extend into updating inventory, making entries in accounts receivable, and immediately informing the head office of every sale. While a great system might involve all those pieces, don't try to do everything at once. What are the minimum objects that you need to get the functionality that you need?

4.1.1.2 Class responsibility collaboration (CRC) cards

The second activity in analysis is *CRC cards,* which are a way of defining the responsibilities for each class that you have defined. CRC cards were invented by Ward Cunningham and Kent Beck as a way of exploring how classes interact with one another and provide services to one another while performing various scenario tasks. CRC cards are really useful because they're concrete (i.e., physical, manipulable) and so easily shared in groups.

Typically, CRC cards are common 3 × 5 index cards (Figure 4–1). Across the top, you write the class name. You make two columns, one for Responsibilities of this class, and another for the Collaborators of this class. That's all there is to a CRC Card.

You are *strongly* encouraged to use real, physical, paper-based 3 × 5 index cards. Part of the fun of CRC cards is arranging them, fiddling with them, and tossing them around. The physicality of the cards is really part of the method. But if you insist on doing things virtually, a **CRCcard** morph is available (by the author and Lex Spoon) for manipulating the cards on-line. The source is available on the CD. Once filled-in, you can create new ones simply by choosing *New Morph* from the World Menu, then choosing **CRCCard** from the *Windows* submenu. See Figure 4–2.

Here's what you do with CRC cards:

- Write the name of each class that you plan to define at the top of its own card.
- If you want, you can start writing responsibilities for that class on the card.
- Invent some scenarios—functions or sets of activities that go together that you will want your set of objects to handle. In UML, these are called *use cases,* and in eXtreme Programming (XP), these are simply called *stories.* If you were

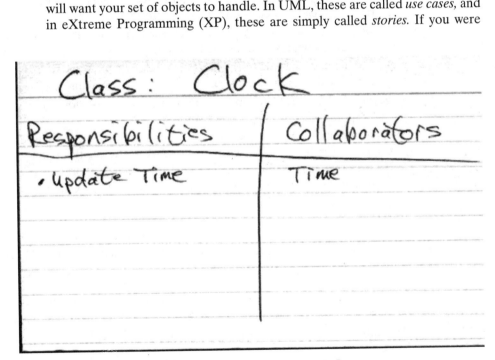

Figure 4–1   A Typical CRC Card

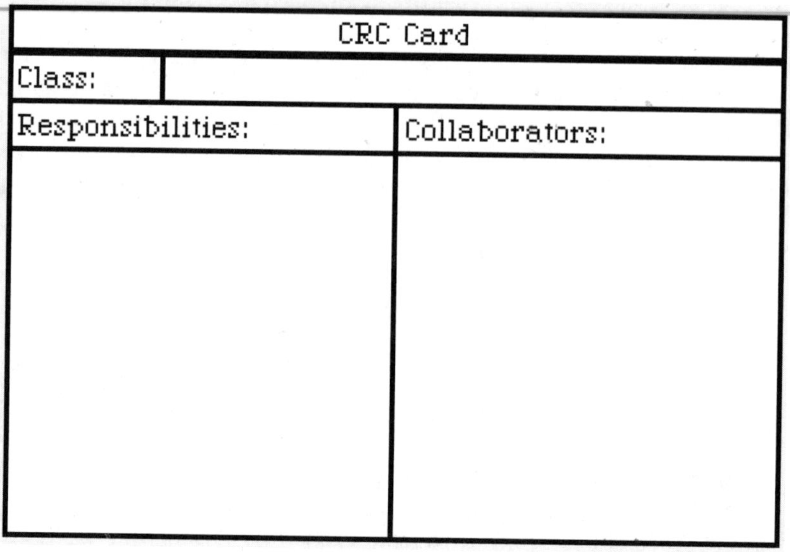

```
┌─────────────────────────────────────────────────────────────┐
│                        CRC Card                              │
├──────────────┬──────────────────────────────────────────────┤
│ Class:       │                                              │
├──────────────┴──────────────┬───────────────────────────────┤
│ Responsibilities:           │ Collaborators:               │
│                             │                               │
│                             │                               │
│                             │                               │
│                             │                               │
│                             │                               │
│                             │                               │
│                             │                               │
│                             │                               │
│                             │                               │
└─────────────────────────────┴───────────────────────────────┘
```

Figure 4–2   A CRC Morph

designing an inventory system, your scenarios might include handling a delivery and collecting materials for an invoice. If you were designing a class-registration system, your scenarios might include checking that a student has the pre-requisites for a class and making sure that there was room in a class.

- Now, play with your cards. Walk through each of your scenarios and use the cards to identify who is responsible for what.
  - What object will get the initial message that starts the scenario process? Lay that card down first on a table or some other large playing surface.
  - What will the object be responsible for? If that information is not written in the responsibilities, write it down now.
  - What other objects will that object need to work with? As you encounter each object in the scenario, lay down its card and iterate through the process. What are its responsibilities? Who will it need to collaborate with?
  - As objects leave the scenario, pick the relevant cards back up. Lay down new cards as their objects enter the scenario.

The CRC cards can help you check that you've covered all your responsibilities, that you understand the interactions between the objects, and that the responsibilities make sense. They have other useful attributes, too:

- The cards form a useful record of your early design thoughts. In a big project, capturing why someone made the design decisions they did can be very useful.
- You can play with your cards in a group! Walking through scenarios with CRC cards can be done with a whole development team or even nonprogramming stakeholders (like, maybe the customer,) gathered around the table. CRC cards

are non-technical, so there is no language or notation to learn. Instead, it's all about talking through the process as objects. Talking with the developers and other stakeholders is a great way of making sure that everyone understands the objectives.

4.1.2 Object-Oriented Design Stage

The output from the analysis stage is a set of object definitions, in terms of their responsibilities and collaborators. These definitions will become *class definitions* through the design stage. We are not actually defining the individual object instances of our eventual system. Rather, we are defining the general behavior for classes of these instances. By making the object definitions into classes, we can create as many of the object as we want, as well as handle growth and complexity in the system.

The outcome of the design stage is a description detailed enough to code from. For this book, the result of the design will have two parts:

- A class diagram, which defines the attributes and services of each class and formally identifies the connections between each class.
- A detailed description of what each service is supposed to do.

There are many different forms of the detailed description. Peter Coad, an author and object-oriented design methodologist, likes an "I am . . ." notation. *"I am a Count. I know how to increment. To increment, do . . ."* Others prefer notations like Activity, Sequence, or Collaboration Diagrams, which are notations in the UML Standard. Still others use flowcharts and pseudocode. In this book, we will forego another notation to settle for a natural-language description.

There are just as many different kinds of class diagrams that one might use as there are forms of detailed description, but there is now an accepted standard for this notation. There is a standard for class diagrams, and many other kinds of diagrams, called UML (for *Unified Modeling Language*). UML was invented by a group of developers who had different methodologies for object-oriented design and were interested in coming up with a single, uniform process. UML has been approved as a standard by the Object Management Group (OMG).

UML is amazingly powerful: It has notations for various stages of analysis (for example, there are notations for describing scenarios) as well as for design stages. In fact, a theorist recently showed that you can actually compile UML correctly to an object-oriented language now! In general, the different class diagrams are fairly similar to one another between different OO methodologies, but it's useful to learn the standard.

4.1.2.1 UML tools

There are several tools out there for creating and manipulating UML diagrams:

- The standard UML tool (literally, the one in which the standard is first implemented) is Rational Rose. A demo version is available for free at

~~http://www.rational.com.~~ While Rational Rose is the most complete implementation of UML, it's also an enormous, expensive, and complicated program.

- Another popular UML tool is Together, by Object International (http://www.oi.com) which is provided by OO guru Peter Coad. A version of Together is also available for free from http://www.togethersoft.com. The neat thing about Together is that it ties the software to the diagrams: Updating one updates the other. Together also comes in an "Enterprise" version, which can support multiple languages, but the free version is specific to either Java or C++ (you get to choose which you want). For creation of UML diagrams, either will work.

- Some of the diagrams in this chapter were produced using BOOST, a tool especially designed for student object-oriented designers and programmers by Noel Rappin. BOOST is written in Java. BOOST is available on the accompanying CD, and is available for download at http://www.cc.gatech.edu/gvu/edtech/BOOST/home.html. BOOST actually supports CRC card analysis as well as class diagramming in design.

- Other diagrams in this chapter were produced using Object Plant, a Macintosh-only tool available at http://www.softsys.se/ObjectPlant/.

We have already seen a UML class diagram in the previous chapter, copied to Figure 4–3. Each class becomes a rectangle in this notation. The class rectangle is split into three parts. The class name appears at the top. The middle section lists the *attributes* of the class, and the bottom section lists the *services* of the class.

4.1.2.2 Relationships between classes

The lines between the class boxes indicate *relationships*. Relationships are about all the different ways in which two objects can interact with one another. How can one object be related to another? There are three main kinds of relationships that we'll talk about:

- The first is a *generalization-specialization* or IsA relationship. This relationship indicates that one object (class) is a specialization of another class, and the other class is a generalization of the first class. The NamedBox IsA Box, which means that the NamedBox is a specialization of the more general Box. The IsA relationship often gets implemented later as a superclass-subclass relationship.

- The second is an *association* or HasA relationship. This relationship indicates that one object has another and uses it. The Box HasA Pen that it uses for drawing. A Car HasA Engine, a Student HasA Transcript, and a Person HasA Job. The UML standard points to another similar relationship: Aggregation. Aggregation is part-whole. The sum is *only* the collection of its parts. Aggregation is symbolized with a diamond. Aggregation is not used often, so we won't say more about it now.

- The third is a *dependency* or TalksTo relationship. We don't have any examples in the Box Microworld, but it's not hard to understand. Sometimes, you have one object that sends a message to another, but it isn't a part-whole relationship. For example, your Computer TalksTo a Printer, though you might be more

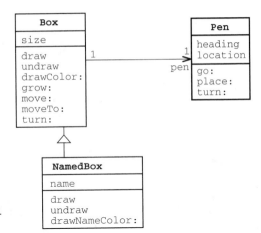

Figure 4–3   Example UML Class Diagram of Box Microworld

tempted to say that your Computer HasA Printer. A dependency relationship is sort of a temporary HasA. It's indicated in UML with a dashed line.

The UML class diagram depicts each of these relationships. The triangle symbol indicates a generalization-specialization relationship. That appears between NamedBox and Box to indicate that the NamedBox **IsA** Box. The line indicates an association relationship between the Pen and the Box.

The association link between Pen and Box tells us three other things, too:

- There are numbers at each end of the line. They indicate that there is one Box (left "1") for one Pen (right "1"). These are the *multiplicities* associated with these objects.
- The word "pen" appears near the Pen class-definition on the right side of the association. This label indicates that the Pen object is referenced by the Box object as **pen**. In some sense, it's a way of identifying attributes outside of the class-definition box.
- There is an arrowhead from Box toward Pen, but not vice-versa. This indicates that the Box can reference the Pen, but that the Pen object doesn't know its corresponding Box. This attribute is called *navigability*. Typically, navigability is defined during the object-oriented *design* stage, because figuring out who needs to reference who is a latter-stage decision.

There is an additional distinction that we will sometimes use in our class diagrams in this book, that is, the distinction between *concrete* and *abstract* classes. A *concrete* class is one from which you will actually create instances. An *abstract* class is one that you create only to define functionality that you will inherit in other classes. You never create instances of an abstract class. In a UML class diagram, an abstract class has the word "abstract" in the top pane of the class box on the diagram.

The UML class-diagram definition includes lots of other distinctions and features that we will not use in this book. That is not to say that the additional distinctions are not useful; however, the philosophy here is to provide a minimal notation. For example, there are also *constraints* in UML. There are frequently constraints on objects, e.g., an Order has more than one Shipping Request associated with it only if one of the Items ordered is back-ordered. UML allows for putting constraint descriptions on a diagram in curly braces.

4.2 YOUR FIRST DESIGN: A CLOCK

Let's do our first design example: A clock. We'll design a good, old-fashioned, uncomplicated clock. It's a simple artifact of which we are all users, so we're all qualified to be valid analysts of it. The goal, however, is to produce something reusable and maintainable so that we can develop more things with it.

4.2.1 Doing it Quickly . . . and Wrong

Let's do a quick design of the clock—which we identify up front will be wrong. Watch for where the design goes wrong.

First, we brainstorm the pieces of a clock. What goes into a clock?

- A face for the clock, to read the time from—leaving open the question of analog or digital clock face, and 12-hour or 24-hour time representation.
- Some kind of internal ticker that keeps the clock moving at a regular interval.
- Probably some internal representation of hours, minutes, and seconds. (Maybe on a lower level than even that?)
- Some way of mapping between the internal ticker into seconds, and then every 60 of those, into minutes, and then every 60 of those, into hours.
- Some kind of knob for setting the clock.

Let's pause there and start filtering. We should filter out the face for the clock and the knob for setting the time, for now. Both of those are about the human-computer interface. Our clock must have a way of presenting the display-able time, and for setting the current time, but the interface to those methods comes later. For now, let's ignore those pieces.

The rest of it, plus the pieces for displaying time and setting the time, seem like a reasonable definition of a Clock class. We can identify several *instance variables:*

- For tracking time: **seconds**, **minutes**, and **hours**.
- For deciding how to display the time (e.g., 12 or 24 hours): **displayFormat**.

Similarly, we can define several methods:

- For accessing the time variables: **getSeconds**, **setSeconds**, **getMinutes**, **setMinutes**, **getHours**, **setHours**

- For ticking the clock: **nextSecond**.
- For getting the time into the appropriate display format: **display** (the time), **setFormat**.
- Maybe something for getting the time into some kind of raw form, and for setting the time: **getTime**, **setTime**.

4.2.2 Object-Oriented Analysis of the Clock

There. Did you see it? Did you notice when we started making design-process mistakes? That last example had several of them:

- When did we decide to do only a single class, Clock? Putting everything in a single class is a bad idea for lots of reasons. It centralizes responsibility and authority, which makes it hard to work on in a group and doesn't take advantage of object-oriented programming. Further, it makes it hard to reuse. Think about a real clock, say, a clock radio that wakes you up in the morning. Don't you think that there are components of that clock (e.g., some chip, some display) that are used in other devices? Shouldn't our clock also be made up of reusable devices?
- We started out with data, listing all the instance variables, rather than thinking about what our class should do, and even before that, what its responsibilities are.
- We jumped to using words that are specific to given programming languages. As long as possible, we should remain language-independent. We should talk about attributes (the ones that might get mapped to instance variables in Smalltalk and Java, or member data in C++) and services (the ones that might get mapped to methods or member functions), because these describe the objects, not the implementations.
- We also started using a get/set kind of notation right away, e.g., **getTime** and **setTime**. While not bad, that notation is more common in Java or C++ than in Smalltalk. It's important to be aware of the idioms of a given language community.

4.2.2.1 Brainstorming a clock

We can use some of those previous analyses, but we really do need to start over. So let's brainstorm again what makes up a clock. But this time, let's consider all the relevant *objects:*

- A **Display**, which would be responsible for displaying the time,
- A **Time**, for tracking hours, minutes, and seconds and their relationships,
- A **Ticker** or **SecondsTicker** (if we're going to use seconds as our smallest grain size for time), for providing constant time pulses,
- A **Clock**, which would be responsible for tracking time and displaying it on request.

Again, we'll pass on the display object for now, as being in the realm of human-computer interfaces. But the rest seem like a reasonable assortment of pieces to be-gin with. Now we need to flesh out the responsibilities of each candidate object and its collaborators. We use the term "candidate" because we can still decide to reject some or add some. CRC cards are good for this.

4.2.2.2 CRC cards for a clock

We need some scenarios to use in our CRC-card analysis. Here are two relevant ones that seem to capture the most critical pieces in our design:

- When the **SecondsTicker** ticks out a time pulse, an internal counter must incre-ment seconds, minutes, and hours as needed.
- When a display is requested, the appropriate format for the display must be determined, and the time must be gathered, then converted (as necessary) to the appropriate format.

Let's play these out using CRC cards. First, we play out a new time pulse.

- Control begins with the Ticker. We'll call it a **SecondsTicker** because we don't really care (here) about time at intervals shorter than a second. It needs to tell the clock that a second has gone by. We write down this responsibility for the **SecondsTicker**, and we note that it needs to collaborate with the **Clock**. See Fig-ure 4–4.
- Now the **Clock** enters the picture. It needs to accept the pulse from the **SecondsTicker**. It doesn't really have a collaborator for that—the **SecondsTicker** is initiating the action. But the **Clock** also must increment the representation of **Time**. This implies that the **Clock** must collaborate with the **Time** object. See Fig-ure 4–5.
- Now **Time** is informed that a second has gone by, so it must increment its sec-onds representation, which may in turn trigger the representations for minutes and hours. **Time** doesn't need any collaborators to do this. Having provided its service to the **Clock**, **Time** leaves the scenario, and then the **Clock** completes its service to **SecondsTicker**, and the **Clock** also leaves the scenario. See Figure 4–6.

✗	CRC		⭘
Class: SecondsTicker			
Responsibilities:		Collaborators:	
Pulse the clock.		Clock	

Figure 4–4   The First CRC Card in the Ticker Scenario

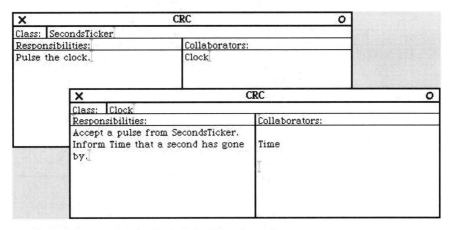

Figure 4–5   Adding the Clock to the Ticker Scenario

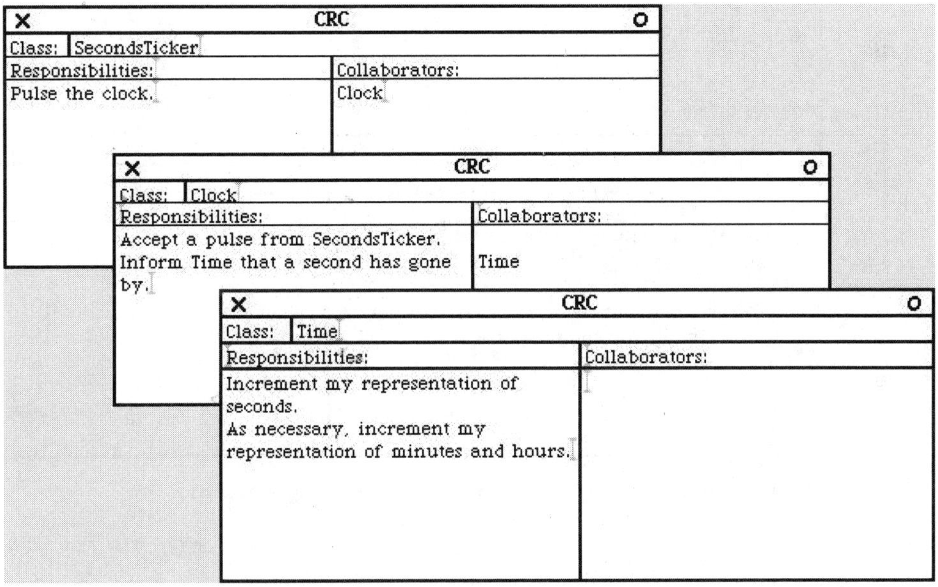

Figure 4–6   Last stage in CRC analysis of Ticker Scenario

We have now defined several roles and interactions between objects. Let's walk through the next scenario and add to these. Then next scenario begins with a request (perhaps from the human interface, perhaps from some other external object that wants to use the time) to display the time:

- When a time display is requested, the **Clock** needs to get the time, so **Time** is a collaborator. Note that **Clock**'s other responsibilities and collaborators remain. (In the end, we must design **Clock** for all its responsibilities.) See Figure 4–7.

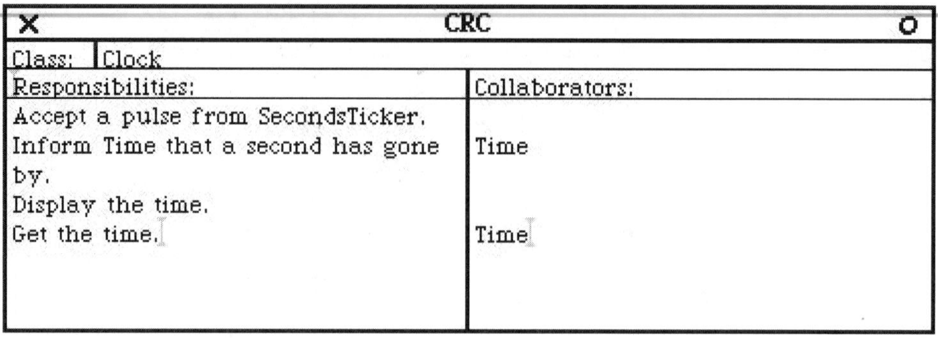

✕	CRC		○
Class: Clock			
Responsibilities:		Collaborators:	
Accept a pulse from SecondsTicker. Inform Time that a second has gone by.		Time	
Display the time. Get the time.		Time	

Figure 4–7   Clock enters the Display Scenario

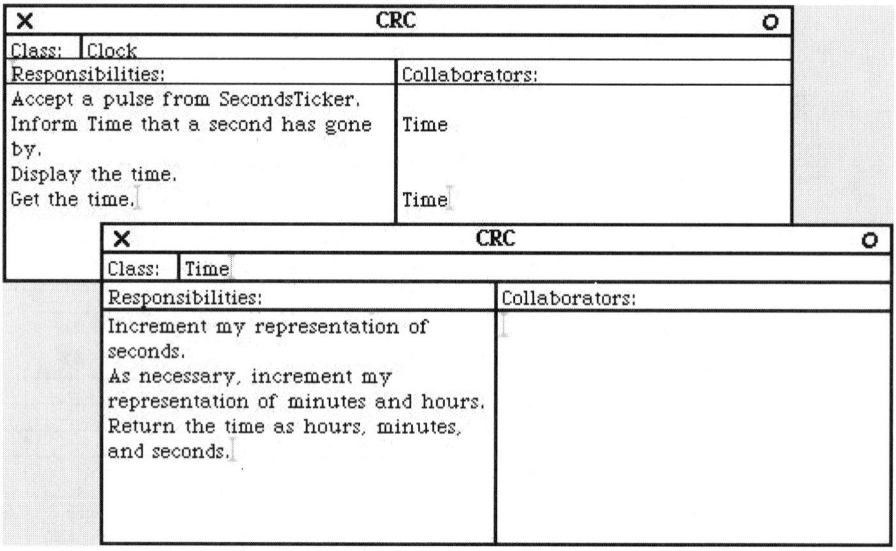

✕	CRC		○
Class: Clock			
Responsibilities:		Collaborators:	
Accept a pulse from SecondsTicker. Inform Time that a second has gone by.		Time	
Display the time. Get the time.		Time	

✕	CRC		○
Class: Time			
Responsibilities:		Collaborators:	
Increment my representation of seconds. As necessary, increment my representation of minutes and hours. Return the time as hours, minutes, and seconds.			

Figure 4–8   Clock collaborates with Time in the Display Scenario

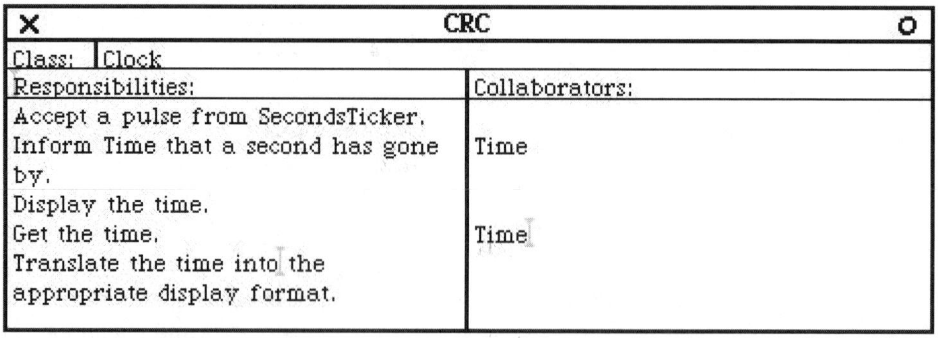

✕	CRC		○
Class: Clock			
Responsibilities:		Collaborators:	
Accept a pulse from SecondsTicker. Inform Time that a second has gone by.		Time	
Display the time. Get the time. Translate the time into the appropriate display format.		Time	

Figure 4–9   Clock completes the Display Scenario

- **Time** must return the time in a format that the **Clock** can manipulate, since it will be the **Clock**'s responsibility to format it. See Figure 4–8.
- **Time** can leave the scenario after returning the raw representation of the time, and the **Clock** must format the time appropriately, and then return it to the caller to be displayed. See Figure 4–9.

4.2.3 Object-Oriented Design of a Clock

At this point, we have some CRC cards that tell us about our classes. We now have a pretty good idea about what each object is going to be responsible for, and what it is not responsible for (that is, what is passed on to its collaborators). We can now talk about what each class *knows* and can *do:*

- **Clock:** The **Clock** has to be able to set the **displayFormat** (and thus know it, too) and return time in a given format. It needs to be able to respond to a **nextSecond**, and pass that on to **Time**. Clearly, it needs to know about **Time**.

Now, according to our scenarios and CRC-card analysis, the **Clock** does not actually collaborate with the **SecondsTicker**, so the **Clock** doesn't really need to know about that object. But thinking about it again, it's clear that we did not include a significant scenario. (This is an excellent example of having to step back to the analysis stage and rethink things from there.) What happens when you *start* the clock? When you start the clock, it's really the clock's job to start the timer. For example, you don't plug in an electric clock into a wall socket and then start up a separate timer — you expect the clock to start any internal timers. How will the clock start the timer if it doesn't know about it? It becomes useful for the **Clock** to know its **SecondsTicker** when you think about starting and stopping the **Clock**. Starting and stopping the clock is really about asking the timer to stop firing:

- **SecondsTicker:** The **SecondsTicker** has to know its **clock** in order to be able to tell it when a second has passed. The **SecondsTicker** has to be able to turn on and off (start and stop). It is probably going to use some kind of external process to generate the timing signals, so it will need to know its **process**.
- **Time:** **Time** must be able to track the hours, minutes, and seconds. It must be able to increment the number of seconds, and to have that addition flow into the other units, too. It doesn't really need to know about any other objects.

We characterize the relationships between the **Clock** and the **SecondsTicker** and between the **Clock** and **Time** each as *association* relationships. The **SecondsTicker** and **Time** are each *used* by the Clock. The **Clock** *has* them. They are distinct entities, but it's also clear that **Clock** is associated with both a **SecondsTicker** and a representation of **Time**.

All of this leads to the UML class diagram in Figure 4–10. Given the UML diagram and the previous CRC analysis, it's possible for someone to move into the language-*dependent* aspects of design and actually program our clock. That's our first complete object-oriented design.

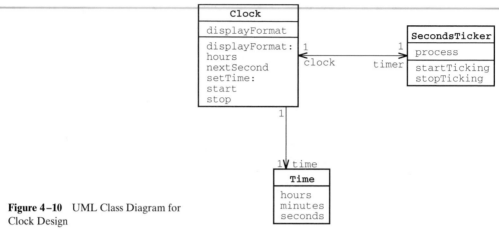

Figure 4–10   UML Class Diagram for Clock Design

Now, in this model, the **Clock** doesn't actually know what hour it is. It can find out by asking its **Time** object. What if you decide that you *want* the **Clock** to know what **hour** it is? What if the user interface that you later connect needs to be able to ask the clock for the hour? What you do then is use a technique called *delegation*. The Clock *can* provide service in response to the message **hour**, but it does it by simply asking its **Time** to provide the **hours**. That's delegation—asking another object to perform the requested service for the requested object.

4.2.3.1 Considering an alternative design

An expert designer actually explores many alternatives to any final design. All the alternatives may not be written down, nor may they even appear in a CRC analysis or UML diagram. But expert designers at least *consider* other ways of doing a design. Their goal is not to come up with a *perfect* design that covers *all* situations; that's usually not possible. But designers are looking for the best solution for the current problem while trying to maintain maximum malleability for the future.

We should do the same. What are the other ways in which we could do the design? Different designs with basically the same functionality are often referred to as different *factorings* of the solution, like when you move variables around an equation without changing its value. Let's brainstorm a bit about different factorings of the **Clock** solution.

What about dropping the **Clock** object and just having the **SecondsTicker** talk directly to **Time**? That removes a middleman, which is often a good idea. However, that kind of a model is somewhat resistant to reuse and not very reflective of the real world. Think ahead to when we create variations of the **Clock**, like the **AlarmClock**. Do we subclass **Time** to create **AlarmTime**? But isn't an **AlarmTime** exactly the same as regular **Time**? (While it may seem that **AlarmTime** is awfully fast when you hit the snooze button, the reality is that it's still about seconds, minutes, and hours.) And when we need **Time** in other contexts (e.g., as a timestamp for when something happens), does it make sense for **Time** in those other contexts to know how to respond to the next second pulse from **SecondsTicker**? Also, think ahead to creating a user

---

CAUTIONARY NOTE:

We don't always put all the accessors in the class diagram, at least not at the object-oriented design (OOD) stage. Obviously, all the accessors that you want have to actually be implemented, but they can be left implicit at the OOD stage.

Similarly, we do not always specify the attributes that are necessary to implement whole-part relationships at the OOD level. It's not incorrect to do so, but it's also okay to leave it to the programmer to figure out how to implement the relationships specified in the model.

SIDE NOTE:

In a sense, *inheritance* is a form of *delegation,* where delegation is implied whenever a message is sent to a subclass and the subclass has not provided a method to override the superclass's method. The key to *polymorphism* is *late-binding,* where one message can be handled by any number of classes and the association of a given class's method to a given message is done as late as possible. Inheritance is enabled by late-binding, and a similar technique is used to enable broader delegation capabilities in some languages.

---

interface on the **Clock**. Does it make sense to have a user interface on **Time**? Maybe it does. The question that you have to ask yourself is whether **Time** and **Clock** are separate objects or really the same.

What about dropping the **Time** object and having the **Clock** know about seconds, minutes, and hours? That's the way that we originally tried to do the design in Section 4.2.1. That could work, and there would be no user-interface problem. But **Time** is still a useful object all by itself, even without the context of a **Clock**. (In fact, that's why there is a **Time** class implemented in the base Squeak image!) **Time** is actually a *reusable* object. It's better to keep it separate and just use its services for the **Clock**.

EXERCISES: REVIEWING THE CLOCK DESIGN

1. Would this design change if we were talking about an analog clock (two or three hands on a face with 12 numbers on it) rather than a digital one? How would it change?
2. How would this design change if we wanted a millisecond resolution on the clock instead of seconds resolution?
3. Implement the methods **halfDayFormat** and **continuousDayFormat**, which switch the **Clock** between 12- and 24-hour time formats. Also implement **isHalfDayFormat** and **isContinuousDayFormat** tests.

SIDE NOTE

The question of whether to make two separate objects or combine them into one comes up frequently for an object-oriented designer. There are two questions you have to ask yourself. Do these two objects have different *behaviors?* Do these two objects have different *data* (attributes), or are they the same data with different values? If they don't have different behaviors and they only differ in values for the same attributes, then combine them. But if they do differ in behavior or attributes, separate them.

4.2.4 Object-oriented programming for the Clock

Now let's build some of those objects we just designed. All of the code that follows is on the CD and on the website. The definition of the class **Clock** is pretty straightforward:

```
Object subclass: #Clock
        instanceVariableNames: 'time timer displayFormat '
        classVariableNames: "
        poolDictionaries: "
        category: 'ClockWorks'
```

So is the definition of the class **SecondsTicker**:

```
Object subclass: #SecondsTicker
        instanceVariableNames: 'clock process '
        classVariableNames: "
        poolDictionaries: "
        category: 'ClockWorks'
```

But in Smalltalk, we don't need to implement **Time**. **Time** is a pre-defined class in Smalltalk, and it already does all the things that we need it to do. We may need to change some of our method definitions as we go along—that's part of the language-dependent aspect of design. But the responsibilities remain the same.

4.2.4.1 Implementing SecondsTicker

Let's talk about what goes on inside the **Clock**, bottom-up, starting with the **Seconds Ticker**. The **SecondsTicker** needs some accessor methods for manipulating its clock instance variable:

```
clock
        ^clock
clock: aClock
        clock ← aClock.
```

But the really tricky part of the **SecondsTicker** is how it ticks off seconds.

Smalltalk already knows all about multi-processing. You can have many different processes running at the same time in Smalltalk. What we need the **SecondsTicker** to do is

- Create a **process** (at this point, not clear what that will be) that sends the **Clock** the message **nextSecond** after each second.
- Stop that process when requested.

This turns out to be pretty easy when using Smalltalk's built-in classes. To create a process, you simply send a block the message **newProcess**. It is created in a frozen (or *suspended*) state. To get the process started, we tell it to **resume**.

We need a process that will wait a second, send a message, then repeat indefinitely. **[true] whileTrue: [ ].** is an effective infinite loop. There is already a class named **Delay** that can create instances for different time durations (as we saw in the last chapter, when we made Joe the Box animate well). When an instance is told to **wait**, it pauses the process for that long.

Processes have *priorities;* a higher priority gets more CPU attention than a lower priority. Our timing process needs to do very little, and only once a second (which, in CPU time, is very infrequently). We don't want our timing process to conflict with other processes, so we'll make it a low priority. The class **Processor** defines a bunch of priority levels. We'll take a low, background priority:

```
startTicking
        "Define a process to send nextSecond once a second forever"
    process := [[true]
        whileTrue:
            [(Delay forSeconds: 1) wait.
            clock nextSecond.]]
        newProcess.
        "Make it not interrupt anything"
    process priority: (Processor userBackgroundPriority).
        "Start the process"
    process resume.
```

Stopping the process is even easier. Because we create a reference to the process in the instance variable **process**, our **SecondsTicker** just has to tell the process to stop, or **terminate**:

```
stopTicking
    process terminate.
```

4.2.4.2 Side trip on Processes

We won't need too much more of **Process** to create **Clock** or any of its descendants, but they are awfully useful, so it's worthwhile to discuss them a bit more. Instances of **Process** are independent flows of control. Processes do not correspond to operating-system processes or threads. They are implemented within only the virtual machine. They are *pre-emptive* between priority levels (i.e., higher levels can interrupt lower levels), and *cooperative* within a priority level. They can be in a suspended state (explicitly put in a suspended state with the message **suspend**), then resumed (**resume**), and also terminated (**terminate**). Priority levels can be set with **priority:**.

Processes can pass information through **Semaphores**. Processes can interact by talking to the same instance of a **Semaphore**. A signal is sent when you send the message **signal** and received when you send the message **wait**. If no signal has been sent when a **wait** message is sent, the sending instance of **Process** will be suspended until a signal is sent. While it may not sound like much, this limited amount of information is enough to implement things like a **SharedQueue**, an object that makes sure that multiple processes can access the same queue safely.

Processes have an **errorHandler** block associated with them. The **errorHandler** block allows us to deal with errors that may occur within the block. Where there is an entire **Exception** hierarchy of classes, error handling is easiest to deal through the use of **ifError:**. Blocks understand **ifError:**, and **ifError:** takes a block with two arguments. The first argument is the error that occurred, and the second is the receiver. The block can take some action to recover or deal with whatever error occurred.

If you have a **Process** running along that you've lost a reference to, it will not get garbage-collected. Once running, the scheduler knows about it, so there will always be one reference to it. You can find all references to all processes by executing:

```
Smalltalk garbageCollect. "Clear out any that need to be collected"
Process allInstances inspect. "View the rest of them"
```

You can then find the one you want (probably near the bottom of the list) and send it **terminate**. Be careful that you don't accidentally **terminate** a process that you want to keep running, like the garbage-collection process! Your processes will usually be some form of "DoIt," while the necessary processes refer to things like **LowSpaceWatcher** and **ProcessScheduler**. (Of course, you can always **terminate** one of those, just to see what happens, then quit the image without saving.)

4.2.4.3 Implementing the Clock class

The **Clock** does very little beside talk to its pieces. First it needs some accessor methods (including one to delegate **hour** to **time**):

```
hours
        ^time hours
time
        ^time
timer
        ^timer
```

Starting and stopping the **Clock** is a matter of setting up and tearing down the timer. The first thing that you may notice is that **start** and **stop** check to see if the **timer** instance variable is **nil** (empty), and if not, the **timer** is asked to stop. (The **timer** instance variable will be **nil** before it is assigned anything.) At the end of **stop**, the **timer** is set back to **nil**. The **timer** must stop, even if (by accident) **start** is executed twice in a row. Once the **timer** process is started, it's very hard to stop unless we explicitly **terminate** it. Executing start a bunch of times in a row, without stopping any of the old timers from ticking, will leave *lots* of old processes floating around, a situation that eats up CPU time and slows down your system. The code is as follows:

```
start
        timer isNil ifFalse:
                [timer stopTicking. "Stop one if already existing."].
        timer ← SecondsTicker new.
        timer clock: self.
        timer startTicking.
stop
        timer isNil ifFalse:
                [timer stopTicking].
        timer ← nil.
```

The rest of the **Clock**'s methods are manipulating the time. Setting the time turns out to be a predefined function in the class **Time**. The method **readFrom:** can understand time in a variety of string formats, such as '13:13' and '12:10 am'. All we have to do is create a **Stream** on the input string. A **Stream** is a kind of object that can be read or written efficiently, one element (in our case, one character) at a time. (We saw streams briefly in Chapter 2 when we looked at how files are manipulated in Squeak.) We need a **ReadStream** for reading the input string, so we simply create a **ReadStream** on our string:

```
setTime: aString
        time ← Time readFrom: (ReadStream on: aString).
```

nextSecond is a little more complicated, though it is also just a single line. There is no predefined method for incrementing seconds in the class **Time**. But there is an ability to add two times together. So, **nextSecond** creates a **Time** instance of only a single second, then adds it to our current **time**, and makes the result the new current **time**:

```
nextSecond
        time ← time addTime: (Time fromSeconds: 1)
```

Another responsibility of the **Clock** is dealing with displaying the time; in the appropriate format. First, we need an accessor method for the **displayFormat**:

```
displayFormat: aType
        "aType should be '24' or '12'"
        displayFormat ← aType
```

The last method is the longest and most complicated: **display**. In **display**, the **Clock** instance gets the hours, minutes, and seconds from the **Time** instance (padding minutes and seconds with 0's). (Recall that the comma is the string-concatenation message in Smalltalk.) If the display format is 24-hour, we drop through to the bottom and just output a string of hours, minutes, and seconds. If it's a 12-hour display format, we have to compute a 'pm' time versus an 'am' time versus a just-after-noon time, which is 'pm' but doesn't require that we subtract 12 from the time. Following is the code:

```
display
        "Display the time in a given format"
        | hours minutes seconds |
        hours ← time hours printString.
        minutes ← time minutes printString.
        (minutes size > 2) ifTrue: [minutes ← '0',minutes]. "Must be two digits"
        seconds ← time seconds printString.
        (seconds size > 2) ifTrue: [seconds ← '0',seconds].
        (displayFormat = '12')
        ifTrue: [(hours asNumber > 12)
                ifTrue: [^((hours asNumber - 12) printString),':',minutes,':',
                        seconds,' pm'].
                (hours asNumber > 12)
                ifTrue: [^hours,':',minutes,':',seconds,' am']
                ifFalse: ["Exactly 12 must be printed as pm"
                        ^hours,':',minutes ,':',seconds,' pm']]
        ifFalse: ["24-hour time is the default if no displayFormat is set"
                ^hours,':',minutes,':',seconds].
```

That's it! Try out your clock with some workspace code. First, set up a clock and tell it to start:

```
cl := Clock new.
cl displayFormat: '12'.
cl setTime: '2:05 pm'.
cl start.
```

Try this a few times to convince yourself that the clock is running: **Transcript show: cl display**. Finally, end the clock with **cl stop**.

EXERCISES ON CLOCK

4. If the **timer** is **nil** during **start**, do we have to stop it? What could be done instead? Implement your solution.
5. Implement **isTiming**, which returns true if the clock currently has a running timer.
6. The **display** code is awful. First, there's a bug in it: 12:01 am will be displayed at 0:01 am. Second, it's too huge. Refactor the code and repair it.

4.3 SPECIALIZING CLOCK AS AN ALARMCLOCK

The next design project is an **AlarmClock**. Our first impulse might be to change the **Clock** class, but that would be a bad idea. Clocks are useful in themselves, and there are clocks in the real world that are not alarm clocks. There are mechanisms for modeling different *kinds* of things in Smalltalk, or in any object-oriented language. In general, it's better to reuse and extend than to redesign and change.

4.3.1 OOA for AlarmClock

An **AlarmClock** is clearly *a kind of* **Clock**, so we model it as a *specialization* (later, when we program it, as a *subclass*). The **Clock** is the *generalization* (*superclass*). We can use a CRC analysis to figure out how the responsibilities of an **AlarmClock** differ from those of a **Clock**.

 The main difference is in what happens in the second during which the alarm should go off. When the current time is the alarm time, how do you detect it? What do you do? See Figure 4–11.

- The **AlarmClock** will depend on its generalization to inherit the standard **nextSecond** behavior, which increments the time.
- The **AlarmClock** needs a new **Time** object, one that represents the alarm time.
- When the alarm time arrives, the **AlarmClock** needs to execute the alarm behavior.

4.3.2 OOD for AlarmClock

We can now think more carefully about the definition of the class **AlarmClock**. It needs to handle responsibility for **nextSecond** itself (and within it, call upon Clock's **nextSecond** behavior). Clearly, it must know an **alarmTime**, so the **AlarmClock** has its

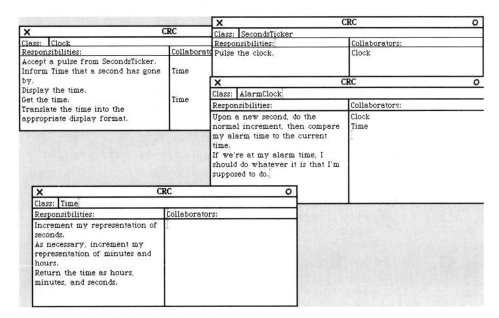

Figure 4–11 CRC Cards for AlarmClock

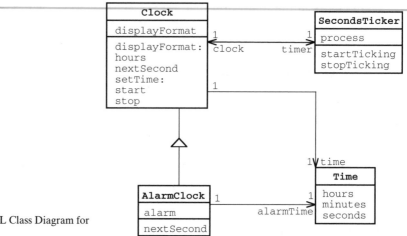

Figure 4–12   UML Class Diagram for
Alarm Clock

own **Time** (HasA relationship). The **AlarmClock** needs to know what its alarm behavior is. For now, we will define that alarm behavior as an attribute, an **alarm**, so that we later have flexibility in what happens upon an alarm. We are leaving open the option of defining an **Alarm** class later, though as we will see, we will end up using the attribute for a language-dependent feature. See Figure 4–12.

The fact that we could use our **Time** class in more than one place (i.e., as the representation of running time in the Clock and as the representation of the alarm time in the **AlarmClock**) is an indication that we are doing well with the design so far. Potential future reuse is a good test of current designs. If we can reuse our objects in new situations, then we did indeed come up with definitions of flexible objects, like the ones that inhabit the real world.

4.3.3 OOP for the AlarmClock

Before we actually implement the **AlarmClock**, let's make the language-dependent decision that we alluded to earlier. The **AlarmClock** must do *something* when the alarm is to go off. In the design, we simply inserted an **alarm** attribute. As we get language-specific, we realize that we can just define the alarm behavior as a *block*. As we program the **AlarmClock**, we will define **alarm** as **alarmBlock**.

The **AlarmClock** class definition is then straightforward, according to the class diagram:

```
Clock subclass: #AlarmClock
        instanceVariableNames: 'alarmTime alarmBlock '
        classVariableNames: "
        poolDictionaries: "
        category: 'ClockWorks'
```

The **AlarmClock** has very few methods. There are obviously some access methods:

alarmBlock: aBlock
>   alarmBlock ← aBlock.
alarmTime
>   ^alarmTime
setAlarmTime: aString
>   alarmTime ← Time readFrom: (ReadStream on: aString).

The interesting part of **AlarmClock** is **nextSecond**. It does the following things:

- It asks its superclass, **Clock**, to handle the basic **nextSecond** responsibility.
- It then compares its **alarmTime** to the current **time**. If they are equal, it's time to fire off the **alarmBlock** by taking its **value**. **value** is the method that asks a block of code in Smalltalk to execute.

nextSecond
>   super nextSecond.
>   (time = alarmTime) ifTrue: [alarmBlock value].

Test the **AlarmClock** with some workspace code. When the alarm goes off, Squeak beeps three times and displays "ALARM!" in the Transcript:

```
cl ← AlarmClock new.
cl setTime: '2:04 pm'.
cl alarmBlock: [3 timesRepeat: [Smalltalk beep. Transcript show: 'ALARM!']].
cl setAlarmTime: '2:06 pm'.
cl start
```

After the alarm fires, the clock is still going. (Does your clock radio stop after you turn off the alarm?) You need to explicitly stop it with a DoIt on **cl stop**.

EXERCISES: BUILDING ON THE ALARMCLOCK

7. How would you implement a snooze button (one that you can press when the alarm goes off to delay the alarm for five or so minutes)?

8. Design and implement an alarm clock for two people who have to get up at different times and want different kinds of alarms, e.g., one wants a different radio station or a beep (try **Smalltalk beep**) instead of a radio wake-up call. How would you differentiate alarm actions and alarm behaviors?

4.4 REUSING THE CLOCK AND ALARMCLOCK

The **AlarmClock** was a reasonable test of the **Clock**'s reusability, but if the design is good, it should also be flexible when the larger system is reused. In this section, we push the design of the **AlarmClock** (and **Clock**) farther by reusing it in yet more designs.

4.4.1 Reuse in a VCR

An **AlarmClock** is itself useful, but we can test this larger design (more than just the single class **Time**) by seeing if we can reuse it in even larger, more complicated projects. Let's start by talking through use of this **AlarmClock** structure in a VCR (video-cassette recorder). A VCR requires something like an alarm clock to start and stop the recorder.

Brainstorming probably would lead to a decision that new objects are necessary: a **VCR** object and a **VCRRecorder**. We can then use CRC cards to work out the responsibilities of each of these objects (Figure 4–13).

A **VCR** has a recorder, and a current channel, and the **VCR** knows how to do things like start the record process, fast-forward, rewind, change the channel, and so on. If we were out to do a really detailed model of a **VCR**, we might want to think about motors that are controlled by fast-forward and rewind, and perhaps even sensors and a tape carriage for handling the recording and playing process. But since our focus is on the starting and stopping of the recorder, we'll leave those others open for now.

The **VCRRecorder** is where the action is. It is the **VCRRecorder** that tells the **VCR** when to record, on what channel to record, and when to stop. Here's the CRC analysis:

- The **VCRRecorder** has an alarm clock for starting the recording session. When it goes off, it tells the **VCR** to go to the appropriate channel and to start recording.
- The **VCR** knows how to change channels and record.
- The **VCRRecorder** also has an alarm clock for ending the recording session. When the alarm goes off, it tells the **VCR** to stop.

This isn't a very sophisticated extension of an alarm clock, but it is interesting for several reasons. First, it shows the power of combining objects in object systems. Look how many levels we now have in our system (Figure 4–14). **Clocks** have **Seconds Tickers** and **Time**. **AlarmClocks** extend **Clocks** and have an additional **alarmTime**. Now **VCR**s have **VCRRecorders** that themselves have two **AlarmClocks**—and each of those has everything that an **AlarmClock** has: a **SecondsTicker** (attribute inherited from **Clock**, and set through initialization) and two **Time** objects. Our model is actually getting fairly complicated, but the complexity is quite manageable. When you're dealing with the **AlarmClock**, you can quite forget that the **SecondsTicker** is there at all. When you're dealing with the **VCRRecorder**, you just create a couple of **AlarmClocks**, and you tell them their alarm times and what to do when the alarms go off.

When you ask object-oriented programmers what is powerful about object-oriented programming, they will often talk about inheritance. Being able to create a new subclass that can do many things as soon as you create it, because of inheritance, is clearly very powerful. But the real workhorse of object-oriented programming is the ability to combine objects: Connecting objects together, having bunches of objects lying underneath easy-to-use surface objects, having collections of heterogeneous objects. That's where the real power of objects to hide complexity lies.

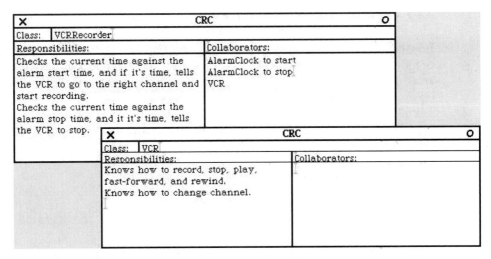

Figure 4–13   CRC cards for VCR and VCRRecorder Objects

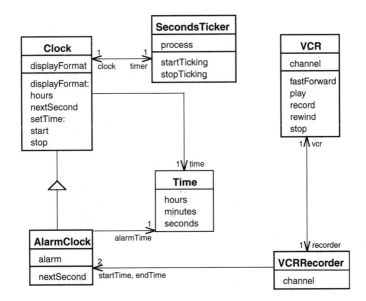

Figure 4–14   Class diagram for VCR design

EXERCISES: CONTINUING THE VCR EXAMPLE

9. If you look at the aggregation in our **VCR**, you'll notice some strangeness. There are actually two **SecondsTickers** in our model, each telling a different **AlarmClock** to tick. In a real **VCR**, these two would probably be combined to create a single timing circuit. How would you change our diagram for a single timer? Would there still be two clocks? Or would it have a new kind of **AlarmClock** that keeps track of multiple alarms?

4.4.2 Reuse in an AppointmentBook

If we can reuse our **AlarmClock** in one situation, that's good. If we can reuse it in two or more, that's better. Our last reuse example of the **AlarmClock** is an **Appointment-Book**. An **AppointmentBook** is a good example because we can actually build and play with it. Unless your computer happens to have a VCR motor and tape-carriage assembly with sensors, you probably can't actually build and use the VCR example.

What are the new objects in an **AppointmentBook**? We can brainstorm a bit here:

- Maybe an **AppointmentBook**, to track appointments.
- A **Calendar**, to associate appointments with their days.
- The former suggests an **Appointment**, which is responsible for alerting the user to a given appointment at the right time.
- Maybe the **AlarmClock**, to trigger the **Appointment**.
- An **AppointmentQueue**, to sort the appointments and set up the **AlarmClock** for the next appointment.

Now, we filter. We want to do this as simply as possible, so that we can set up a demonstration. But we want it to be able to extend later. Let's choose to eliminate the **Calendar** and the **AlarmQueue**. Instead, we'll associate an **AlarmClock** with *each* **Appointment**. It's somewhat inefficient, but it's an inefficiency that can be corrected later. It's simple and allows us to get started quickly. We'll give the **AppointmentBook** the responsibility to alert all the **Appointments** for a given day, which could be triggered by a **Calendar** object if we ever added one.

A complete class diagram appears in Figure 4–15.

- **Appointments** know their alarm and the date on which they should be active. They don't need to know their time—that's *delegated* to the **alarm**.
- **AppointmentBook** knows all the appointments, and it is responsible for turning them on for a given day (and off at the end of the day), and to make an appointment for a given day.

The class diagram in Figure 14 shows how we can aggregate across the existing objects to define the **Appointments** and **AppointmentBook**. Aggregation is an important way to scale up object systems.

CAUTIONARY NOTE

We don't always want to model the whole. That is, we may be able to get by just by defining appointments without an appointment book. If the parts define all of the whole, and we define all the parts, we don't also need to model the whole. In this case, the **AppointmentBook** does more than just collect all the **Appointments**, so we define it separately.

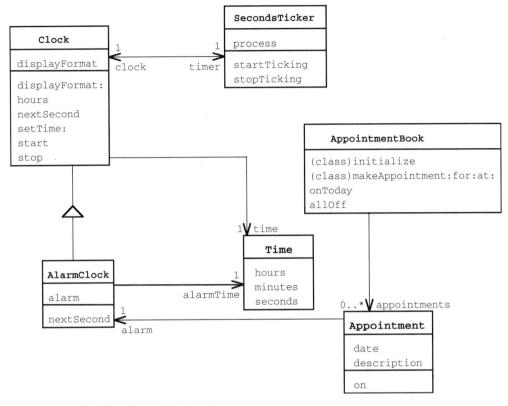

Figure 4–15   Class diagram for Appointments

EXERCISES: ON THE APPOINTMENTBOOK ANALYSIS

10. We skipped the CRC Card analysis in the previous **AppointmentBook** example. Fill it in.

11. The **AppointmentBook** shouldn't be responsible for creating well-formed appointments. Instead, the request to make an appointment should be delegated to the **Appointment** class. How would you model that?

13. Now that we've done it the short way, figure out how to add a **Calendar** and an **AlarmQueue** that uses only one **AlarmClock**.

4.4.2.1 Programming the AppointmentBook

We start out by implementing the two new classes that we need.

```
Object subclass: #AppointmentBook
        instanceVariableNames: 'appointments '
        classVariableNames: ''
        poolDictionaries: ''
        category: 'ClockWorks'
```

```
Object subclass: #Appointment
        instanceVariableNames: 'alarm description date '
        classVariableNames: "
        poolDictionaries: "
        category: 'ClockWorks'
```

4.4.2.2 Implementing the AppointmentBook with Collections

The **AppointmentBook** has a couple of techniques in it that we haven't previously seen, so we'll discuss that one first. To begin with, an **AppointmentBook** must be explicitly initialized. The initialize method sets up the **OrderedCollection** of appointments.

An **OrderedCollection** can be thought of as an array that grows to fit as many elements as are placed in it. Smalltalk has many such collections classes (e.g., **SortedCollections**, **Arrays**, **Sets**, **Bags**). Each has its own characteristics, and the implementation of each is optimized for the kind of characteristics that it supports. For example, **Sets** are unordered and allow no duplications, while **Bags** are unordered and allow duplications.

In fact, it's not obvious that an **OrderedCollection** is the right vehicle for storing the collection of **Appointments** in an **AppointmentBook**. However, **OrderedCollections** provide an amazingly wide variety of services, so they are often a good choice for early implementation and prototyping. Later, a more optimal collection can be chosen. We have

initialize
```
        appointments ← OrderedCollection new.
```

We provide an accessor for the **appointments**, particularly for user interfaces that may want to display all of the appointments:

appointments
```
        ^appointments
```

When we are making an appointment via the **AppointmentBook**, we create an **Appointment** instance, fill it with the appropriate values, and then add it to the **appointments** collection. You will also notice here a reference to the **Date** class. Smalltalk's **Date** class understands how to manipulate dates and answer questions about dates (e.g., "What day of the week was July 4, 1776?" (**Date readFrom: (ReadStream on: 'July 4, 1776')) weekday**, which prints as **Thursday**). We use it for the **date** instance variable in **Appointment**, and we use its ability to parse dates to create the appointment. Again, we must hand it a **Stream**, not a **String**, so we create one on the fly:

makeAppointment: aDescription for: aDate at: aTime
```
        | a |
        a ← Appointment new.        "Make an appointment, and set its attributes"
        a description: aDescription.
        a date: (Date readFrom: (ReadStream on: aDate)).
        a alarm: aTime.
        appointments add: a. "Store it"
```

Note that our **AlarmClock** doesn't know anything about dates, only about time. It doesn't know how to go off on a given day and time, only how to go off at a given time. So turning on the alarm when the appointment is created doesn't work. We can only set the alarm on a given day. That's what **onToday** does:

onToday
```
(appointments select:
      [:each | each date = Date today])
         do: [:each | each on].
```

This is a fairly complex piece of code, even if it's only one statement, so let's go slowly through it in its two major pieces:

- **(appointments select: [:each | each date = Date today])**: All **Collections** in Smalltalk understand methods that allow one to iterate over a **Collection** and do something to or with each element in the **Collection**. **select:** is a method that evaluates a block for each element in the collection, then returns a new collection with just those elements that returned **true** for the block, as seen in Chapter 2. In this piece of code, we are selecting all of those appointments whose date is today.
- **do: [:each | each on]**: In this piece, we are walking over the appointments that are due today, and telling each that it is **on**.

Recall that each appointment has its own **AlarmClock**, which keeps ticking even after the appointment is done. We need a way to turn them all off again:

allOff
```
appointments do:
      [:appointment | appointment alarm stop].
```

EXERCISES: IMPROVING THE APPOINTMENTBOOK

14. We turned on *only* the appointments that were due on the given day, but we turned off *all* alarms. That's both ineffcient (we did the selection in the first case, but processed all appointments in the second), and non-orthogonal (we tell the **appointment** on, but we tell the **alarm** stop). Which way do you like better? Why? Fix the wrong method.

4.4.2.3 Implementing the Appointments

The **Appointments** keep track of the information for each individual appointment in an appointment book. The most important responsibility for an appointment is to track the time, date, and description of each appointment:

date
```
^date
```

```
date: aDate
        "Set date of appointment."
        date ← aDate
description
        ^description
description: aDescription
        description := aDescription.
```

Setting the alarm time is a little tricky. Instead of just recording the time, we use the instance variable **alarm** to actually hold an instance of **AlarmClock**, and delegate tracking the alarm time to it:

```
alarm: someTime
        alarm ← AlarmClock new.
        alarm setAlarmTime: someTime.
```

We provide an accessor method to access the **AlarmClock** instance.

```
alarm
        ^alarm
```

Finally, the method for turning on the alarms is called simply **on**. It creates an **alarmBlock** for the alarm, sets the **AlarmClock**'s current time to the real time, and starts the **AlarmClock**:

```
on
        "The appointment is today, so turn on alarm."
        alarm alarmBlock: [3 timesRepeat: [Smalltalk beep.].
                Transcript show: 'Appointment: ',description.
                alarm stop.].
        alarm setTime: (Time now printString).
        alarm start.
```

We can test the **AppointmentBook** now:

```
b ← AppointmentBook new initialize.
b makeAppointment: 'Testing!' for: '9/27/98' at: '2:34 pm'.
b onToday.
```

When you're declaring the end of the day, be sure to use **b allOff**, or else you'll be leaving seconds timers running around.

EXERCISES: EXTENDING THE APPOINTMENTBOOK

15. Write a **time** method that returns the time of the appointment. (Hint: Delegation!)
16. Why don't we set the **alarmBlock** at the time to which the alarm is set in the **Appointment** instance?

4.5 IMPLEMENTING MODELS

The mapping from a class diagram to a program is fairly straightforward, but there are some decisions to be made. Probably the easiest part of the mapping is from attributes and services to instance variables and methods, but even there, some variations exist. For example, if you were modeling a class of students, you might want to have an attribute called **studentCount** to track the number of students in the class. But when you actually implement this, you may just want to define a method **studentCount** that returns the size of the collection storing the students. That way, you don't have to maintain the count during each addition and deletion, and the count is still fast and up-to-date.

The mapping of classes in the class diagram to actual classes is pretty clean, until you need interactions between objects of the same type. For example, if you had a **LinkedListNode** that pointed to itself, mapping that in a traditional class diagram would be a little confusing. The problem is that the class diagram describes classes; it doesn't do a great job of describing individual objects. You need to keep this distinction in mind when creating the mapping. In UML, sequence and collaboration diagrams do a better job of showing how individual objects relate to one another.

Generalization-specialization relations (*IsA*) always get mapped as superclass-subclass relations, but association (*HasA*) relations can be mapped in a variety of ways:

- The fact that a part (say, tires) is part of a whole (say, a car) doesn't actually tell you anything about who needs to know about what. Does the tire need to send messages to the car? If so, it needs some kind of instance variable that refers to the whole, and it needs to be initialized to set that reference to its car. Does the car need to send messages to its tires? Then the car needs to be able to reference the tire objects. But you don't always need to go both ways. In UML, this issue is called navigability.
- If there is a many-to-one relationship, then you will probably need some kind of collection to manage the relationship. If a course is composed of students, the course object will probably need a collection of students. In our earlier examples, the appointment book had a collection of appointments that were composed within it. But it isn't always true that you need a collection if you have more than one part composed within a whole. For example, consider our alarm clock, which had two instances of **Time** within it: One for the current time (inherited from **Clock**), and one for the alarm time. In this case, two separate instance variables modeled the relationship better than a collection of **Time** objects.

There are lots of other variations for object-oriented design, and lots of other mappings from a design to a programming language. Any good book on UML identifies a number of other kinds of relationships between objects, as well as other aspects of design to consider. For example, we haven't considered the best way to involve stakeholders (the people who care about the result of a design) in a design process, nor have we considered modeling *roles,* that is, the different kinds of users. The issues covered in this chapter are a good start on design, but there's a lot more to learn about doing good design.

4.6 RULES OF THUMB FOR GOOD OBJECT-ORIENTED DESIGNS

The process described in this chapter *can* lead to good object-oriented design, in which a good design is reusable and maintainable. Through the chapter, we've identified several key aspects of a good design:

- It's general and is based on real-world artifacts. That makes the design more reusable.
- It defines objects as nouns, not functions or managers.
- The relationship between a subclass and a superclass is always an IsA relationship.
- It avoids computer science terms like "linked list." The real world doesn't have linked lists in it. Implementations of models of the real world do.

But this is only a partial list. There are many other characteristics of good designs. In this book, we can touch on only a handful of them through the examples and exercises.

There are lots of *rules of thumb,* or *heuristics,* that you can use to measure the quality of your design. They don't always work—sometimes, there are very good reasons for breaking a standard "rule" of design. But they work in most cases and can help in measuring up your design.

Here are several useful object-oriented design rules of thumb:

- Almost no good design consists of a single class. The real world isn't made from a single object. A program that has a single class with many services and attributes looks like a procedural program jammed into an object-oriented language.
- In a good design, information access is enough. Objects don't need information that they can't access. Objects can get to the information they need either directly or by asking one of the objects that they *can* access directly.
- Responsibility, control, and communication are distributed in good designs. One object will not do everything.
- There should be little or no redundancy: Code should appear only once. Use inheritance or delegation so that you do not have to replicate code.
- There is a correct level of detail for any model, and it depends on what you need. Yes, everything in the world is made of molecules, but most problems don't require you to model each and every molecule. Create models for the things that you need.

4.6.1 Reconsidering Joe

Now let's think back to Joe the Box. What can we say about its design now that we've done some more design thinking?

- While it's okay that **Box** is a concrete class and **NamedBox** is also a concrete class, we could also have designed them differently. Think about an *abstract* class **Box** that defines a set of functionality that specific kinds of boxes (like **NamedBox**) implement or redefine. Perhaps **PlainBox** is the concrete subclass of **Box**.
- One disadvantage of the concrete-class implementation is that we are hiding the fact that **draw** and **undraw** must be implemented by subclasses in order to override default drawing. If **Box** were abstract, **draw** and **undraw** could be explicitly undefined, to inform subclasses that implementing drawing is their responsibility.
- The methods defined in Box are mostly *polymorphic*. The methods **move:**, **grow:**, and others are defined once in **Box** but are then inherited by others. They do the same thing, no matter what kind of **Box** you're addressing. The messages **draw** and **undraw** are also polymorphic, but those require new implementations in each subclass.

4.7 TOOLS AND STRATEGIES: PROGRAMMING IN GROUPS

Your code for exercises might be growing large enough that you want to work with someone else. How do you work together? How do you merge code? How do you keep track of your changes, as opposed to someone else's? The issue gets even more complicated when your changes appear in multiple classes. How do you file out all of your changes in multiple classes to give to someone else?

Smalltalk programmers have always worked together in collaborative groups, so the support for programming in groups in Squeak has its roots in the earliest Smalltalk-80. The basic two ideas are *projects* and *change sets*:

- A project stores the state of a complete Squeak desktop, including all the windows (and in Morphic, all morphic objects), as well as the currently active change set. When you change projects, whether by entering or exiting, the global state is saved into the project being exited, and loaded from the one being entered. We have already seen a project and have entered and left. Whatever changes you make to classes while within a project get associated with the change set for that project.
- A change set is a collection of changes to the system. Changes include class changes, method changes, class removals, and method removals. All of these changes impact the *whole* system, e.g., you can't have one version of a method in one change set and another version of the same method in another change

set. But you can fileOut all of the changes of one change set at once. You can also copy changes between change sets, compare change sets, and generally manage change sets.

4.7.1 Creating Projects and Change Sets

You have already seen how to create a project, enter it, and exit it. You can do this from any project. Projects can be nested within projects, and you can jump from any project to any other.

Change sets go along with projects, but they don't have to. You can create change sets, and declare that new changes go to the new change set, from any project whatsoever.

There are two tools available in the *Open...* menu for managing changes: *simple change sorter* and *dual change sorter*. The simple change sorter (Figure 4–16) lets you see the list of change sets in the current system (upper left hand corner), the list of classes in the selected change set (upper right), the list of methods changed in the selected class (center pane), and the actual code in the lower pane. From any change sorter, you can use the yellow-button menu on the change-set pane to create a new change set, file out all the changes of a change set (so that someone else can load in all the things you've changed in a given project), or even choose to send changes to a different change set. Even within a single project, you can choose to make changes go to a different change set.

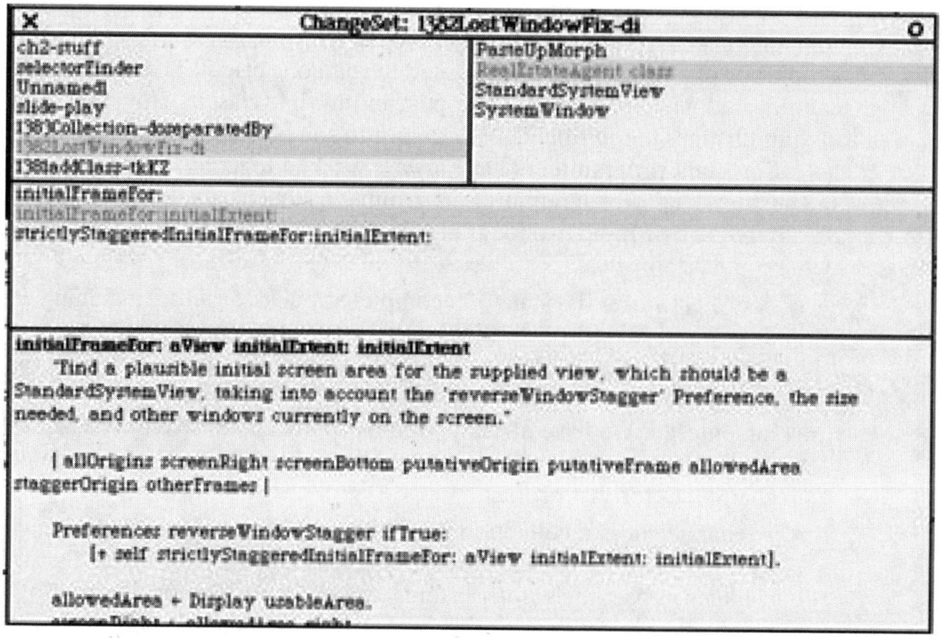

Figure 4–16 Simple Change Sorter

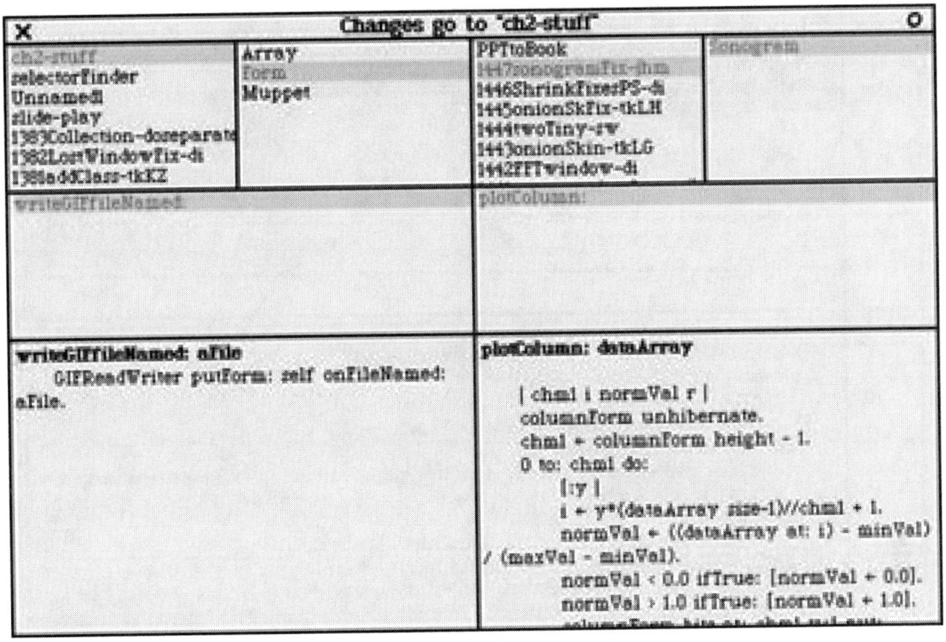

Figure 4–17   Dual Change Sorter

The dual change sorter (Figure 4–17) allows you to look at two change sets at once. With two change sets open at once, you can copy changes from one to the other, submerge one change set into another, or even subtract all the changes from one change set that are also in the other change set. By manipulating change sets, you can find any particular changes that you need to include in what you give to your collaborators.

Change-set files are a little different from the ".st" files in filing out classes or categories. When a change set is filed out, the filename ends with ".cs" rather than the ".st" from filing out the class or method. A changeset fileOut contains the name of the change set and the date and time of the file out. The time stamp makes it easier to track versions of changes.

It's also possible to attach a preamble or postscript to a change set. The preamble appears at the top of a change set, and a postscript appears at the end. In a preamble, you can put in a comment describing the change set, or even provide some set-up code, e.g., check that a prerequisite class is defined in the image before the change set is loaded in. In a postscript, you can clean up things, or perhaps start some of the newly-loaded code.

4.7.2 Working with Someone Else's Changes

When someone else gives you a change set, you could simply file it in via the file list. But you might want to check it first, to see how it differs from what you already have (beware of someone overwriting your methods!) and even just to see what it includes.

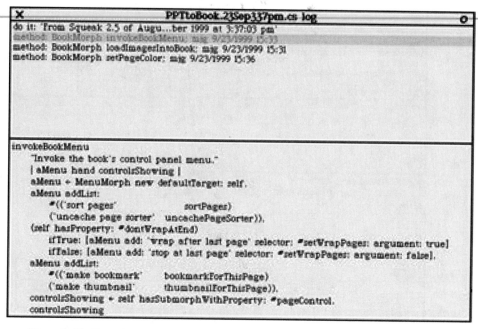

Figure 4–18   Browsing changes from a change set file

From the file list, you have several options from the yellow-button menu when a code file (.cs or .st) is selected:

- You can *File into a new change set*. This option puts all of the new changes into one change set that you can easily inspect using a change sorter.
- You can *Browse* changes (Figure 4–18). This option puts up a window in which you can inspect each separate change that the change set will make to your system if you file it in. You can choose to file in any one or any set of the changes in the change browser. In addition, you can use the yellow-button menu to select just those that are already in your system (conflicts), or those that are not. (Notice that you can see the initials of the author, as well as the time and date, for each change.)
- Perhaps the most powerful option is the ability to *Browse code* (Figure 4–19). The Package Browser allows you to walk through the code that's in the selected file just as if it were already in your System Browser. As you select each method, it tells you if the method is already in your image or not. If it is, strikeouts and color coding show you how the new method differs from the method that's currently in your system. As in the changes browser, the package browser lets you file in any particular methods or classes that you choose.

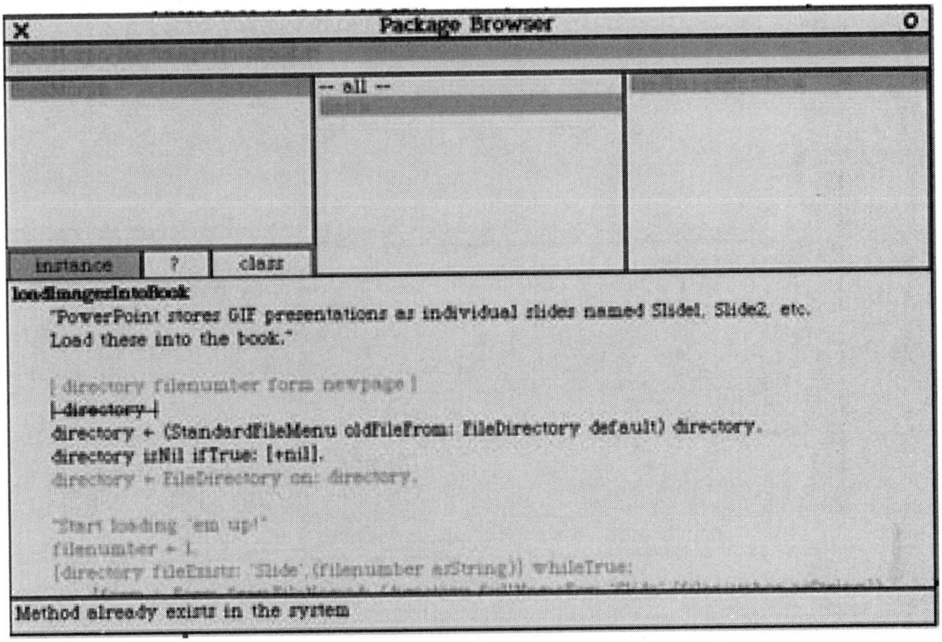

Figure 4–19   Browsing Code from a Code File

4.7.3 Recovering from Someone Else's Changes

You have now filed in someone else's code, but missed one critical method, so now all of your code is broken. (Or maybe you just made a really bad change, and now you realize that you hadn't filed out the previous, almost-working version.) You really want to turn back the clock to an earlier version of the method.

Fortunately, the changes file really does capture *all* changes in the system, which includes all those previous versions of a given method. From any method list (e.g., an implementors list, a System Browser, wherever), you have a yellow-button menu item *Versions...* The recent versions browser shows you all the versions of the same method in your changes file (Figure 4–20). Selecting an older version shows you with color and strikeouts how the selected version differs from your current version. You can copy anything you want out of any older version and paste the changes into your browser to reaccept them.

If you open up the *Preferences* (under the *Help* menu item in the Desktop or World menus), you can choose to *useAnnotationPanes.* In several of the browsers (especially Senders and Implementors), when annotation panes are selected, you are shown a pane between the list of methods and the code that gives useful information about the selected method. This information typically includes the initials of the author, the timestamp, the number of implementors of this method, the number of senders, and which change set the method came from (Figure 4–21). What gets dis-

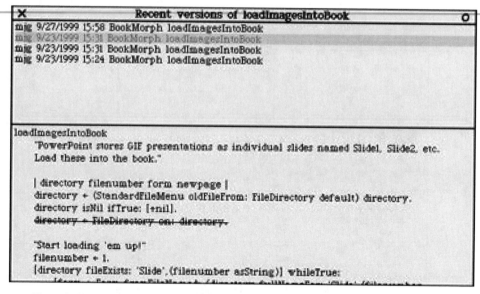

Figure 4–20   Recent versions of a method

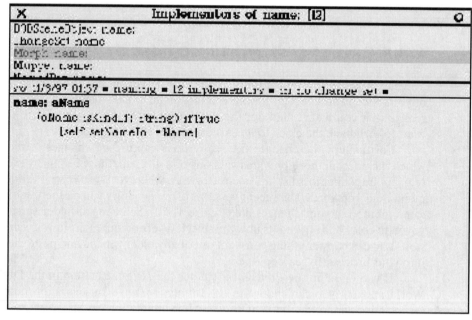

Figure 4–21   Implementors browser with Annotation Pane

played in the annotation pane can actually be configured with an easy drag-and-drop interface, which is brought up when you DoIt on **Preferences editAnnotations**.

REFERENCES

An excellent and practical introduction to UML (many more diagrams than what we covered here) is *UML Distilled: Applying the Standard Object Modeling Language,* Second Edition, by Martin Fowler and Kendall Scott (Addison Wesley, 2000).

Perhaps the best book on design in Smalltalk is Chamond Liu's *Smalltalk, Objects, and Design* (Prentice-Hall, 1996). The form of Smalltalk that he focuses on is IBM Smalltalk, but the core language is the same, and the discussion of design issues is very nice.

One of the critical themes in object-oriented design today is *design patterns,* that is, identifying common kinds of objects and relationships between these objects. The book that started this theme is *Design Patterns: Elements of Reusable Object-Oriented Software* by Erich Gamma, Richard Helm, Ralph Johnson, and John Vlissides (Addison Wesley, 1995). A Smalltalk-specific companion to the book has been written by Sherman R. Alpert, Kyle Brown, and Bobby Woolf, called *The Design Patterns Smalltalk Companion* (Addison Wesley, 1998). While design patterns are pretty abstract ideas for beginners, the idea of patterns is an important concept for more advanced study of object-oriented design.

An important new movement in object-oriented programming is *eXtreme Programming (XP)*. Started by Kent Beck, Ron Jeffries, and Ward Cunningham (recall that Cunningham and Beck also invented CRC Cards), XP suggests specific practices to improve coding performance and quality. There's a great collection of on-line references starting at http://www.c2.com/cgi/wiki?ExtremeProgrammingRoadmap and there's a good book by Kent Beck *Extreme Programming Explained: Embrace Change* (Addison Wesley, 1999).

5

Building User Interfaces in Squeak

5.1 ISSUES IN BUILDING A USER INTERFACE

Designing user-interface software really has two aspects to it:

- How do you create user-interface software that you can maintain well, is truly object-oriented, is easy to build, and is easy to change in pieces without impacting everything?
- How do you create user interfaces that people can actually use?

This chapter addresses only the first question. The second question is much more complicated and will be touched upon in the next chapter. This chapter deals with the characteristics of user-interface software that is easy to build, is object-oriented, and is maintainable.

These goals do not always fit together easily. It's possible to build interfaces quickly, but in throwing the pieces together, the programmer might not also create a clean structure that is easy to manipulate years later. In terms of creating object-oriented and maintainable software, there is a mechanism called *model-view-controller (MVC) paradigm* that has served well over the years—but it's not easy to understand and use. MVC basically describes a user interface in terms of a *model* of the real world, which is presented in a *view*, with user input handled by one or more *controllers*.

Much of the work going on in user-interface software today emphasizes ease of use, but not the engineering issues. In a lot of new user-interface toolkits or prototyping tools, you embed the code that defines the model or application inside the view. For example, you may put a script behind a button that does something to a data structure when the button is pressed. Now, where's the model? Scattered all over the various UI components. Where's the view? Well, it's there, but it's completely and inextricably linked to the model. This is hard to maintain. Squeak offers a new mechanism called *Morphic* that provides both ease of use and the possibility of good engineering. This chapter presents both MVC and Morphic.

But what makes Squeak particularly effective in exploring UI construction is that one can use *either* MVC *or* Morphic — or something else entirely! Squeak provides all of the primitives for creating whatever UI paradigm or toolkit you might wish to explore, MVC and Morphic being two examples. This chapter begins by doing exactly that—building a piece of a UI toolkit from scratch. The reason is not that you will often build a UI toolkit, but if you see the issues underlying a structure like MVC, it can help in understanding any individual toolkit.

5.2 DEVELOPING MODEL-VIEW-CONTROLLER

The core idea of MVC is that we need to separate our *model* of the real world from the user interface *view*. The reality of any application is that both the model and the view are going to change over time. The model is going to change (e.g., we may be using a **Clock**, but decide later that we want to use an **AlarmClock**.) Our *view* is going to change between an analog and digital clock, or between a kind of knob and kind of button. We don't want to be tweaking the model every time we change the view, and we don't want to have to change the view when we swap out the model.

How close can we get to this goal? Can the model know *nothing* of the view? Can the view know *nothing* of the model? We probably can't fulfill both possibilities, but the MVC structure will get us as far as we can get towards that goal. In this section, we build a user interface for our clock. We're going to do it not once, not twice, but three times. Each time, the interface we build will be essentially the same, but we will try to improve on the maintainability and object-oriented-ness of the system. Each time, the user interface will look essentially the same (Figure 5–1), but the underlying mechanism will change fairly dramatically. The features are as follows:

- The text at the top is the running clock.
- The buttons on the bottom increment or decrement the hours, and increment or decrement the minutes. The idea is to use these to set the time.

5.2.1 Round 1: No Separation At All

Let's make the first pass by simply tacking a user interface onto our existing **Clock** structure. The code for this version of the user interface is on the CD and on the Web as *clock-ui1.cs*.

We begin by considering how we need to revise our existing design. We won't do a CRC Card analysis because, strange as it seems, we've already *decided* to do this wrong. We won't add any new classes. Instead, we'll simply throw everything into the **Clock** class. But in so doing, we might get a clearer idea of what we really do need in our analysis.

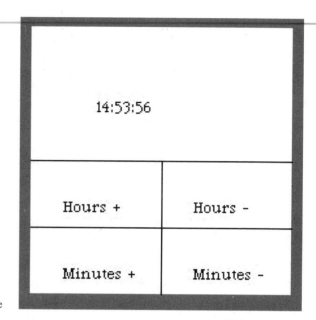

Figure 5–1 A Clock User Interface

We can identify several pieces that we'll need to add to **Clock** in order to get the interface in Figure 5–1:

- We need some way to define all the pieces of our interface: The text is for the clock, the buttons for changing the time, and the blank area handles everything. This will include adding one new instance variable: The upper-left-hand-corner **position** of the clock, in order to place all other interface components against a set point.
- We will need to do something to make sure that the time updates every second.
- We will also need to deal with the user's actions, which are typically called interface *events*, such as clicking on a button. Somehow, we must catch the event and handle it appropriately (e.g., incrementing the minute if the user clicks on the *Minutes+* button).

All of this leads to the class diagram in Figure 5–2. (You *should* look at the long list on **Clock** and wonder "Do we really want all of that in one class? Does all of this belong here?") We'll add the position **instance** variable (and the accessor methods for it), and a method to **openWindow** that places all the interface components. We'll add the methods **addHour**, **addMinute**, **subtractHour**, and **subtractMinute** to make it easier to build the buttons. We'll have to modify **nextSecond** to send the message **timeDisplay**, which will update the display. We'll handle the user's events in **catchEvents**.

We start implementing these changes by updating our definition of the **Clock** class:

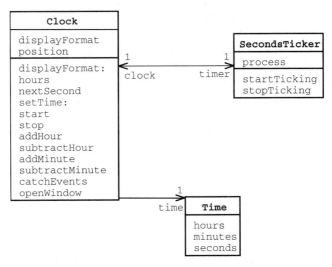

Figure 5–2   Class Diagram for Round One of Clock UI

Object subclass: #Clock
    instanceVariableNames: 'time timer displayFormat position '
    classVariableNames: ''
    poolDictionaries: ''
    category: 'ClockWorks'

The new position instance variable will track where the clock's window will go. We'll need accessor methods for the new variable:

position
    ^ position
position: aPoint
    position := aPoint.

Once the position is set, we can actually open a window on a clock:

openWindow
    | pen |
    "Open the blank frame"
    (Form extent: 200@200) fillWhite displayAt: position.

    "Draw the Buttons"
    pen := Pen new.
    pen up. pen goto: (position x) @ ((position y)+100). pen down.
    pen north. pen turn: 90.
    pen go: 200.
    pen up. pen goto: (position x) @ ((position y)+150). pen down.
    pen go: 200.

```
pen up. pen goto: ((position x)+100) @ ((position y)+100). pen down.
pen turn: 90.
pen go: 100.
'Hours +' displayAt: ((position x)+25) @ ((position y)+125).
'Hours -' displayAt: ((position x)+125) @ ((position y)+125).
'Minutes +' displayAt: ((position x)+25) @ ((position y)+175).
'Minutes -' displayAt: ((position x)+125) @ ((position y)+175).
```

This is a fairly complex piece of code, so let's walk through it a bit:

- The expression to create a blank (white) frame is one that we saw before, in Joe the Box.
- The **Pen** expressions create the boxes below the time display that suggest the "buttons."
- The final four lines create the labels on the buttons.
- Note that all the coordinates are offset from the position instance variable. The buttons start about 100 pixels below the upper-left-hand corner of the display.
- Note also that there is nothing in here that says anything about the text to appear in the upper part of this "window".

To make the text display work, we're going to need to modify **nextSecond** and create a method to actually paste the time display into our makeshift window:

nextSecond
```
        time := time addTime: (Time fromSeconds: 1).
        self timeDisplay.
```
timeDisplay
```
        "Erase whatever time was there before"
        '        ' displayAt: position + (50@50).
        self display displayAt: position + (50 @ 50).
```

The code so far will make the window appear with the time display in the middle of it. As each second goes by, the time will update in the window. We have yet to deal with the buttons. Simply clicking inside our boxes won't do anything yet.

We need a piece of code called an *event loop*. An event loop waits for user-interface events, figures out who needs what event, and then passes the event to the appropriate interface component. An event loop is actually a very important invention for user interfaces. Previous to event loops, interfaces would be written with the computer in charge, by dictating when input was to occur from what device (e.g, by providing a command-line prompt to say "Okay, now *you* type something.") An event loop changes everything: Now the user is in control, and the computer waits for an event it can handle and then handles it when it arrives.

Here is an event loop for our first user-interface system:

catchEvents
```
        | hourPlus hourMinus minutePlus minuteMinus click |
        "Define the rectangles where we care about mouse clicks"
```

```
hourPlus := (position x) @ ((position y)+100) extent: 100@50.
hourMinus := ((position x)+100) @ ((position y)+100) extent: 100@50.
minutePlus := (position x) @ ((position y)+150) extent: 100@50.
minuteMinus := ((position x)+100) @ ((position y)+150) extent: 100@50.

"Enter into an event loop"
[Sensor yellowButtonPressed] whileFalse: "Yellow button press ends the clock"
["Give other processes a chance, and give user a
chance to pick the mouse button up."
(Delay forMilliseconds: 500) wait.
(Sensor redButtonPressed) ifTrue:
        "Red button press could go to a button"
        [click := Sensor mousePoint.
        (hourPlus containsPoint: click)
                ifTrue: [self addHour].
        (hourMinus containsPoint: click)
                ifTrue: [self subtractHour].
        (minutePlus containsPoint: click)
                ifTrue: [self addMinute].
        (minuteMinus containsPoint: click)
                ifTrue: [self subtractMinute].]].
```

Let's walk through this fairly lengthy code. The method starts out by defining four rectangles, one for each of our buttons. These are exactly the same rectangles that we defined when we drew the buttons. (You should be thinking, "Do I really have to do this twice?") Then there's a loop waiting for the yellow button to be pressed, which is the signal that (we'll decide) indicates the end of the clock processing. Until the yellow mouse button is pressed, we look for the red button to be pressed. If there is a red mouse-button press, we get the mouse-point position, and see if it's within one of our four rectangles. If the mouse press is in one of them, we execute the appropriate method for the clock to add or subtract time. The small **Delay** at the top of the loop is to prevent a single mouse click from being executed several times (due to the loop's being faster than the human) and allowing other processes to sneak in.

We haven't actually created these four methods yet, but they are fairly straightforward:

addHour
```
        time := time addTime: (Time fromSeconds: 60*60)
```

addMinute
```
        time := time addTime: (Time fromSeconds: 60)
```

subtractHour
```
        time := time subtractTime: (Time fromSeconds: 60*60)
```

subtractMinute
```
        time := time subtractTime: (Time fromSeconds: 60)
```

SIDE NOTE

This event loop triggers a button press upon clicking *down* with the mouse. Most interfaces actually trigger the event upon *releasing* the mouse button. This gives the user the opportunity to move the cursor after pressing down *before* triggering a button. The previous event loop could be written to support mouse releases rather than mouse-down events. The key is to track the state of the mouse so that the release can be detected.

To make our first user interface work, we execute code that looks like this:

```
c := Clock new.
c position: 100@10.
c setTime: (Time now printString).
c openWindow.
c start.
c catchEvents.
```

The clock will then start running. You can click on the buttons to change the displayed time. (Remember that you're modifying your **Clock** instance—you're not changing your system's time.) To stop the event loop, use your yellow button anywhere. The clock will keep running. To stop the clock, use **c stop** in your workspace.

EXERCISES: IMPROVING ROUND ONE

1. Change the event loop to process on mouse releases, not mouse downs.
2. Figure out why the clock is still running after the yellow-button press, and change the code above (hint: in the event loop) so that the clock stops when the user interface stops.

5.2.2 Round 2: Separate Windows and Buttons

While this user interface has the advantage of working, it has a great many disadvantages. Here are a few:

- We've had to modify the **Clock** class a great deal. There's no separation between view and model here. To change the layout of the window, for example, we have to change the window-drawing code as well as the event loop. To change the window from a digital to an analog display, we might as well start from scratch.
- The **Clock** suddenly has to know all kinds of things it shouldn't care about, from the position of the window in space to user-interface events. Responsibilities are clearly wrong here.
- There is nothing reusable here. The next user interface is going to be just as hard as the first with this structure.

Let's start making it better by separating the two most obvious components: The **ClockWindow** and the **ClockButtons**. It's pretty clear that we need these components. A CRC Card analysis would lead to the determination of these responsibilities:

- The **ClockWindow** should be responsible for assembling the user interface and displaying the time.
- The **ClockButtons** should handle displaying themselves and triggering the appropriate action in the clock.

We can move from these descriptions to a class diagram with more details of how to actually make this work (Figure 5–3). We can move the **position** instance variable and the **timeDisplay** method from **Clock** into **ClockWindow**. We're moving the window-opening and event-catching methods, too, but the names change. **ClockWindow** has an **openOn:** method, which takes a parameter of a clock to use as its model. Instead of **catchEvents**, we'll have a **processEvents** method, which seems to be more accurate.

We need to add to **ClockWindow** an instance variable that references the **Clock**, which we'll name **clock**. We need this because **ClockWindow** now knows how to do the **timeDisplay**, but we request the **timeDisplay** during **nextSecond**, which is in **Clock**. Thus, at least for this round, the **Clock** has to know the **ClockWindow**.

The **ClockWindow** knows its **position**, its **clock**, and its **buttons**. It needs to know about its buttons in order to check them and pass control to them if they get a mouse click. The rest of **ClockWindow**'s methods are just accessors.

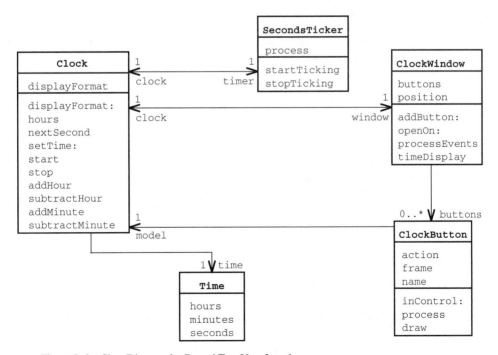

Figure 5–3   Class Diagram for Round Two User Interface

The **ClockButton** is another new class that handles drawing, checking for clicks, and executing some action for the on-screen button. We can talk about each responsibility separately:

- The **ClockButton** knows how to **draw** itself, and to do that, it knows its **frame** (the rectangle where it is displayed) and its **name** (to display its label).
- The **ClockButton** can tell whether it is **inControl:** of a given mouse click, by checking the position against its **frame**.
- If the **ClockButton** does have control, it's asked to **process**, which involves telling its **model** to execute a given **action**. We'll talk more about the **action** later, because it's quite important for having flexible MVC components. (There are **Button** classes in Squeak, but if we used those to start, we'd never get the chance to roll our own and understand it well.)

The code in this section is available on the CD and on the Web as *clock-ui2.cs*. We'll start out by redefining the **Clock** class, and defining **ClockButton** and **ClockWindow**:

```
Object subclass: #Clock
        instanceVariableNames: 'time timer window displayFormat'
        classVariableNames: ''
        poolDictionaries: ''
        category: 'ClockWorks'
Object subclass: #ClockButton
        instanceVariableNames: 'model frame action name '
        classVariableNames: ''
        poolDictionaries: ''
        category: 'ClockWorks'
Object subclass: #ClockWindow
        instanceVariableNames: 'position clock buttons '
        classVariableNames: ''
        poolDictionaries: ''
        category: 'ClockWorks'
```

The **Clock** still knows about its **window**, which is unfortunate, but we'll clear this up later. At least it no longer has to know about a **position**. The **Clock** is nearly back to its basic responsibilities, with the **ClockWindow** taking care of the user interface issues.

Let's start by looking at how we create windows in this version of the user-interface code:

```
openOn: aModel
        | button |
        position isNil ifTrue: [self error: 'Must set position first.'].

        "Set this model as this window's clock"
        clock := aModel.

        "Open the blank frame"
```

```
(Form extent: 200@200) fillWhite displayAt: position.

"Draw the Buttons"
button := ClockButton make: 'Hours +'
        at: ((position x) @ ((position y)+100) extent: 100@50)
        for: aModel
        triggering: #addHour.
self addButton: button.
button := ClockButton make: 'Hours -'
        at: (((position x)+100) @ ((position y)+100) extent: 100@50)
        for: aModel
        triggering: #subtractHour.
self addButton: button.
button := ClockButton make: 'Minutes +'
        at: ((position x) @ ((position y)+150) extent: 100@50)
        for: aModel
        triggering: #addMinute.
self addButton: button.
button := ClockButton make: 'Minutes -'
        at: (((position x)+100) @ ((position y)+150) extent: 100@50)
        for: aModel
        triggering: #subtractMinute.
self addButton: button.
```

This is a significant piece of code, so let's walk through the pieces:

- The method starts out by checking to make sure that the **position** is set. If it's not, we will not be able to position everything else, so it's worth checking.
- Next, the argument **model** is set to be the window's **clock**.
- The method clears a frame, as before.
- Each button is created as an instance of **ClockButton**. We specify a name for each button, its frame (a rectangle is specified as an upper-left corner and a distance to the lower-right, the extent), and the model and action message that it sends. The pound sign is necessary for defining a *symbol*. **#addHour** is a *symbol*. A symbol is a kind of special **String** that the Smalltalk knows, which can be the name of a method. Internally, there can be only one instance of each kind of symbol, so all references point to the same thing. That makes lookup especially fast.
- As the buttons are created, they are added into the button list.

While most of the accessors of **ClockWindow** are fairly straightforward, it's worth taking a peek at **addButton**:

addButton: aButton
```
buttons isNil ifTrue: [buttons := OrderedCollection new].
buttons add: aButton.
```

Notice the first line: We check if **buttons** is already set up as an **OrderedCollec-**

tion, and if it is not, we set it. This isn't the best way of initializing an instance variable; it's better to do it in an **initialize** method. This is called *lazy initialization.* There is an advantage to this method if it's difficult to initialize an object or if the class variable is not used often and is huge. In general, though, it's not the cleanest way to initialize a variable.

Processing the event loop becomes a very different activity when the window and buttons are all separate:

```
processEvents
        "Enter into an event loop"
        | click |
        [Sensor yellowButtonPressed]
        whileFalse: "Yellow button press ends the clock"
                ["Give other processes a chance,
                and give user a chance to release the mouse button."
                (Delay forMilliseconds: 500) wait.
                (Sensor redButtonPressed)
                ifTrue: "Red button press could go to a button"
                        [click ← Sensor mousePoint.
                        buttons do: [:b |
                                (b inControl: click) ifTrue: [b process]].]].
```

The main loop here is the same, but the body of that loop is different. Now, we simply ask each button "Do you want control of this mouse click?" and if it does, we tell the button to **process**. It's a very simple structure that distributes responsibility from the window into the buttons.

Obviously, we'll have to handle that responsibility in the buttons. Let's begin going through the **ClockButton** to see how it's implemented. The basic creation method for buttons is a class method. This means that you create ClockButton instances with a specialized send to the class itself:

```
make: aName at: aRect for: aModel triggering: aMessage
        | newButton |
        newButton ← self new.
        newButton name: aName.
        newButton frame: aRect.
        newButton model: aModel.
        newButton action: aMessage.
        newButton draw.
        ^newButton.
```

Drawing a button is pretty straightforward: We simply use the **Pen** code we wrote earlier, but we parameterize the positions differently:

```
draw
        | pen |
        pen := Pen new.
        pen color: (Color black).
```

```
pen up. pen goto: (frame origin).
pen north. pen turn: 90. pen down.
pen goto: (frame topRight).
pen turn: 90. pen goto: (frame bottomRight).
pen turn: 90. pen goto: (frame bottomLeft).
pen turn: 90. pen goto: (frame origin).
name displayAt: (frame leftCenter) + (25@-10).
        "Offset in a bit, and up a bit for aesthetics"
```

This code is pretty self-explanatory, because **Rectangles** have a lot of nice methods for getting their coordinates, such as **origin**, **topRight**, and **bottomLeft**. Basically, we just move the pen around the points of the frame, starting at the **origin** (top left). The little fudge factor in the positioning of the label, **name**, is just to make the label look a bit better. Try it with and without the fudge factor to see why it's there.

inControl: and **process** are both one-liners. **inControl:** simply tests whether the click point is within the **frame** of the button; if it is, **process** tells the model to perform the given **action**:

```
inControl: aPoint
        ^frame containsPoint: aPoint
process
        model perform: action
```

Before we explain how **process** *does* work, let's consider how it *might* work. Imagine that **process** does nothing at all, by default. Instead, you create a separate subclass for the **HoursPlusButton**, for the **HoursMinusButton**, and so on. In each subclass, you override the default **process** method in the superclass, and provide a **process** method that does the appropriate action for *Hours+*, *Hours-*, and so on. What would each of these subclass **process** methods look like? For **HoursPlusButton**, it would just say **model addHour**. That's it, just two words.

The original user-interface components for MVC in Smalltalk-80 *did* work like this—you subclassed components for each specific use. But since the subclasses were *so* similar, it became clear that it would be possible to parameterize the superclass so that each use would simply be an instance with different instance variables. We call these new kinds of user-interface components *pluggable,* because they have plugs (parameters) for the various important parts of the user interface. Our **ClockButton** is pluggable. The **action** is a plug.

What makes pluggables work, in general, are blocks and the **perform:** message. **perform:** is an interesting message. The message **perform:** takes a symbol as an argument, then sends the symbol as a message to the receiving object. Since the symbol could have been created dynamically (e.g., by assembling the string and then converting it to a symbol with **asSymbol**), using **perform:** is like generating code (at least, a message-send) on the fly. The action message could be anything, even input from the user that's been translated into a symbol. When asking an object to perform a message, we want the powerful structure that dynamic languages like Smalltalk provide. It can be slower than a normal message-send in a method—a compiler can optimize most message-sends, but can't do it as easily when the send is created with

perform:. However, the flexibility of **perform:** is important in order to create pluggable components.

We'll move the text display into the **ClockWindow**. The **ClockWindow** will clear the existing text, then ask the **clock** what the **display** time is, and then display it:

```
timeDisplay
    "Erase whatever time was there before"
    '        ' displayAt: position + (50@50).
    (clock display) displayAt: position + (50 @ 50).
```

And we'll change **Clock** to ask the **ClockWindow** to do the text display:

```
nextSecond
    time ← time addTime: (Time fromSeconds: 1).
    window timeDisplay,
```

We can create this clock with workspace code like the following:

```
c := Clock new.
w := ClockWindow new.
w position: 100@10.
c setTime: (Time now printString).
w openOn: c. c window: w.
c start.
w processEvents.
```

Notice that the user interface *looks* exactly the same, but we know that the underlying mechanism is now radically different. To stop this click, you click with the yellow button to stop the event loop. Then do **c stop** to stop the clock.

5.2.3 Round 3: Separating Even the Text

Round Two is clearly a much nicer user-interface model, but it's still not as good as it could get. Let's consider its strengths and weaknesses:

- Clearly, we have a much nicer separation between user interface components (views) and the model. Except for handling the text display, the clock doesn't know anything about its window or the buttons that impact it. The window only needs to know about the clock with respect to getting the time to display.
- Though they're named **ClockWindow** and **ClockButton**, these are fairly generic pieces now. Those buttons could appear as part of anything, and send any message to any object. The window isn't a window in the sense of being draggable, nor is it integrated with other windows, but it is a frame in which things can be placed. Both are nice starts toward generic UI components.
- The text is a real problem. Not only does it force us to spread around more information than we might like (Why should the clock know its window? Why should the window know about anything other than its components? Why

should it have to know about the clock?), but it also deeply constrains the UI structure. Imagine converting all of this into an analog clock, with a dial and two hands. The window and buttons would work almost as-is—*almost*. But the text display of the clock is hardwired in.

Separating the text display of the time is going to be tricky. We have to have some way for the clock to tell its view (whether a textual display or an analog dial) when the time has changed, so that the view can update. But we don't really want the clock to know about its view, or even its *views*—plural. If we do this right, it is imaginable that we could have two (or more) different displays on the same clock. But in order to do this right, we certainly don't want the window to be hard-wired to display the clock. How, then, does the window find out when it has to update?

The original Smalltalk developers had this same problem. They wanted a mechanism for building user interfaces that was efficient and flexible, yet maintained an object-oriented nature. What they came up with was the rest of the Model-View-Controller paradigm. We've already met two of the three pieces, and the third one isn't all that critical in what we're doing:

- The Model is the object from the problem domain. It's where the services and attributes core to the problem are stored.
- The Views are the objects that the user interacts with. Buttons, text areas, graphs, and other kinds of interaction objects are views.
- The Controller is essentially the event loop. It is the controller that collects user-interface events (through the **Sensor**), then hands them off to the view (e.g., mouse clicks on a button) or to the model (e.g., keyboard input). The controller is probably the most complicated piece of the three, but fortunately, it's the one that requires changes the least. Typically, a mouse click is a mouse click, and only unless you want something to happen only upon a more unique combination, like control-A-shift-mouse click, should you care about modifying the controller.

By separating these three pieces, we can modify any one without modifying the others. The model can change, but the user interface remains the same. The interface can change without changing the underlying model. Changing the controller apart from the others is also useful—you can decide to trigger something upon mouse click or upon control key. The decision can be made later.

The MVC structure doesn't solve the text-update problem alone. The text-update problem is handled by the *dependency* mechanism that was built into Smalltalk to make this kind of update work within MVC. The dependency mechanism allows views to *update* upon *changes* in the model. The dependency mechanism can actually be used to handle any kind of dependency relationships—not just those between views and models. It certainly works really well for this connection:

- Views make themselves *dependent* on a model object. The code for creating a dependency is **model addDependent: view**. How the dependency is recorded is unimportant in the paradigm. Suffice it to say that there is more than one way that it happens, depending on the superclass of the model, but in no case does the programmer of the model class ever have to maintain a record of its dependents. For the most part, the model can ignore that any views exist.

- Models simply announce when something has changed. The code to announce a change to all dependent views is **self change: #something** where **#something** should inform the view of the *aspect* of the model that changed. (**#something** doesn't have to be a symbol—it could be a string or something else. Using a symbol is efficient and keeps the information-passing to a minimum.) If a model (say, a **Passenger**) has many attributes, one view may care only about one aspect of the model (say, its destination), while another view may care only about another (say, its payment type). Announcing that something has changed is a pretty lightweight operation. It's reasonable to sprinkle announcements liberally throughout the model wherever a view *might* care about a change.

- Behind the scenes, the change: method informs all the dependent views to **update:** with the aspect information as an argument. The author of a view needs to create an appropriate **update:** method for her view. The update methods can decide if they care about that aspect, and if so, they can ask their model for whatever information they need.

Any object can be dependent on any other object in Squeak, which tells you that the basic methods for **addDependent:**, **change:**, and **update:** are defined in **Object**. Dependencies are stored in a global **Dictionary**. However, **Model** also understands **addDependent:** and **change:**, and it implements them more efficiently—dependencies are stored in a local variable rather than in a global **Dictionary**. You can create your problem domain models as subclasses of **Object** to start, but you can subclass **Model** (with no change) for more efficiency later.

Let's use the MVC structure to create our Round Number Three user interface for the **Clock**. We need to introduce a **ClockText** class, that's clear. It must respond to **update:**. In order to **update:**, it needs to know the **position** it must draw to, the **model** it has to get information from, and the **query** message that it must send for the information to display. The **Clock** no longer needs to know about the **ClockWindow**. And the **ClockWindow** doesn't need the **Clock** anymore—only the **ClockText** will be requesting information from the **Clock**. All of this leads to the class diagram in Figure 5–4.

The code for Round Number Three is available on the CD and on the Web as *clock-ui3.cs*. We begin by redefining the classes **Clock** and **ClockWindow**, and adding our new **ClockText**:

```
Object subclass: #Clock
        instanceVariableNames: 'time timer displayFormat '
        classVariableNames: ''
        poolDictionaries: ''
        category: 'ClockWorks'
Object subclass: #ClockText
        instanceVariableNames: 'model position query '
        classVariableNames: ''
```

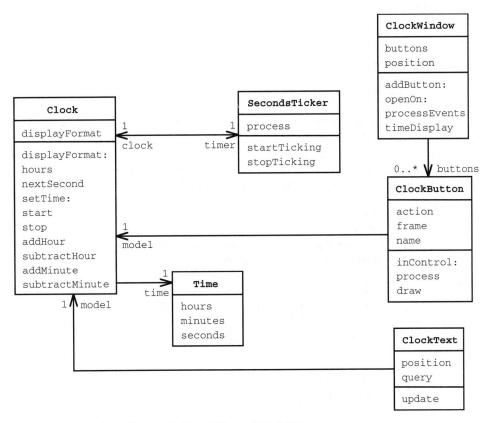

Figure 5–4   Class Diagram for Round Three of Clock UI

```
        poolDictionaries: "
        category: 'ClockWorks'
Object subclass: #ClockWindow
        instanceVariableNames: 'position buttons '
        classVariableNames: "
        poolDictionaries: "
        category: 'ClockWorks'
```

We need to modify the **Clock** to announce a change in the time upon **nextSecond**. Unlike the previous versions of **nextSecond**, this change is quite simple, can be added or changed easily (e.g., involves no new instance variables), and doesn't really affect the design of our problem domain object:

nextSecond
        time ← time addTime: (Time fromSeconds: 1).
        self changed: #time.

The **ClockText** object maintains a **model** instance variable. When the model is set, we create the dependency between the text area and the clock:

model

```
^model
```

model: aModel

```
model := aModel.
aModel addDependent: self.
```

When **nextSecond** occurs, every view (dependent) on the clock is asked to update. Our text area cares about only the time changing, even if there were other aspects of the clock to care about. The text area remembers the **query** message to ask the model in order to get whatever it needs to display. We can ask the model to **perform:** the **query** message, and tell the result to display itself:

update: anEvent

```
anEvent = #time ifTrue: [
'         ' displayAt: position . "Erase whatever time was there before"
(model perform: query) displayAt: position.]
```

To make it easier to set up a text area, we create a class method that creates a text area and sets it up appropriately:

at: aPosition on: aModel for: aQuery

```
| text |
text := self new.
text position: aPosition.
text model: aModel.
text query: aQuery.
^text
```

Finally, we can write a new opening method for our window that sets up the text area. The **openOn:** method is very similar to the one in Round Two, but we don't need to set the **ClockWindow**'s **clock** variable, and we do have to set up the **ClockText**. Notice that the clock doesn't retain any connection to the text area. It doesn't need one—once the text area is set up, the window doesn't need to deal with it at all. (In a *real* window, the window would care about its subviews for things like updating upon moving or resizing, but it's not an issue with our pretend window.) The code is as follows:

openOn: aModel

```
| button |
position isNil ifTrue: [self error: 'Must set position first.'].

"Open the blank frame"
(Form extent: 200@200) fillWhite displayAt: position.

"Setup the textArea"
ClockText at: (position + (50@50)) on: aModel for: #display.

"Draw the Buttons"
button := ClockButton make: 'Hours +'
```

```
            at: ((position x) @ ((position y)+100) extent: 100@50)
    @for: aModel
        triggering: #addHour.
self addButton: button.
button := ClockButton make: 'Hours -'
        at: (((position x)+100) @ ((position y)+100) extent: 100@50)
        for: aModel
        triggering: #subtractHour.
self addButton: button.
button := ClockButton make: 'Minutes +'
        at: ((position x) @ ((position y)+150) extent: 100@50)
        for: aModel
        triggering: #addMinute.
self addButton: button.
button := ClockButton make: 'Minutes -'
        at: (((position x)+100) @ ((position y)+150) extent: 100@50)
        for: aModel
        triggering: #subtractMinute.
self addButton: button.
```

Running the Round-Three version of the code is pretty similar to Round Two. Remember, still, to stop the clock with **c stop** after ending the event loop:

```
c := Clock new.
w := ClockWindow new.
w position: 100@10.
c setTime: (Time now printString).
w openOn: c.
c start.
w processEvents.
```

5.2.4 Strengths and Weaknesses of Model-View-Controller

MVC is the dominant metaphor for UI construction today. It's at the heart of how we think about user-interface toolkits today. Even the latest user-interface toolkits, like the Java Swing toolkit, are essentially MVC-based systems. Let's consider the strengths and weaknesses of MVC:

STRENGTHS

- Clean object-oriented structure that minimizes information-sharing. The model knows essentially nothing of the views. The views don't need to poll the model, and as we've seen, they can be designed to be quite generic.
- Can support multiple views on the same model. An **update:** message goes to *all* dependents, even if they're in different windows. One could imagine having a single **Patient** class, for example, with separate views for doctors (who need to see test results and specify diagnoses and treatments), nurses (who need to see and implement treatments), and billing office staff (who don't need to see the diagnosis, but do need to know the costs of tests and treatments). The model doesn't have to be changed at all to support any number of views.

WEAKNESSES

- Inefficient. The view gets told to update, and then it has to ask the model for the value, and then it updates. Having the model *tell* the view what to change would be more efficient, but less object-oriented. If the model knew what the view wanted, then there would be an information dependency between them, in which changing one might require changes in the other.

- Especially inefficient for multiple views. Let's say a doctor changes something on a patient's record (adds a test, for example). That view changes the model, which then triggers an update, and all views (say, the laboratory's for what tests to run, the nurse's for what tests to check on, and the billing office for what to charge) now get the update, and request what is, probably, the same piece of information. Why couldn't the doctor's view tell all the others' views directly? To do that would require views to know something about each other, which is a less clean structure, but more efficient.

- Gets very complicated if you want to have a view dependent upon multiple models. Imagine that you have a nurse's view that wants to show all of the status information for the patients in a three-person room. When the view gets informed that the patient's prescription has changed, *which* model does the view request information from? You can handle this by creating *application models*—models that are dependent upon a set of problem domain models. The views get built on the application models. In the example, you'd create a **Room** object, which was itself dependent on the three patients and whose responsibility would be to figure out which patient announced the update. The nurse's view is dependent on the **Room**.

The problem is that it's hard to deal with MVC's weaknesses without destroying its object-oriented clarity. That's an open research problem today. Some UI researchers are exploring ways to allow the programmer to work in pure MVC while improving the efficiency at compile time. Other researchers are looking for alternatives to MVC, such as constraint-based systems.

EXERCISES: REBUILDING THE CLOCK INTERFACE

3. Now, try writing a graphic text area that displays an analog clock, then update the **Clock-Window** to use that.

4. Find a user-interface toolkit (one that you've used before, or one that you are using for another project) and figure out how it handles model-view communication. Odds are good that it is using a change-update mechanism.

5.3 BUILDING PLUGGABLE USER INTERFACES IN SQUEAK

Since the previous sections shows that it is clearly possible to build generic user-interface components, it should come as no surprise that there are pluggable user-interface components built into Squeak. The first versions of Squeak did not have them—they were based on Smalltalk-80 *before* pluggable interface components were created. Pluggable UI components were introduced soon after the Morphic user interface was added to Squeak. (More on Morphic later in this section.)

Building your interface with pluggable components has both strengths and weaknesses. An important strength is that, for many common interfaces, using pluggable components means that creating a user interface is *much* simpler. You may need to create *no* classes besides your model classes.

A weakness of pluggable components is that *only* standard interfaces can be created with them. If you wanted to have something animate inside a pluggable interface, or have scrollbars change their shape or color dependent on their content, you can't do it with pluggable interfaces. To do more unusual things, you'll need to either build your own pluggable interfaces or do it in Morphic.

Three kinds of pluggable components in Squeak get used the most. Each component comes in both a View (to be used in MVC) and a Morph (to be used in Morphic) variation. All three require a model to be specified for their use. Each provides a number of slots for selectors (messages to be sent to the model). Any selector can be set to **nil** (i.e., unspecified), which means that that specific functionality is not enabled.

- **PluggableButtonView** (**PluggableButtonMorph**): PluggableButtons normally keeps track of a state selector and an action selector. The action selector is the message to send the model when the button is selected. The state selector is used to ask the model if the button should currently be on or off. There are also selectors for asking the model for a yellow-button menu to display and for asking the model for a label (if the button's label needs to dynamically update). There are options to make the button work on mouse-down rather than the standard mouse-up, to ask the user if they're sure, and to use a shortcut character for triggering the button. PluggableButtons are often used with instances of **Switch** that can handle tracking boolean state. (For an example of using **Switch** with a PluggableButton, see the **example** class method in **PluggableButtonView**.)

An example of use is the code in the **Browser** that creates the class switch button:

```
aSwitchView ← PluggableButtonView
        on: self "The browser is the model"
        "It's 'on' if the class messages are being shown"
        getState: #classMessagesIndicated
        "When triggered, class messages should be shown"
        action: #indicateClassMessages.
aSwitchView
        label: 'class';        "Label"
        window: (0@0 extent: 15@8); "Size of view"
        "Make sure that no text gets whumped"
        askBeforeChanging: true.
```

- **PluggableTextView (PluggableTextMorph)**: PluggableText areas can keep track of up to four selectors. One selector retrieves the text to be displayed from the model. Another submits new text to the model when the user accepts the text. (Setting this selector to **nil** makes the text essentially read-only.) There are also selectors for getting the current text selection and for a yellow-button menu. PluggableText areas are often used with instances of **StringHolder**, which can handle model-like access to a string.

    An example of using Pluggable Text View can be found in Celeste, the e-mail reader in Squeak:

```
"Set up a StringHolder as a model"
textHolder ← StringHolder new .
textHolder contents: initialText. "Set the initial value"

textView ← PluggableTextView
on: textHolder "The textHolder is the model"
text: #contents "Ask for #contents when need the text"
"Send #acceptContents: with the text as an argument to save"
accept: #acceptContents:.
```

- **PluggableListView (PluggableListMorph)**: PluggableLists can keep track of up to five selectors. The main three get the contents of the list, get the currently selected item, and set the currently selected item. There is also a selector for a yellow-button menu. The fifth selector processes a keystroke typed in the list, and the selector must take an argument of the keystroke. There is also an option to **autoDeselect** which allows you to turn off selection by clicking on an item twice.

    The code that creates the message category list in the **Browser** looks like this:

```
        "Browser is the model"
messageCategoryListView ← PluggableListView on: self
"messageCategoryList returns the categories in an array"
        list: #messageCategoryList
"messageCategoryListIndex returns an Integer of the current sel"
        selected: #messageCategoryListIndex
"when the user changes the selection, messageCategoryListIndex is sent"
        changeSelected: #messageCategoryListIndex:
"MessageCategory has its own menu"
        menu: #messageCategoryMenu:.
```

5.3.1 Creating Pluggable Interfaces in MVC

Let's use the pluggable user-interface components in Squeak to create an MVC-based interface for the **Clock**. The code for this is available on the CD as *clock-pluggable.cs*. We'll put the method in **ClockWindow**, though it really could go into **Clock** — nothing of the **ClockWindow** will be used anymore. The code for creating the window will look like this:

CAUTIONARY NOTE

Be sure that you are in an MVC project or at the top level (i.e., not in any project) when running this example. You won't see the MVC window if you do this from Morphic.

```
w := ClockWindow new.
w openInMVC.
```

This is a very long method because of all the pieces that need to be created. In order to describe it, text will appear in the middle of the method, in this normal text font:

openInMVC
```
        | win component clock textArea |
        "Create the clock"
        clock := Clock new.
        clock setTime: (Time now printString).
        clock start.
```

Because the window is being opened separately from the **Clock**, it will be the window-opening method's responsibility to create the clock, set the time, and get it started:

```
"Create a window for it"
win := (StandardSystemView new) model: self.
win borderWidth: 1.
```

StandardSystemView is the main window class in MVC. A **StandardSystemView** takes care of things like displaying a title bar and a close box—and handling them appropriately. It also manages interactions with the main-window scheduler, which creates the illusion of overlapping windows. Creating and using a StandardSystem View is necessary to create the window itself.

```
"Set up the text view and the various pieces"
textArea := PluggableTextView on: clock text: #display accept: nil.
textArea window: (0@0 extent: 100@100).
win addSubView: textArea.
```

The PluggableText area code follows. The model will be the **Clock** instance that was created earlier. The text to display will be whatever the clock responds from the message **display**. We do not want the user to be able to edit the text, so we set the accept selector to **nil**. We specify the size of the text area to be 100 pixels horizontal by 100 pixels vertical. Finally, the window adds the new text area into it as a subview. The code looks like this:

```
component := PluggableButtonView new
        model: clock;
        action: #addHour;
        label: 'Hours +';
        borderWidth: 1.
component window: (0@100 extent: 100@50).
win addSubView: component.
```

The button for incrementing the hours is created here. Its model is the **Clock** instance, with the action method to add an hour. It has a label, and a border, which will be one pixel wide. The position of the button is specified to be essentially the same as what it was in our previous user interface. The window is told to add the button.

We create the other three buttons similarly:

```
component := PluggableButtonView new
        model: clock;
        action: #subtractHour;
        label: 'Hours -';
        borderWidth: 1.
component window: (100@100 extent: 100@50).
win addSubView: component.
component := PluggableButtonView new
        model: clock;
        action: #addMinute;
        label: 'Minutes +';
        borderWidth: 1.
component window: (0@150 extent: 100@50).
win addSubView: component.
component := PluggableButtonView new
        model: clock;
        action: #subtractMinute;
        label: 'Minutes -';
        borderWidth: 1.
component window: (100@150 extent: 100@50).
win addSubView: component.
```

We need a button in this interface that wasn't in the previous ones. Since the clock is no longer accessible once the window is created, we need some way to stop it. We'll build a button for stopping the clock.

A better way to do this is to stop the clock upon closing the window. The model of the **StandardSystemView** is sent the message **windowIsClosing** when it is to be closed. The message breaks MVC in some ways: What if there are multiple views open on the same model? Which one is closing? For now, we'll just create a stop button:

```
component := PluggableButtonView new
        model: clock;
        action: #stop;
        label: 'STOP';
        borderWidth: 1.
```

```
component window: (0@200 extent: 200@100).
        win addSubView: component.
```

The following code sets the label for the window and defines a minimum size (the window is opened by asking its controller to open):

```
win label: 'Clock'.
win minimumSize: 300 @ 300.
win controller open
```

While this is a pretty long method, it is a *single* method. No new classes are needed to implement this user interface. It also has a good bit of flexibility built into it. The window can be dragged around and even resized, and it will work just fine.

We do have to make one change to **Clock**. Pluggable components don't allow us to use any changed aspect. We have to do something that they expect. For Pluggable-Text areas, the text knows to care about the **update:** message if the aspect is the same as the get-text selector. This means that **nextSecond** has to announce a change to **display** in order to get the text to update appropriately:

nextSecond
```
        time ← time addTime: (Time fromSeconds: 1).
        self changed: #display.
```

The completed window looks like Figure 5–5. Go ahead and try it from the code. Be sure to hit the Stop button before closing the window.

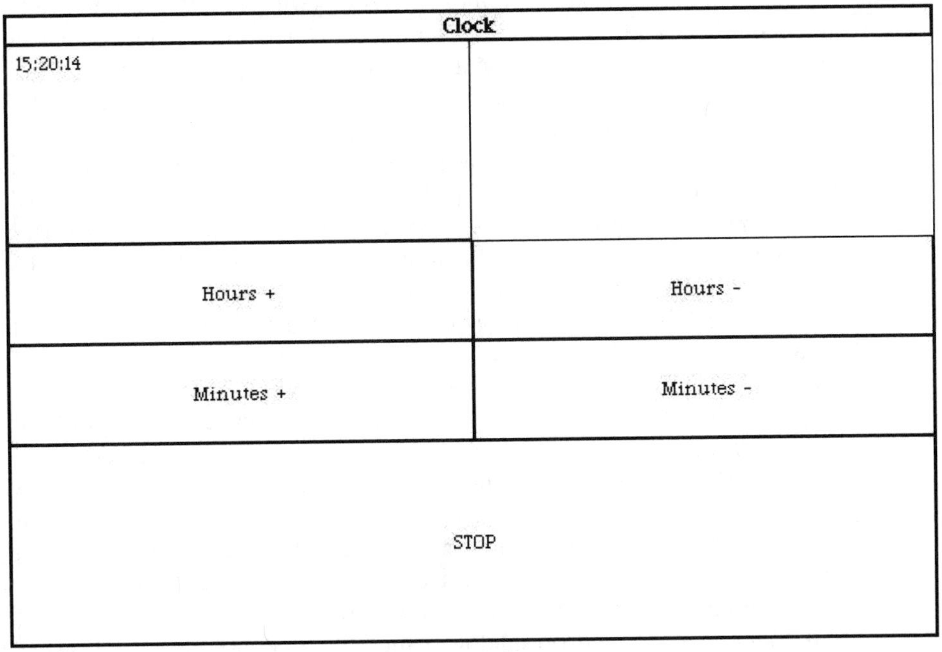

Figure 5–5   Clock UI from Pluggable Components in MVC

5.3.2 Creating Pluggable Interfaces in Morphic

Morphic is a very different model from MVC for doing user interfaces. In this section, we'll do the same interface, using the same pluggable components with an MVC architecture, but in Morphic. But first, we'll introduce and try out Morphic.

CAUTIONARY NOTE

There is a mixed use of terms in Squeak that may be confusing. The original window model (the structure by which all interfaces were built) in Smalltalk was called MVC (for Model-View-Controller). MVC is also a *paradigm,* a way of thinking, about building user interfaces. It is possible to use the MVC *paradigm* in a Morphic project, but objects that rely on the MVC *window model* must be run at the top level or in an MVC project. We'll try to make it clear as we go along.

5.3.2.1 Introducing Morphic

At this point, even if you have a slow computer, try out Morphic. From the Desktop Menu, choose *Open* and *New Project (Morphic)*. Click in the new Project Window. Use the red button to open a World menu, where you can access tools via the *Open* window (just as in the Desktop menu).

You might also choose *authoring tools...* (which wasn't in the Desktop Menu) and open the Standard Parts Bin. You'll see a window like Figure 5–6. Click on any one of the components of this window, drag it out, and drop it on your desktop.

You start to see immediately how Morphic is different from the MVC window model. *Any* object can be a "window" in Morphic — even stars and ellipses. Anything can lie on the desktop, can be resized, can be dragged around, or can be laid on top of another window or Morphic object.

Morphic was invented for the Self programming language. Self is, in several senses, a successor language to Smalltalk. Self explored just how efficient an object-oriented programming language could be without sacrificing pure object-oriented semantics, that is, *everything is an object.* Self was a project at Sun Microsystems Laboratories by David Ungar and Randall Smith. The Morphic user interface was developed by Randall Smith and John Maloney in Self, but John left that project and joined Apple as Squeak was just getting started, and he brought Morphic with him.

Every display object in Morphic is a Morph. That's a key design element in Morphic. Every object in Morphic — every window, menu, and graphical widget — is a subclass of the class **Morph**, and inherits a set of standard behaviors and interfaces.

Morphic objects are *concrete, uniform,* and *flexible,* as the original design goals for Morphic stated. Morphic objects are concrete in that they can be moved around and manipulated in ways similar to the real world. Click down on a Morphic object and drag it. Notice the drop shadow behind the object (Figure 5–7). That's the kind of concrete realism that the Morphic designers wanted.

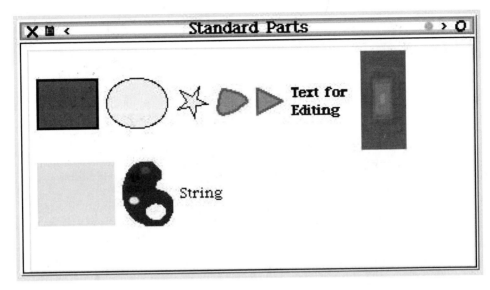

Figure 5–6   Standard Parts Bin in Morphic

Figure 5–7   Moving with Drop Shadow

Morphic objects are uniform in that they all have a basic structure and can be manipulated in the same basic ways. Each Morphic object can be selected (Table 1) to bring up a set of *halos* (colored dots) that allow the selected Morphic object to be manipulated in a standard set of ways, including resizing, rotations, and dragging. A standard set of halos is shown in Figure 5–8. (The difference between *pick-up* and *move* is that pick-up moves the target morph *within* its owner Morph, while move lifts the target morph from its owner.) You can get help on the meaning of any halo by simply resting your cursor above the colored dot (don't click down) and waiting a moment. A pop-up balloon explains the halo (as is seen for the red Menu halo in Figure 5–8.) Perhaps not all of the halos make sense right now (like making a tile or opening a viewer), but those will be explained later.

Table 1   Morphic Selection in Various Systems

System	Morphic Selection
Macintosh	Command-Click
Windows	Alt-Click
UNIX	Right-Click

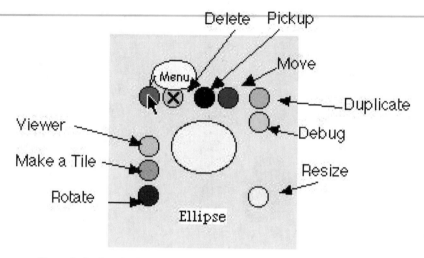

Figure 5–8   Standard Morphic Halos

Go ahead and try resizing or rotating some morphs. You may be surprised to find that everything (including menus and windows!) responds to those halos. Try keeping a menu up (by clicking on *keep this menu up* on any menu), selecting it, and then rotating it.

Note that sometimes when you select (depending on where you click), you may click on a sub-element of the object, like a menu item inside of the menu. *Morphs can be composed to create new morphs.* That's another key design feature of Morphic. When you Morphic-select on a morph, you get the bottommost morph first. If you keep repeating the selection, though, you select the parent morph, and its parent, and then cycle around back to the bottommost morph.

Not all objects have the same halos. As is seen in Figure 5–9, editable strings have some extra halos that do morph-specific things. But the main halos are uniform, and manipulation with halos is a constant across Morphic.

There are two morph-specific menus associated with any morph. One is accessed from the red (upper left) halo. The second is accessed by using control-click (the same for all platforms) on the morph itself. In general, the red-halo menu tends to have more programmer-specific commands (e.g., a debug menu, items to control the **Pen** that draws the morph), while the control-click menu tends to have more end-user facilities (e.g., features to name the object and save the object).

We have already seen some of the flexibility of Morphic. Every object can be resized and rotated—and most morphs still work in a rotated form! As we'll see in Section 5.4, the flexibility (and uniform structure) of Morphic extends into every morph.

There are many other morphs built into Squeak than just those few in the Standard Parts Bin. The way to get to all of them is via the *New Morph* menu, available from the World Menu (Figure 5–10). All morphs are available through this menu. The submenus in the New Morph menu are the names of the class categories for the morph's classes, e.g., the class category *Morphic-Books* becomes the *Books*

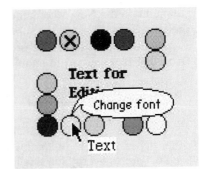

Figure 5–9 Halos on an Editable String Morph

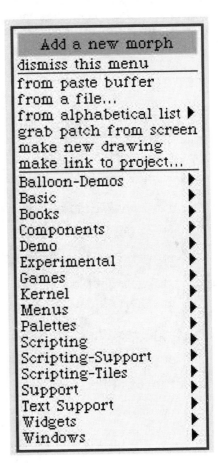

Figure 5–10 New Morph Menu in Squeak 2.7

submenu on the New Morph menu, and the classes defined in that category become the morphs available in the submenu.

Another way to access morphs is through *flaps*. There is a Preference available (from the Help menu) to enable global flaps, *useGlobalFlaps* (Figure 5–11). (Help

---

SIDE NOTE

The other flaps contain tools, menus, and some useful buttons and menus in the *Squeak* flap. As everything else in Squeak, everything about flaps is completely malleable. Try Morphic-selecting a flap tab, then choosing the red halo menu. You'll find that flap tabs are positionable, can be triggered on something other than mouse-over, and can change their names or colors. The *About Flaps* button in the *Squeak* flap gives more information on using and creating flaps.

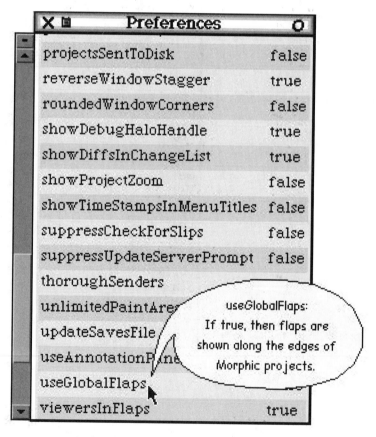

Figure 5–11   Preferences window, with useGlobalFlaps help available

Figure 5–12   Supplies Flap in Morphic

is available from pop-up balloons here, as for halos.) When the flaps are enabled, they appear along the edges of the screen in a Morphic project. The bottom flap is called *Supplies,* and it contains standard morphs, like those in the Standard Parts Bin. By default, the flap will open when the cursor passes over the flap tab (Figure 5–12). Morphs can then be dragged and dropped onto the desktop.

5.3.2.2 Doing pluggable components in Morphic

An important aspect of Morphic is that it is easy to learn if one is coming from the MVC window model, where the same kinds of pluggable-components programming that we saw in the older UI structure is still available in Morphic. You can bring up the Morphic version of our ClockWindow right now with these workspace expressions:

```
w := ClockWindow new.
w openAsMorph.
```

Notice that this will work in an MVC project, as well as in Morphic! When you open a morph from MVC, a miniature Morphic world (a Morphic window) is opened, with the morph inside it. This provides for a lot of flexibility while moving into Morphic.

Let's walk through the **openAsMorph** method for **ClockWindow**:

```
openAsMorph
    | win component clock |

    "Create the clock"
    clock := Clock new.
    clock setTime: (Time now printString).
    clock start.
```

We start out the same way—creating the clock, setting its time, and starting the clock:

```
    "Create a window for it"
    win := SystemWindow labelled: 'Clock'.
    win model: self.
```

Instead of creating a **SystemView**, as we did in the MVC model, we create a **SystemWindow**. A **SystemWindow** is a morph that provides all the standard window functionality: A close box, a collapse box, and a title bar. Note that you do not *have* to use a **SystemWindow** in Morphic—anything can be a window. But if you like the basic window structure, **SystemWindow** is a good starting place:

```
"Set up the text view and the various pieces"
component := PluggableTextMorph on: clock text: #display accept: nil.
win addMorph: component frame: (0.3@0.3 extent: 0.3@0.3).
```

Creating the **PluggableTextMorph** is obviously *very* similar to the **Pluggable-TextView** that we saw earlier. The same **on:text:accept:** message is used to create the instance. There are three significant differences:

- Notice that we don't define a **window:** for the view (that is, the frame where the component will be displayed). Instead, we specify the frame when we add the morph into the **SystemWindow**.
- Instead of **addSubView:**, we use **addMorph:frame:** to put the morph into a specific place in the window. Note that we don't *have* to specify a frame. You can just use **addMorph:** to add the morph. You use tools such as **AlignmentMorph** in order to get the structure that you want if you just toss the morph in without specifying a frame. (We'll talk more about **AlignmentMorph** later in this section.)
- Notice that the frame is not specified as a rectangle made up of points on the window. Instead, the frame is defined in terms of *relative* positions, where **0@0** is the upper-left-hand corner and **1.0@1.0** is the lower-right-hand corner. The rectangle defined for the **PluggableTextMorph** starts at ⅓ of the window's horizontal and vertical size, and extends for another ⅓ (to **2/3@2/3**). The relative size will be respected through all resizing

Creating the buttons is very much the same in the Morphic version of the **Clock** user interface as in MVC, modulo those same three changes as described above. In each case, we define a morph and we *don't* define a view-window, but we *do* define a frame when we add the morph to the whole window:

```
component := PluggableButtonMorph new
        model: clock;
        action: #addHour;
        label: 'Hours +';
        borderWidth: 1.
win addMorph: component frame: (0@0.6 extent: 0.5@0.2).
component := PluggableButtonMorph new
        model: clock;
        action: #subtractHour;
        label: 'Hours -';
        borderWidth: 1.
win addMorph: component frame: (0.5@0.6 extent: 0.5@0.2).
component := PluggableButtonMorph new
        model: clock;
        action: #addMinute;
        label: 'Minutes +';
        borderWidth: 1.
win addMorph: component frame: (0@0.8 extent: 0.5@0.1).
component := PluggableButtonMorph new
        model: clock;
```

```
        action: #subtractMinute;
        label: 'Minutes -';
        borderWidth: 1.
win addMorph: component frame: (0.5@0.8 extent: 0.5@0.1).

component := PluggableButtonMorph new
        model: clock;
        action: #stop;
        label: 'STOP';
        borderWidth: 1.
win addMorph: component frame: (0@0.9 extent: 1@0.1).
```

Opening the Clock window is even easier in Morphic than it is in the MVC window model. All morphs understand how to **openInWorld**. We don't have to mess with controllers. We simply tell the window to open:

```
win openInWorld.
^win
```

The resulting window appears as in Figure 5–13. Notice that the basic structure is exactly the same as in Figure 5–5, the MVC window model version. It's exactly the same *except* for the big black stuff around the text area. That is actually *nothing*. There is no morph there, and that black stuff is what the **SystemWindow** shows when there is no morph to display.

We'd like a better looking window than that. What we need is some kind of

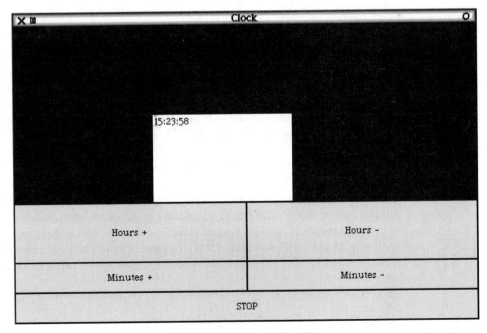

Figure 5–13   First Version of Pluggable Clock UI in Morphic

filler, which is where **AlignmentMorph** comes in. An **AlignmentMorph** is especially designed to fill in a space and to align things nicely within that space.

The method that follows differs from **openAsMorph** only in that it fills *all* the top ⅔ of the **ClockWindow** with an **AlignmentMorph**. The **PluggableTextMorph** is then added to the **AlignmentMorph**. We tell the fill to center the morphs placed in it from the **#bottomRight**. That doesn't mean that objects appear in the bottom-right quadrant. Rather, it indicates that the positioning will be from the bottom (if orientation is vertical) or right (if orientation is horizontal). The result is in Figure 5–14. The method is

openAsMorph2

```
| win component filler clock |

"Create the clock"
clock := Clock new.
clock setTime: (Time now printString).
clock start.

"Create a window for it"
win := SystemWindow labelled: 'Clock'.
win model: self.

"Set up the text view and the various pieces"
filler := AlignmentMorph newRow.
filler centering: #bottomRight.
win addMorph: filler frame: (0@0 extent: 1.0@0.6).
component := PluggableTextMorph on: clock text: #display accept: nil.
filler addMorph: component.
"ALL OF THE REST IS JUST LIKE openAsMorph"
```

We can get a different position for the text area by telling it to use center as **#center**. The result is in Figure 5–15. We can also get a different look by changing the *orientation* of the **AlignmentMorph**. Try **filler orientation: #horizontal** (or change it dynamically by Morphic-selecting the **AlignmentMorph** in the **ClockWindow**, and then using the red-halo-menu to change the orientation.)

Basically, an **AlignmentMorph** has two roles:

- To lay out the component morphs (submorphs) in a row or column, possibly resizing the submorphs as necessary.
- To resize itself (as necessary) based both on the sizes of the submorphs and on whether or not it's contained in *another* **AlignmentMorph**. You can tell an **AlignmentMorph** to be **rigid** (never resize), **spaceFill** (make itself as big as its enclosing **AlignmentMorph** will allow) and **shrinkWrap** (make itself as small as it can be), and each of these can apply to the horizontal or vertical dimensions.

The options are laid out in the initialize method of **AlignmentMorph**:

```
orientation ← #horizontal.     "#horizontal or #vertical "
centering ← #topLeft.          "#topLeft, #center, or #bottomRight"
```

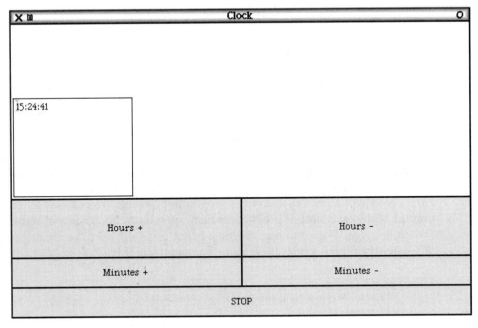

Figure 5–14   Cleaning up the Pluggable Morphic UI

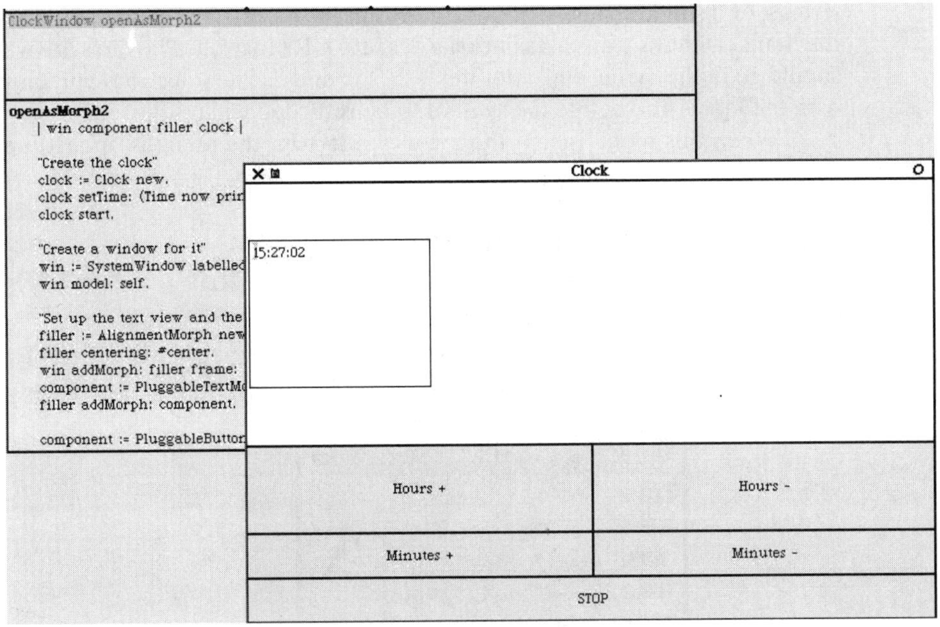

Figure 5–15   Exploring Variations on the AlignmentMorph

```
hResizing ← #spaceFill.      "#spaceFill, #shrinkWrap, or #rigid"
vResizing ← #spaceFill.      "#spaceFill, #shrinkWrap, or #rigid"
```

You can use multiple **AlignmentMorphs** to get the effect that you want. To center something in the middle, simply put **AlignmentMorphs** to either size and let them be space-filling. To force something to the right, put a space-filling **AlignmentMorph** on the left.

5.3.3 Menus and Dialogs in a Pluggable World

Menus can actually be handled exactly the same way in both MVC and Morphic models, and they're very easy. While there is a wide variety of Menu classes, there are a couple of classes that serve as programmers' tools. You can set them up (even on the fly, upon a button press), and then open them up. They will return a value when selected. For example, the menu that pops up over the messages pane in Celeste (the e-mail reader in Squeak) is created like this:

```
CustomMenu
        labels: 'again\undo\copy\cut\paste\format\accept\cancel
compose\reply\forward' withCRs
        lines: #(2 5 6 8)
        selections: #(again undo copySelection cut paste format accept cancel compose reply forward)
```

The labels are the words in the menu. Labels can be defined as an array of strings, or a single string with carriage-return (CR, ASCII 13) characters separating the items. **withCRs** translates backslashes into CRs for you. The lines are where lines should go in the menu, e.g., after items 2, 5, 6, and 8. The selection symbols match up with the labels and define the symbol to be returned when selected.

When this menu is sent the message **startUp**, the menu is opened up and the

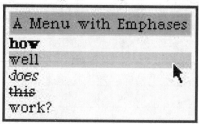

Figure 5–16   A Menu with Emphases

PopUpMenu notify: 'Your system will now crash'
Your system will now crash
OK

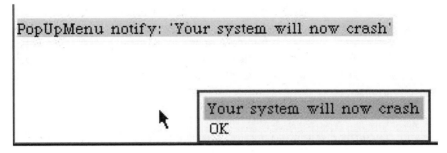

Figure 5–17 Using a PopUpMenu to Inform the User

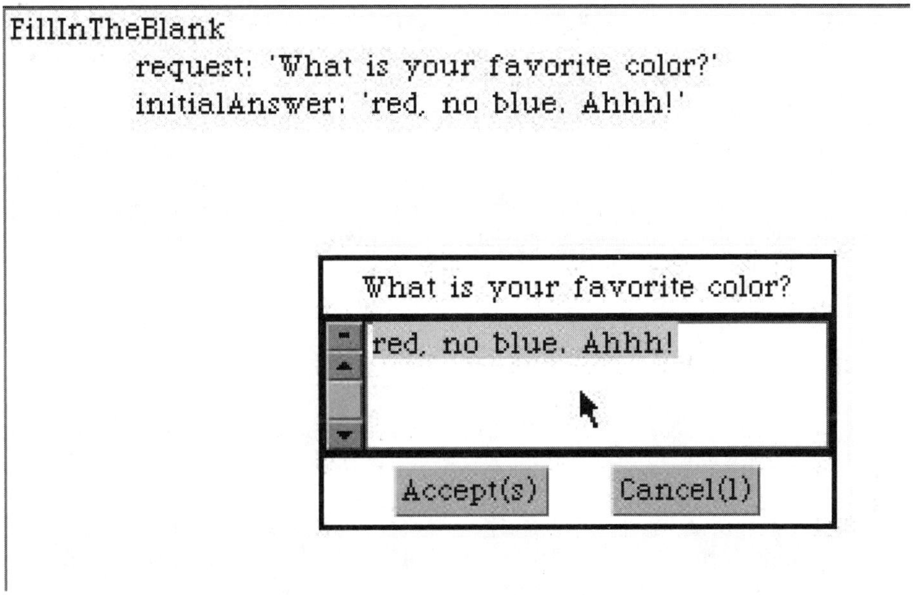

FillInTheBlank
request: 'What is your favorite color?'
initialAnswer: 'red, no blue, Ahhh!'
What is your favorite color?
red, no blue, Ahhh!
Accept(s)
Cancel(l)

Figure 5–18 Querying the User with FillInTheBlank

user makes a selection. The selection symbol is then returned for later processing. One can also **startUp: initialSelection**, so that a given item starts out selected. If no item is selected, the menu returns **nil**.

You don't have to create all of the labels, lines, and selection symbols in one fell swoop. There is also an **add:action:** method for adding a word and a corresponding symbol to a menu, and an **addLine** method for inserting lines.

There are several useful menu classes that provide particular kinds of menus. An **EmphasizedMenu**, for example, allows you to add emphases to your menus, such as bold and italics, as in Figure 5–16. **PopUpMenu** provides some of the default dialogs that you might expect to use to inform the user of important events (Figure 5–17). **FillInTheBlank** is classified as a menu, but it's really the provider of various query-the-user dialogs, such as **request:** (Figure 5–18).

If you know that you will only be using your menu in Morphic, you can use the class **MenuMorph** and **GraphicalDictionaryMenu**. **MenuMorph**s understand some Morphic-specific features, like **addStayUpItem** (which allows a menu to stay available for later mouse clicks). When a **MenuMorph** is being constructed, it is also possible to specify **balloonTextForLastItem:** to set up help for users. **GraphicalDictionaryMenu** knows how to display forms for items, which can be a useful alternative in many situations.

EXERCISES: WORKING WITH PLUGGABLE INTERFACES

5. Redesign the **ClockWindow** so that there is no Stop button and the **Clock** is stopped as soon as the **ClockWindow** is closed.

6. Get rid of the **ClockWindow** class and make the user interface work from **Clock**.

7. Use pluggable components to make a simple Rolodex. Create Rolodex cards that contain name, address, and phone-number information. Provide a scrolling list of names, and when one is selected, display the information in a text area.

8. Use pluggable components to make a simple calendar system. Provide a multi-pane list browser for picking a year (within, say, a ten-year range), a month, and a date. (Be sure to fill in the date pane only when the year and month are selected!) Allow the user to fill in text-pane notes for the given date. Use a **Dictionary** to store the text information, with the dates as the indices.

5.4 BUILDING MORPHIC USER INTERFACES

The real strength of Morphic lies in the creation of Morphic interfaces within Morphic. Morphic interfaces don't necessarily have to follow the MVC paradigm, but they can. Morphic interfaces can also be assembled rapidly through simple dragging and dropping. We have already seen that one morph can be *added* to another. From within Morphic, we say that one morph can be *embedded* within another.

In this section, we'll explore how to work with morphs from the user-interface perspective, and then from the programmer's perspective. We'll use the same example, a simple simulation of an object falling, to explore both sides. Along the way, we'll describe the workings of Morphic.

5.4.1 Programming Morphs from the Viewer Framework

The Viewer framework (sometimes called the *etoys system*) has been developed mainly by Scott Wallace of the Disney Imagineering Squeak team as an easy-to-use programming environment for end users. It's not a finished item, and it may change dramatically in future versions of Squeak. But as-is, it provides us a way of exploring Morphic before we dig into code.

We're going to create a simulation of an object falling. Our falling object will be a simple EllipseMorph. Our falling object will have a velocity (initially zero) and a constant rate of acceleration due to gravity. We'll use pixels on the screen as our distance units.

If you recall your physics, the velocity increases at the rate of the acceleration constant. For our simulation, we'll only compute velocity and position *discretely* (i.e., at fixed intervals, rather than all the time, the way that the real world works). Each time element, we'll move the object the amount of the velocity, and we'll increment the velocity by the amount of the acceleration. This isn't a very accurate simulation of a falling object, but it's enough for demonstration purposes.

For example, let's say that we run our discrete simulation every second. Let's say that the velocity was currently 10 and the acceleration was 3. We say that the object is falling 10 pixels per second, with an acceleration of 3 pixels per second per second (that is, the velocity increases by 3 pixels per second at each iteration, which occurs every second). When the next second goes by, we add to the velocity so that it's 13 pixels per second, and we move the object 13 pixels (because that's the velocity). And so on.

We'll also create a *Kick* object. When the object is kicked, we'll imagine that the object has been kicked up a few pixels, and its velocity goes back to zero. Strictly speaking, an upward push on the falling object would result in an upward velocity that would decrease as gravity pulled the object back down. (This is simplification for the sake of a demonstration.)

Create three morphs (from the *New Morph* menu, or from the Standard Parts bin, or from the Supplies flap): A **RectangleMorph** (default gray), an **EllipseMorph** (default yellow), and a **TextMorph** (appears in Supplies and Parts as "Text for Editing"). We're going to use the rectangle and text as our Kicker, and the ellipse as our falling object.

We'll start out by creating our Kicker button. Click on the text so that you can edit it, and change it to say "Kick." Now Morphic-select it, and drag it (via the black *Pick Up* halo) into the rectangle (Figure 5–19). Use the control-click menu to *embed* the text into the rectangle. After you choose the *embed* menu item, you will be asked to choose which morph you want to embed the text into. Choose the **RectangleMorph**. (As we'll see later in this chapter, the other option, a **PasteUpMorph**, is actually the whole Morphic world. It is possible to embed morphs into the desktop of a Morphic World.) Once embedded, they move as one morph (Figure 5–20).

Now, let's start programming our two morphs. Morphic-select the ellipse and choose the center-left (turquoise) halo, the *View me* halo. When you do, a *Viewer* for the ellipse will open (Figure 5–21).

The Viewer is a kind of browser on a morph. It allows you to create methods for this morph, create instance variables for the given morph, and directly manipulate the morph. Click on one of the yellow exclamation points—the command, whatever it is (say, *Ellipse forward by 5*), will be executed, and the morph will

Figure 5–19 Dragging the TextMorph into the RectangleMorph

Figure 5–20 Once Embedded, They Drag Together

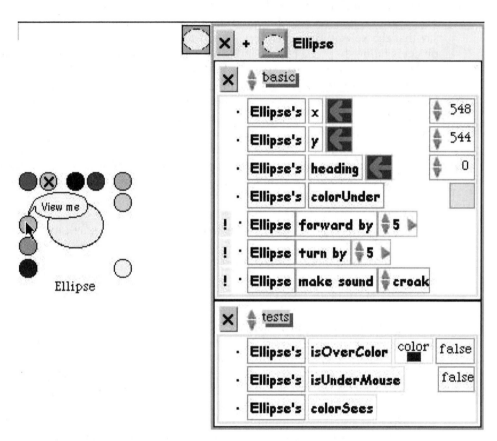

Figure 5–21 Opening a Viewer on the Ellipse

move five pixels. Directly change the number of the x or y coordinate, and the morph will move.

To prepare for what we want to do, change the heading of the ellipse to 180. That means its heading will be straight down. That's important because objects fall down. If the heading were zero, our object would fall up.

5.4.1.1 Adding an instance variable

We are going to need a velocity for our falling object, so let's add an instance variable to our ellipse. Click on the small tile of the ellipse inside the viewer itself. (The leftmost tile of the ellipse in Figure 5–21 is actually a tab. Click on it, and the viewer will slide to the right. Click it again to open the viewer back up.) A

SIDE NOTE

Take note of what we're doing here: We're adding an instance variable *directly to an instance,* not to the *class.* The Viewer system offers a different kind of object-oriented programming, called *prototype-based objects.* Each of the morphs is a prototype that can be given variables and methods *directly.* It is possible to then create new instance morphs from these prototypes. Squeak is still *class-based*—the prototypes are created by defining *Player* classes on the fly for each Viewer object, where the Viewer object is the one and only instance of that class. Prototype-based systems can be easier to build in, but may not be as easily maintained as class-based systems.

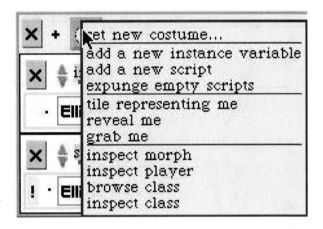

Figure 5–22 Adding an Instance Variable to a Morph

pop-up menu will provide a number of programming items, including a new instance variable (Figure 5–22). Choose *add a new instance variable* and enter the name as *velocity.*

The viewer will then update to show the new instance variable (Figure 5–23). This instance variable can be accessed or set, just like any other instance variable. In a few steps, we'll use it in an equation for changing the velocity by the amount of a gravitational constant.

5.4.1.2 Making our ellipse fall

We can then begin to program our falling object. Click on the "forward by" tile and drag it off the viewer. Drop it anywhere on the desktop, and a script object is formed (Figure 5–24).

Let's make this script run all by itself. We'll trigger it when we click the mouse down upon the ellipse. Click and hold on the word *normal.* You'll get a pop-up menu of the conditions on which the script should run (Figure 5–25). Choose *mouseDown* (Figure 5–26).

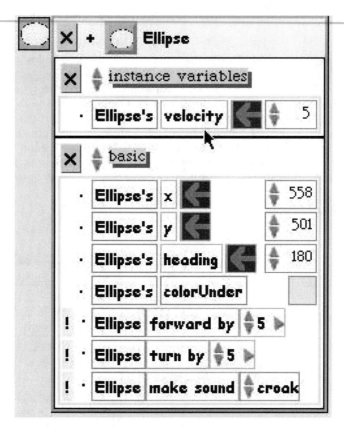

Figure 5–23   Ellipse's Viewer with the new Velocity
Instance Variable

Figure 5–24   Creating Our First Viewer
Script

   Now, click on the ellipse. Each time that you click on it (actually, as soon as you click down on it), it should jump forward five steps. You can play with the amount of the jump in the script1 window.

   When an object falls, it should move as much as its velocity, using the simplified model of physics that we're using. So, instead of the constant in the script, we need to reference the velocity instance variable that we've built. That's fairly easily done. Click on the velocity tile in the ellipse's Viewer, and drag it over the constant in the script (Figure 5–27). Now, when you click down on the ellipse, it moves forward as much as the value of the velocity.

   The next step is to make the velocity increase at each time interval. Go back up

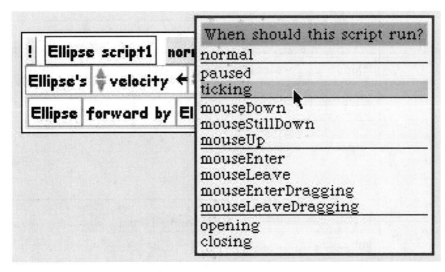

Figure 5–25   Changing the Conditions of the Script

Figure 5–26   How the Script Window Changes

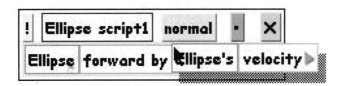

Figure 5–27   Dragging the Velocity over the Constant

to the Viewer and click-and-drag on the arrow next to the velocity. You're now grabbing a set of tiles for *setting* the velocity. Drag them into your script window, just above the *forward by* tiles. (You'll find that the other tiles literally move out of your way as you drag in your tiles.) You'll now be setting the velocity to 1 (Figure 5–28). Now click on the little green arrow next to the 1. The line will expand to *1 + 1* (Figure 5–29). Go back up the Viewer and drag the velocity instance-variable tile over the second 1 (Figure 5–30). You've now constructed the falling script. Your rate of acceleration is 1, and the velocity will increase by that number during each time interval.

You can really make this work now. Change the *mouseDown* trigger on the

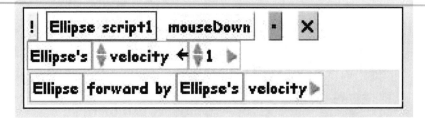

Figure 5–28 Setting Velocity to 1

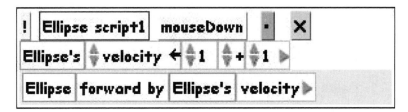

Figure 5–29 Setting Velocity to 1 + 1

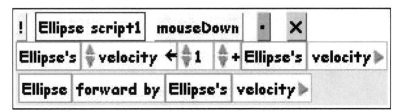

Figure 5–30 Setting Velocity to 1 + Velocity

script to *ticking.* A ticking script fires continuously at a regular interval. (You can change the interval by clicking on the *Ellipse script1* tile and choosing the menu item there.) You will find your ellipse falling ever more rapidly toward the bottom, and then bounce when it gets to the bottom. (That's default Viewer behavior.) You can set the script back to triggering *normal* (which means that it just sits) to stop the falling and also to be able to move the ellipse elsewhere.

Feel free to explore values different from 1 for the acceleration constant. You can make small changes by clicking on the up or down arrows next to the 1, or click right on the 1 and type whatever you want. Be careful how large you make it, though! Remember that this value is the amount of change of the *velocity,* so it compounds quickly.

If you want, you can now *name* your script. Click on the *Ellipse script1* tile, and choose *Rename this script* (Figure 5–31). You might call it *Fall.*

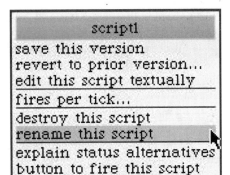

Figure 5–31 Changing the Name of a
Script

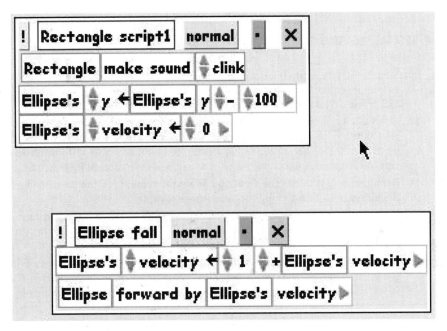

Figure 5–32 The Final Scripts

5.4.1.3 Building the kicker

Now let's build the kicker. Open up a Viewer on your kicker rectangle. Drag out the
tile that has the rectangle making a sound, and drop it to make a new script. With
this start, whenever we "kick" the ellipse, a sound will be made. Feel free to use the
up and down arrows on the sound tile to explore other sounds, and pick the one that
makes sense as the "kick" sound to you. (Later in the book, we talk about how to record new sounds to use in the sound tile.) Go ahead and make this script work on
mouseDown. You can click the kick rectangle to hear the sound.

When we kick the object, the object should move up a few pixels (the effect of
our kick), and the velocity should be set to zero. Your final script should look like the
top of Figure 5–32. Set the kicker's script to fire on *mouseDown* and the falling ob-

ject's script to fire on *ticking*, and you should then have a working simulation of a falling object that you can kick.

You can save these morphs and share them with others as they are. Control-click on any of the morphs and choose *Save morph in file*. You can name the file, and its file extension will be ".morph". You can send this file to others (via email or even on the Web). Others can load it back into their image. From the file list, when you select a morph file, your yellow-button menu will let you file in the morph and recreate it—scripts and all.

The references between objects may get messed up in this process. For example, the kicker's script will probably need to remapped to the falling object. That's what the *Make A Tile* halo (just under the Viewer halo) is good for. Simply make a tile and drag it into each of the "Ellipse" tiles in the kicker's script.

EXERCISES: IMPROVING THE VIEWER FALLING OBJECT

9. Should the kick script belong to the kicker or the falling object? We currently have it as the kicker, but maybe the falling object should figure out how it should fall, and the kicker should just tell the falling object to fall. Rebuild the system that way.

10. Our velocity is really the *vertical* velocity. Add *horizontal* velocity to the object. Create a launcher that fires out the falling object at a given vertical and horizontal velocity. If you do it right, the object should fall in an arc. (Remember why from your physics? Recall that the horizontal velocity remains constant and isn't affected by gravity.)

11. Remembering your physics, figure out how you need to set things up, without changing the kicker, such that kicking the object stops it dead.

12. How would you make the falling object fall *up,* that is, fall as if the gravitational pull was from the top of the screen rather than from the bottom? (Hint: The gravity's impact in our simplistic simulation is through the acceleration on the object.)

13. Brainstorm a bit over class-based versus prototype-based object systems. When would you want to use one over the other? Consider at least these two scenarios: (1) You are trying to find the implementor of a given behavior and (2) you are trying out a new idea.

5.4.2 Programming Basic Variables and Events of Morphs

The previous section gave you a sense of how easy it can be to manipulate morphs. When you are working through how you want your interface to work, this is a great process. You can quickly assemble a morph that you want, and even test out its functionality. However, it gets hard to make many of them, or to create abstractions over them (e.g., subclasses, abstract classes), or to control things like connections between objects. Also, the Viewer system doesn't yet provide all the tools of text-based programming, such as a debugger.

Typically, you should still use text to build your more complex systems. The transition between the tiling world and the scripting world isn't as complex as you might think. If you click on the *script1* tile, you get a pop-up menu that allows you to view your script textually (Figure 5–33). This provides you the opportunity to see the mapping from the Viewer system into the text world.

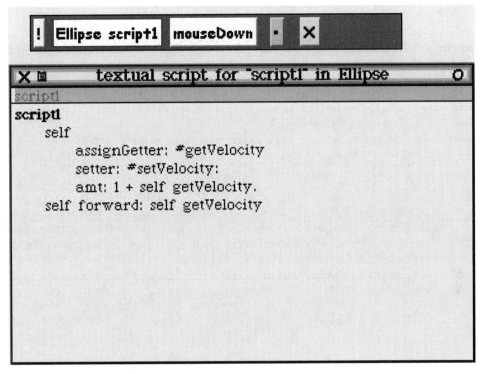

Figure 5–33   Viewing a Tile Script as Text

But the text world is clearly more complicated than the tile world. We need to know some more things about Morphic in order to dig into programming there. This section introduces the key instance variables, events, and methods needed to program in Morphic.

5.4.2.1 Instance variables and properties

The following table summarizes the instance variables that are common to every morph. Each of these can be set and accessed using the normal Smalltalk conventions. The **bounds** variable is accessed using the **bounds** method and set using the **bounds:** method. One of the interesting things about Morphic is that any change is immediately apparent in the system. Changing the **bounds** makes the morph change its size immediately. You don't have to do any kind of refresh to make it show.

The last instance variable, **name**, is a bit of a trick. Yes, you can use **name:** on any morph, but if you look at the definition of the class **Morph**, you won't find **name** there. Instead, there is another instance variable, named **extension**, that refers to an instance of **MorphExtension**, and it is the **MorphExtension** that knows how to be named.

What's going on here is a cost-savings technique. Every object on the screen in Morphic is a morph. Morphs must therefore be cheap to have around. Thus, extra things like **name** (not every morph needs a name) are *extensions*. If you set the name

Instance variable	Meaning
bounds	The rectangle defining the shape of this morph. Change the bounds to resize or move the morph. (**fullBounds** is the bounds of the morph and all of its submorphs. They're usually the same.)
owner	The containing morph. It's **nil** for the World, but is otherwise the morph in which **self** is embedded.
submorphs	The morphs inside me, typically changed with **addMorph:**
color	The main color of the morph.
name	Morphs can be named, and that's what shows up at the bottom of the halos when you Morphic-select an object.

of a morph, it will check to see if it has an extension, will create one if it doesn't (see the **Morph** method **assureExtension**), and will then set the name in the extension. The name accessor asks the extension for the name. This is an example of the *delegation* introduced in Chapter 2.

MorphExtension provides many other instance variables, some of which are shown here:

Instance variable	Meaning
balloonText, balloonTextSelector	Any morph can do **self extension balloonText: 'This is all about me . . . '** and will set the balloon help for themselves. A morph can also set its **balloonTextSelector**, which will be used to access balloon text dynamically.
visible	Determines whether a morph is visible.
locked	Manipulate with **lock** and **unlock**. A locked morph can't even be selected.
sticky	A sticky morph can't be moved. Change it with **toggleStickiness**.

There are other interesting instance variables in **MorphExtension**, but these are the most critical, save one: **otherProperties**. There is built-in space for additional properties in **MorphExtension**, so there is no need to add additional instance variables.

otherProperties is a **Dictionary**. You can add properties with **setProperty: toValue:**, retrieve them with **valueOfProperty:**, and ask if a property is there with **hasProperty:**. The name of a property is typically a symbol, and the value can be anything you want. The properties won't be as fast to access as an instance variable, but this allows for great expandability without ever changing the basic structure of **MorphExtension** instances.

5.4.2.2 Morphic events

Programming user interfaces in Morphic is much easier than under the MVC window model. Conceptually, the complicated controller part is built into the toolkit. A few predefined user-interface events are passed on to morphs that want them. The basic model is that a morph is asked if it wants to handle a particular kind of event, and if it does, the event is sent by calling a predefined method in your morph. (**Morph**, of course, defines all of these and will catch them if your subclass doesn't override them.)

The object passed around is a **MorphicEvent**. A **MorphicEvent** understands many of the same things as **Sensor**, but encapsulates the event into an object. You don't poll **MorphicEvent** the way that you do **Sensor**. Instead, you can ask a **MorphicEvent** whether **redButtonPressed** is **true** if it's a mouse event (**isMouse** would return true), or you can ask the **MorphicEvent** what the **keyCharacter** is (if **isKeystroke** is true).

The following table summarizes how to handle the most common kinds of events.

Event you want your morph to handle	How to handle it
MouseDown	Have a method **handlesMouseDown:** that takes a **MorphicEvent** as input, and return **true**.
	Have a method named **mouseDown:** that takes a **MorphicEvent**, and deal with the mouse down as you wish.
MouseUp and MouseOver (mouse passes over the object)	Similarly, have a **handlesMouseUp:** or **handlesMouseOver:** method, then a **mouseUp:** and **mouseOver:** method.
MouseEnter and MouseLeave	Return **true** for **handlesMouseOver:**, then define **mouseEnter:** and **mouseLeave:**.
MouseMove (within the morph)	Return **true** for **handlesMouseDown:**, and then implement **mouseMove:**
Key Strokes	When your morph should capture keystrokes, return **true** for **hasFocus**, then accept events in **keyStroke:**. When the focus is changing, your morph will be sent **keyboardFocusChange:**, **true** for receiving and **false** for losing.

There are more subtleties to the Morphic event-handling model. For example, if a morph's extension defines an **eventHandler**, then your events can be delegated to the object referenced by the **eventHandler**. There are also events associated with mouse clicks starting text entry or not, accepting drag-and-drop, and catching whether the mouse is already carrying an object when it enters the bounds of the morph. More details on these can be found in the event-handling category of **Morph** instance methods, but the previous ones are the most common cases.

5.4.2.3 Animation

One of the most interesting things about Morphic is that it makes animated user interfaces very easy to build. To make your morph animate, you need to implement just one method, **step**, and optionally one other method, **stepTime**. Note that

- At regular intervals, the method **step** is called on all morphs. In your morphs' **step** methods, you can change the appearance, update the display, poll a model to ask for its current values, or do whatever else you'd like.

- The default step frequency is once per second. **stepTime** can return a different value, the number of milliseconds between each time you want **step** to be called.

An easy-to-understand example of using **step** and **stepTime** is the **ClockMorph**. The **ClockMorph** is a subclass of **StringMorph**, and all it does is display the time. The **stepTime** method simply returns 1000 — the clock updates once a second (1000 milliseconds). The **step** method simply sets the contents of the string (**self**) to the current time. That's all that's needed to create an updating string with the time.

5.4.2.4 Custom menus

There is a custom menu associated with each morph, available from the control-click menu or from the red-halo menu. You can easily add morph-specific items to this menu, by overriding the method **addCustomMenuItems: aCustomMenu hand: aHandMorph**. This method is called whenever the menu is requested by the user (via control-click or red-halo click). Simply use **add:action:**, **add:target:action:**, and **addLine** methods to add additional items to the menu that's being handed to the method.

Most of the time, you will want to allow your morph's superclass a chance to add its menu items, via **super addCustomMenuItems: aCustomMenu hand: aHandMorph**. But if you'd like to limit the menu items a user sees, you don't need to call the superclass. The menu will still have many generic **Morph** items in it, though.

For an example menu customization, **ImageMorphs** provide user-accessible manipulations through this method:

```
addCustomMenuItems: aCustomMenu hand: aHandMorph
        super addCustomMenuItems: aCustomMenu hand: aHandMorph.
        aCustomMenu add: 'choose new graphic...' target: self action: #chooseNewGraphic.
        aCustomMenu add: 'read from file' action: #readFromFile.
        aCustomMenu add: 'grab from screen' action: #grabFromScreen.
```

5.4.2.5 Structure of Morphic

The Morphic world may be clearer if some of the internal structure is described. It's important to realize that, just as everything in Squeak is an object, everything in Morphic is a morph (i.e., an instance of a subclass of **Morph**). This includes the desktop itself and even the cursor.

The desktop itself, the World, is an instance of the class **PasteUpMorph**. There are many **PasteUpMorph**s around. The Standard Parts Bin and the flaps are **PasteUpMorph**s. **PasteUpMorph**s are general "playfields" (as some of them are named) that can hold other morphs.

The World **PasteUpMorph** does something very important: It runs **doOneCycleNow** repeatedly. This method updates the cursors, processes user-interface events for the given cursor, runs step methods, and updates the display. The method **doOneCycleNow** is as follows:

doOneCycleNow

> "Do one cycle of the interactive loop. This method is called repeatedly when the world is running."

> "process user input events"
> self handsDo: [:h |
>   self activeHand: h.
>   h processEvents.
>   self activeHand: nil].

> self runStepMethods.
> self displayWorldSafely.
> StillAlive ← true.

Notice that the previous paragraph (and code) make it clear that events are handled *for each cursor*. A Morphic world can have multiple cursors at once. Each is an instance of **HandMorph**. It is **HandMorph** that sends the events to morphs. Because of this implementation, it is possible to have multiple users interacting in the same Morphic world. There is an option under the *Help* menu from the World Menu called *Telemorphic* that lets you connect multiple users to the same image, each with his or her own cursor.

The **HandMorph** provides many core behaviors to Morphic. As can be seen in the earlier code, it's the **processEvents** method in **HandMorph** that deals with sending the appropriate messages to the appropriate morphs when user input comes in. It's also the **HandMorph** that creates the control-click menu, in the method **buildMorphMenuFor:**. The **HandMorph** puts up the halos, builds the halo menus, and even builds the World Menu. So, if you want to change the halos or core menus of the system, you start by modifying or subclassing **HandMorph**.

The process of displaying the world safely (**displayWorldSafely**) leads to asking each submorph of the world to **drawOn:** the world's **Canvas**. The **drawOn:** method is the hook for creating your own look to Morphs, if you want something different from a composition or slight modification to the base morphs. **drawOn:** takes a **Canvas** object as its argument. An instance of **Canvas** knows how to draw basic objects (like rectangles and ovals) as well as arbitrary **Form**s.

5.4.3 Programming A Morphic Falling Object

Let's redo the falling-object simulation, but this time from textual Squeak. The idea is to create the same kind of interaction as in the Viewer version, but to use the Morphic programming structure described in Section 5.4.2. By creating a textual version, we have objects that we can build upon later in other contexts. This code is on the CD as *programmedFall.cs*.

We won't go through a CRC-Card analysis here, because we already know what basic objects we want. We need a kicker and a falling object. We will shift responsibilities a bit from the Viewer version: It's the falling object that knows how to be kicked. The kicker just tells the falling object to kick.

Because the textual version will not make the code as accessible as it is in the Viewer version, we'll need to add some user interface to do the kind of exploration that a user might want to do. Probably the most common manipulation will be to change the gravitational-acceleration constant. In terms of responsibility, it seems natural to let the falling object hold a menu item for allowing the user to change the gravitational constant. But given that our falling object will be moving constantly, it's easier on the user to stick it in the kicker.

Just to make the falling object a little more interesting, we'll create it as a subclass of ImageMorph. An ImageMorph can hold any kind of Form, which means that we can have any kind of falling object we wish. Think about what kind of images you might want to have crashing on your screen, with a clear user interface for kicking those objects.

A UML diagram of our classes appears in Figure 5–34. We'll create a **Kick-ButtonMorph** as our kick button, and a **FallingImageMorph** as our falling object. The **KickButtonMorph** will keep track of the **ball** that it kicks. It will have hooks into the user interface, for the gravity-setting menu item (**addCustomMenuItems:hand:**) and for capturing button clicks (**mouseDown:**). The **FallingImageMorph** will keep track of its **gravity** (more correctly, the constant acceleration due to gravity) and **velocity**, provide setters and getters for these, and implement a **kick** method. It will have a **step** method that will implement falling.

We can now begin implementing our classes with some class definitions. While we said that the falling object would be a subclass of **ImageMorph**, we didn't talk yet about what the kicker would be subclassed from. A good solution is to do in code just what we did via direct manipulation of the morphs: We'll start from a **RectangleMorph**. We'll override **initialize** so that our **KickButtonMorph** gets the label that we want.

Notice that there *is* a **SimpleButtonMorph** that would make sense to subclass from. Similarly, there are many button subclasses that would be useful to explore and subclass. However, they make it *too* easy—if we used one of those, we would never deal with mouseDown or set our own label. We would only provide an action method. While that's what you'll do in normal practice, we'll unpack the details a bit here to show how the button is constructed:

```
ImageMorph subclass: #FallingImageMorph
        instanceVariableNames: 'velocity gravity '
        classVariableNames: "
        poolDictionaries: "
        category: 'Morphic-Demo'
RectangleMorph subclass: #KickButtonMorph
        instanceVariableNames: 'ball '
        classVariableNames: "
        poolDictionaries: "
        category: 'Morphic-Demo'
```

5.4.3.1 Implementing the falling object

Let's start out by implementing the basic falling procedure. We know what this looks like from our Viewer implementation, and we know from our discussion of Morphic

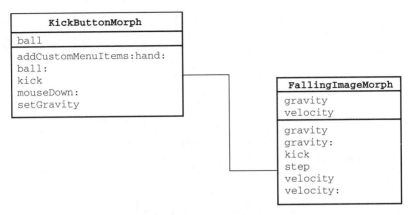

Figure 5–34   UML Class Diagram for Textual Falling Object Simulation

animation that we fall in a **step** method. Falling is a process of incrementing the velocity by the acceleration due to gravity and then moving the object down by the amount of its velocity:

step

velocity ← velocity + gravity. "Increase velocity by gravitational constant"
self bounds: (self bounds translateBy: (0@(velocity))).

As mentioned earlier, the position and size of a morph are determined by its **bounds**. If we move the **bounds**, we move the object. The **bounds** is a **Rectangle**. To move a rectangle is to *translate* it, and the method **translateBy:** handles the translation. The amount of translation is a **Point**: The amount of horizontal translation and the amount of vertical translation. To move an object down, then, we translate it by **0 @ velocity**.

We don't want the step to happen too often, so we'll provide a **stepTime** method. We'll use one second as the step interval, so that our velocity is in the simple units of pixels per second, and our gravity constant is pixels per second per second:

stepTime

"Amount of time in milliseconds between steps"
^1000

Next, we need the ability to kick the object. Kicking, as we defined it earlier, sets the velocity back to zero and moves the object back up 100 pixels. Again, this is a translation, and in this one the vertical coordinate is negative because it's a move up:

kick

velocity ← 0. "Set velocity to zero"
self bounds: (self bounds translateBy: (0@(100 negated))).

Finally, let's provide an initialize method that sets the velocity and acceleration to a reasonable state:

```
initialize
        super initialize. "Do normal image."
        velocity ← 0. "Start out not falling."
        gravity ← 1. "Acceleration due to gravity."
```

We will need methods for getting and setting the gravity, if not the velocity, too. Those are left as an exercise for the reader.

5.4.3.2 Implementing the kicker

The main requirement for the kicker is that it be able to kick an object, so let's begin with that. We'll trigger the kicking action on mouse-down, which means that we have to announce that our morph will handle mouse-down, and then provide a **mouse-Down:** method:

```
handlesMouseDown: evt
        "Yes, handle mouse down"
        ^true
mouseDown: evt
        self kick.
```

Kicking is pretty easy when the kicked object implements the kicking:

```
kick
        ball kick.
```

That's enough to allow for kicking. We'll need to be able to set the ball to be kicked (**ball:**), but we have enough now to start our simulation. However, if we created our objects right now, our kicker would only be a raw rectangle without a label. If we want to have a different look, we should override the **initialize** method.

The initialize method first does whatever rectangles do for initialization, then sets up a label. Our label will be a string (StringMorph) saying "Kick the Ball." StringMorphs know their size (extent), so we'll set the kicker's extent to match it. Then we'll place the string into the rectangle, and place the center of the button wherever the mouse is. The code is as follows:

```
initialize
        | myLabel |
        super initialize. "It's a normal rectangle plus..."

        myLabel ← StringMorph new initialize.
        myLabel contents: 'KickTheBall'.
        self extent: (myLabel extent). "Make the rectangle big enough for the label"
        self addMorph: myLabel.
        self center: (Sensor mousePoint). "Put it wherever the mouse is."
```

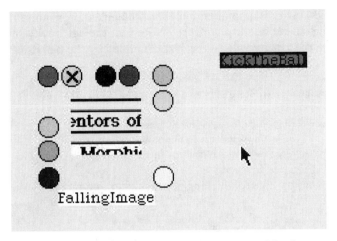

Figure 5–35   FallingImageMorph and KickButtonMorph

5.4.3.3 Running the text falling simulation

In a workspace, we can now run our simulation. We need to create each object, initialize it, and open it in the world. We need to tell the kicker what its ball is. We'll set the form for the falling object to be selected by the user, so when you execute the following code, you'll have to click and drag a rectangle of interesting display before it'll run (feel free to replace that with a form of your own choosing):

```
aBall ← FallingImageMorph new initialize.
aBall newForm: (Form fromUser). "Here's where you select a form"
aKicker ← KickButtonMorph new initialize.
aKicker ball: aBall.
aBall openInWorld.
aKicker openInWorld.
```

With this, you can bounce the ball around (Figure 5–35). (Though it probably doesn't look like a ball, unless you selected one.) However, all you can do is bounce the ball here—not much more exploration than that.

5.4.3.4 Changing the gravitational constant

As seen in our original design, we plan to make a menu item available that will change the gravitational constant for the falling object. We can do that pretty easily. First, we add it to the control-click menu:

```
addCustomMenuItems: aCustomMenu hand: aHandMorph
    super addCustomMenuItems: aCustomMenu hand: aHandMorph. "Do normal stuff"
    aCustomMenu add: 'set gravity' action: #setGravity.
```

Then we provide a method for setting the gravity. Setting the gravity will use a **FillInTheBlank** to let the user know what the current gravity is and to input a new gravity. The gravity is a number, but **FillInTheBlank** accepts an initial answer and returns a string, so we need to convert. (Note that the **setGravity** method doesn't actually change the gravity value—that's still handled by the **ball** itself.) The code is

```
setGravity
        "Set the gravity of the ball"
        | newGravity |
        newGravity ← FillInTheBlank request: 'New gravity'
                initialAnswer: ball gravity printString.
        ball gravity: (newGravity asNumber).
```

Now, try control-clicking on the kicker and changing the gravity for the falling object.

5.5 TOOLS AND STRATEGIES: USING MORPHS THAT YOU HAVEN'T MET YET

Squeak 2.6 contained 225 ancestors of the class Morph (determined by PrintIt on **Morph allSubclasses size**), and more appear with every new fileIn, new release, and new update. Documentation for each and every morph will fill a book of this size— and would be obsolete almost as soon as the book was published. Therefore, it's important to figure out how to use morphs that you haven't used before.

Here is one useful strategy:

- Just like for any other object, start out by checking out its class comment (if any) and class methods. Example methods help a lot, but even class methods that create useful instances can tell you a lot about using a morph.
- Find someplace where the morph is being used. A good way to do that is to figure out an instance or class method that would almost certainly be necessary for good use of the morph (an accessor method, perhaps), then find all of its Senders.
- Finally, just try it. Send the class **new initialize openInWorld** and see what happens. If you get an error message, it will probably relate to something missing. By tracking back through the errors, you can probably figure out what it expects.

Let's use this strategy on a couple of morphs and see how well it works. We'll figure out how to use the **PolygonMorph**. There is no class method, and there are no example methods. But there are two instance-creation methods. One of them looks like this:

```
vertices: verts color: c borderWidth: bw borderColor: bc
        ^ self basicNew vertices: verts color: c borderWidth: bw borderColor: bc
```

By requesting the senders of this message, we can find examples of objects using **PolygonMorphs** (Figure 5–36) It looks like the vertices are an array (probably

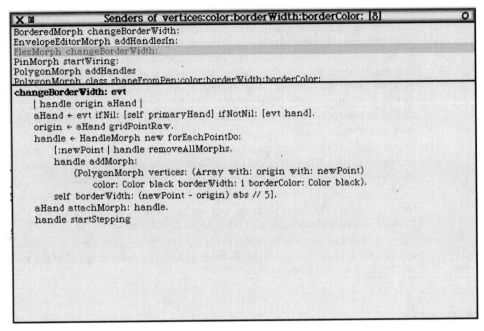

Figure 5–36   Senders of PolygonMorph Instance Creation Message

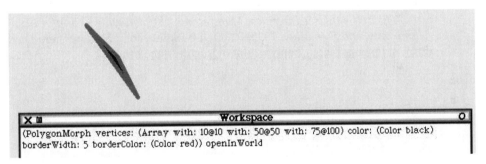

Figure 5–37   Testing Out PolygonMorph

of Points), the colors are just instances of Color, and the border width is an integer. So we can go ahead and try it with some workspace code, just making up values for the parameters. If we get it wrong, we'll get a debugger that will let us play with values. But even the first try creates a real polygon (Figure 5–37).

EXERCISES

14. Without changing any of the code (that is, using only the interface provided for the user), how do you make the falling object in the text version completely stop?

15. Extend the text falling object so that objects have horizontal velocity, too. Add a Cannon button that fires the falling object with a specified horizontal and vertical velocity.

16. In the real world, each object does not have its own gravitational constant. A famous example was created by Randy Smith (who later co-developed Self and Morphic!) called *ARK,* Alternate Reality Kit. In the ARK, all objects had the same gravitational constant, as well as constants that relate to friction with the desktop. All of the constants could be lowered or raised at once. Try implementing a piece of ARK: Create global gravitational constants, with several falling objects that manipulate them. Perhaps you might also allow kickers to manipulate the falling objects that they are touching or are nearest to. (Hint: **World submorphs** lists all the objects in your current world. Their **bounds** gives you their locations.)

17. Create an object that continually updates (via **step**) but responds to user actions. Create an eyeball (a dark ellipse inside a light ellipse) whose position moves the pupil toward the current position of the mouse. (*Hint:* Sensor still works in Morphic.)

18. Try to figure out some of the other useful morphs built into Morphic, such as **Graph-Morph** and **JoystickMorph**. Create a simple tool that will take a minute of positions from the **JoystickMorph** and plot them in the **GraphMorph**.

19. There is already a **SimpleSliderMorph** in Squeak, but it's only vertical and doesn't allow us to easily change the look of the slider (e.g., have the slider wider than the track). Create a more powerful **SliderMorph**.

REFERENCES

John Maloney recommends this paper as a good description of the design philosophy of Morphic.

The Self-4.0 User Interface: Manifesting a System-wide Vision of Concreteness, Uniformity, and Flexibility, 1995, Randall B. Smith, John Maloney, and David Ungar
http://self.sunlabs.com/papers/self4.0UserInterface.html

6

Designing User Interfaces in Squeak

As mentioned in the last chapter, there are basically two challenges to building interfaces for users:

- How do you create user-interface software that you can maintain well, that is, makes it easy to change pieces without impacting everything?
- How do you create user interfaces that people can actually use?

The last chapter addressed the first point. This chapter addresses the second. This chapter is *not* a replacement for a human-computer interface design class. User-interface design is a challenging and complex task, perhaps even more an art than a science. The goal of this chapter is to provide some insights into process and issues. You now know how to build user interfaces. You should give some thought to how to do it well, that is, how to avoid annoying your users. The most important point of this chapter is the heading of the very next section.

6.1 KNOW THY USERS FOR THEY ARE NOT YOU

The most important thing to learn about user-interface design is that the user for whom you are designing is almost always *not* you. The real users may not even be *like* you. This means that, whenever there is a question about what to put in the user interface or what the users want, *you* are not the best authority on the subject. In fact, you may be the *worst*.

Most users are not computer programmers. They don't know anything about how computers work—nor do they want to. You, on the other hand, know a lot about how computers work and you know how to program them. Your expectations and desires are very different from those of most users.

On the other hand, users other than you know lots of things that you don't. Users know their jobs and have the knowledge needed to do their jobs. Let's take a concrete example. You wouldn't presume to know anything about how to do open-heart surgery, and you wouldn't expect a medical doctor to know anything about object-oriented design. So, when a question arises on how best to organize or search for drugs in a prescription database to be used by medical doctors, who's better equipped to answer the question: You, who know databases, or the doctors, who know their jobs? The doctors are the experts on how they want to find drugs and how they expect them to be organized.

At conferences on user-interface design, you can find people wandering around with badges saying "Know thy users for they are not you." This is one of the most important maxims of user-interface designers, and is probably the hardest lesson to learn in the field. You, as a prospective interface designer, know computers, and you've used lots of interfaces. When a question arises about how to do something, you feel like you have lots of experience and knowledge to draw from. And you do—but it's probably wrong for the *users*. Your users are not you.

6.1.1 How Do You Decide Among User Interface Alternatives?

The question of who the user is and what the user may want arises when there is more than one way to do something. When you have alternatives to choose between, the deciding factor is what's best for the users. Ninety percent of the time, the users can tell you exactly what is best for them. Most users are adults who know their jobs and know what they want.

There are some times, however, when the user does not know what she wants. Maybe it's because the user has never used a computer tool for the given task. Maybe because the task, on the computer, will be completely new. In that case, you *will* have to make the choice yourself—but you do it from understanding of the users' *tasks*. What is it that users will have to do?

Again, the user is not you. You cannot know what the users' tasks are until you talk to users, watch them, and get to know them. Your perception of the task can be *very* different from the users' perception.

Consider two interfaces for a clock. The first is the basic ClockMorph built into Squeak (Figure 6–1). The second is the Clock user interface that we built in the previous chapter (Figure 6–2). Which one is better for the user? Which one is better for the user's tasks with a clock? We'll argue before the end of the chapter that Figure 6–2 is very possibly the worst possible user interface for a clock.

6.2 UNDERSTANDING THE USER

The first question you should always ask about a user interface that you are being asked to design is "Who is my user?" Who is it that will be using this tool?

There are lots of ways of modeling a user, including several formal methods on

4:19:40 pm

Figure 6–1   ClockMorph from Squeak

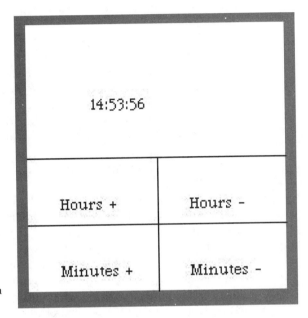

Figure 6–2   Clock User Interface from
Previous Chapter

what to ask the user about. The key issue is to match the users' skills (and later, the task) to the user interface that you are going to design. You want to figure out what the users can and cannot do, then make sure that your interface allows the user to perform the task, within his or her skill set.

Users' skills are pretty hard to pin down, and sometimes you have to ask questions that may not make much sense at first glance. You need to ask users about what they know how to do as it pertains to your program. Let's consider some sample questions.

How old is the typical user? A graduate student at Georgia Tech once developed a program to help first graders learn mathematics where the very first screen was full of text instructions—which first graders were incapable of reading. There's a reason why video games in arcades go into "demo mode" when not being used. Video games don't come with instruction manuals, and not all video game enthusiasts know how to read. A "demo mode" gets around this problem.

On the opposite end of this question are the senior citizens who may no longer be able to read small fonts or manipulate a mouse to click on a small target. As people get older, vision acuity often fades, and hand-eye coordination may become more difficult. There are technologies where this can come into play, such as the small fonts on ATMs or the fuzzy fonts on television-based Web browsers. If your user population is very broad (e.g., a kiosk in the mall that anyone should be able to walk up to and use), you must consider the limitations of each end of your user age range.

What do your users know about? There are some terrific programs for teaching physics that provide the user with all kinds of interesting worlds to explore, for example, worlds where Hooke's law is invalid, or where a different gravitational constant applies. Unfortunately, newcomers to physics classes know neither Hooke's law nor what a gravitational constant is. For these students, the wonderful program is useless because they can't figure out what to do with it.

Terminology on menus, buttons, and help screens is only one area in which the users' past knowledge plays an important role. There are other programs where knowledge of a *process* is critical. For example, there are programs in which data must be prepared in some way before it can be processed. If you don't know the order of operations, you cannot use the program.

A classic example along these lines is a spreadsheet. When you open a spreadsheet application, what should you do? You have a blank sheet of cells sitting in front of you. If the user doesn't have prior knowledge of spreadsheets, how could an interface help the user figure out what to do first?

What does the user want to do? Perhaps this is the most important question to ask a user, not just for the answer, but in the way that the answer is phrased. If a medical doctor says that she wants to "Find all the generics for suphedrine," that tells you that she wants to "find drugs," but also that she's looking in terms of a specific medication that she already knows. If you had created the user interface in terms of "Medications for runny noses," your interface would not only get in the way of the doctor who *already knows* what medication she wants, but it would also be an insult to the doctor who has already matched symptom to drug.

6.2.1 Understanding the Task

Asking what the user wants to do is one part of understanding the user's task. The challenge to understanding the user's task is that not all of it may be explicit in what users say. As people become expert at their tasks, their knowledge of the tasks becomes implicit. People say, "I don't know how I do it—my fingers seem to know." You may have to discover some of the user's task by watching them, or even just looking around where they perform their task. Context of the task can tell you a lot.

Questions the context might be able to answer include "*When* do you perform your task? *What* do you need to do your job?" Some studies of jobs like airport-tower controller have found that users use surprising sources of information. In one study, airport-tower controllers explained their tasks in terms of computer monitors and paper forms, but when observed, interface designers found that the tower controllers kept *looking out the window!* A quick glance out the window told them more about who was on the ground, how busy the terminals were, and where the most open terminals were—far more quickly than hunting through the forms and the monitors. This kind of observation pays dividends when it comes to creating a new interface that actually *does help* the users with their jobs, by providing them with the knowledge that they really need.

Another important attribute of the task that the user may not be able to tell you explicitly is how often they try to achieve various goals. For example, users will often emphasize the time-critical and urgent aspects of their jobs. "When X happens, I have to do Y and Z, immediately!" But they may not tell you that X happens only once a month. It *is* important to support the users in their time-critical and urgent tasks, but it's also important to know that the urgent tasks don't make the everyday, mundane tasks easier.

Imagine a fire alarm that was so sensitive that just running by it would fire off the alarm. That would certainly make calling the fire trucks as easy as possible. However, just walking down that hallway would become tricky, and you'd have to be careful not to go too fast, or to hold down the "not a real alarm" button as you walked by. This would be an awful interface, since it would sacrifice the ease of everyday tasks for the ease of unusual but urgent tasks.

6.3 MATCHING USERS TO INTERFACE: AVOIDING USER ERROR

There are *lots* of ways of constructing an interface. Various interaction styles and widgets were introduced in the last chapter. A brief list includes the following:

- Buttons to click on, radio and checkbox buttons to select
- Text areas
- Various kinds of direct manipulation, from drag-and-drop to resizing windows
- Menu selections
- Dialog boxes with buttons, text areas, and such
- Natural language
- Command languages like UNIX shell

How do you pick among these? Obviously, you use your knowledge of the users and their tasks, but the match between users and interaction styles may not be obvious. It is definitely true that not all matches make sense.

For example, consider command languages as an interaction style. For expert users, command languages are great. Users of Microsoft Windows and Apple MacOS can't hope to do as much with as few keystrokes as a UNIX shell expert. The UNIX shell is just amazing for providing a succinct and programmable interface. But UNIX shell for new or casual (infrequent, logging on once every few days) users is a terrible idea. ("What does *rm* do again?")

On the other hand, expert users get frustrated when forced to use just an iconic and menu-driven interface. They want the speed and flexibility of shortcuts like command languages. Expert users use the system often enough that they won't forget obscure commands. Novice or casual users, on the other hand, need to see things rather than have to remember obscure details.

In general, computers are good at remembering things, but people are not. Command languages are great if users are with them often enough to remember the commands. For everyone else, provide icons, visible menus, and dialogs that make it clear what's to be done and when. User-interface designers talk about "making knowledge visible." Make the state of the program, the options for what to do next, and how to go about those options visible in the interface.

SIDE NOTE

Shortcut keys in laboratory tests, believe it or not, are *always* slower than mouse-driven menu actions! Bruce Tognazzini in his book *Tog on Interface* writes (p. 26): "We discovered, among other things, two pertinent facts: Test subjects consistently report that keyboarding is faster than mousing. The stopwatch consistently proves mousing is faster than keyboarding." While taking your hands off the keyboard does slow you down, using the mouse is cognitively easier than remembering the right shortcut key. There is a real time loss spent remembering the shortcut key, but people are completely unaware of the time loss—they literally have a kind of "amnesia," Toganazzini claims. Note, however, that these tests are being conducted with users in novel applications. After years of use, some keyboard shortcuts may become automatic and not require any mental search.

You should make decisions about interaction mechanisms based on what people expect. For example, if you're building an on-line form that takes the place of an existing paper-based form that people know and have used for years, make the on-line form look like the paper-based form! That way, people will know what's expected and how to use it.

Where there are applicable guidelines for user interfaces on your platform, you should follow them. IBM, Apple, and others have developed notable guidelines for creating user interfaces. The reason to follow the guidelines is not to create a standard, corporate look to the interfaces, but to give people what they expect. If people expect dialog boxes to have the OK and Cancel buttons in certain places, they will be confused if you decide to put them elsewhere. Do what people expect.

In general, your choice of interaction mechanisms should be made to *avoid user error.* You can give command languages to novices, but you can also expect to have lots of user error and frustration. However, if you map that command language to menus and dialog boxes, you'll have less error; however, it may still be frustrating for the user if you basically provide all the same functionality, but in the menu bar. If you figure out the users' tasks, then provide menus that correspond to users' operations in those tasks, and you bring up dialog boxes when necessary with options that relate to the task, then you will probably have even less error and frustration. Design your interface to reduce users' errors.

One way to reduce users' errors is to *avoid modes.* If you've ever used the UNIX *vi* editor, you experience modes all the time. In *vi,* you are either in "insert mode" where typing enters new characters into the file, or you are in "command mode" where typing controls the cursor, deletion, changes, and insertions. (There are actually some additional submodes that we'll skip.) For example, a "k" in command mode moves the cursor up a line, a "d" deletes a character, and a "w" writes the file. Serious *vi* users can tell you what damage typing their name in command mode will do. A mode means that users have to figure out what's valid when, and recall which mode they're currently in. Modes can lead to errors.

There's a general rule for interface designers that says to *put the knowledge in the world.* If there's something that a user needs to know, make it visible somewhere on the screen. If you *have* to have a mode, put a clearly-visible indicator that tells the user the current mode. When there are choices for the user in the interface, use lists or menus to convey the choices, rather than requiring the user to invent them. Making things visible also invites exploration, since all the possibilities are available.

Finally, design *expecting* user errors. That's why *undo* is such an important user-interface advancement. Everyone makes errors. Making recovery from errors a graceful and omnipresent option is an important goal for a good user interface.

6.4 A USER-INTERFACE DESIGN PROCESS

For object-oriented design, we identified a process that made it more likely that we would produce a good (reusable and maintainable) product. For user-interface design, there are again several kinds of processes which make the claim that following the process will lead to a better design. In this section, we present two of these.

The first user-interface design process is the *waterfall method.* The waterfall method sets up a series of steps that, if executed properly, lead to a good design with a single pass through the process. The waterfall method typically has stages that look like this:

- **Requirements specification:** Elicit the user's needs, analyze the task, and define what the user interface must do.
- **Architectural design:** Figure out *how* the user interface provides the necessary functions.
- **Detailed design:** Refine the overall architecture into detailed descriptions that a programmer can code.
- **Coding and unit testing:** Build the user interface and test the low-level components as they are developed.
- **Integration and testing:** Integrate the low-level components and test them.
- **Operation and maintenance:** Actually use the system, and maintain it over time.

The problem with the waterfall method is that it assumes an accurate requirements specification. That may not be possible in all cases, especially for novel technology. User-interface researcher John Carroll of Virginia Tech has pointed out how interfaces and systems impact users' activities and goals. Early requirements-specification based on users' original goals may not be correct any more when they actually start using the system. For many interfaces, this may not be a problem, as in situations when one system is being replaced with a new one. But when technology is new, Carroll's point is critical.

The second user-interface design process that we'll discuss is *iterative design and prototyping.* The idea in this model is to *plan* on repeating the process until a usability goal is reached. There are lots of variations on this approach, some of which take the entire waterfall method as a subset of the process. The general structure can be understood as follows:

- **Requirements gathering:** Do an analysis of the users and their tasks, similar to the first step above. One additional goal is deciding just how usable the system needs to be. Can users perform certain tasks within a certain amount of time? That's a measurable usability goal.
- **Build a prototype:** The process of building a prototype could be all the rest of the steps above.
- **Evaluate the prototype:** Trial the prototype. Actually test it with users and see if the usability goal is met. If you meet the goal, you're done.
- **Iterate:** If the prototype doesn't meet the goal, iterate on it. Maybe you have to go back and fix the goal and requirements. Maybe you have to rebuild the prototype from scratch. Maybe you only have to tweak the prototype. Whatever level you decide to return to, you nave to evaluate the candidate interface before calling it done.

6.5 CRITIQUING OUR CLOCK INTERFACE

Given all of the above, let's consider Figure 6–2 and decide the quality of the interface that we invented in the last chapter for the clock. We are all users of clocks, so it's fair to use ourselves as the users for this interface. What are the tasks for which we use a clock? Your list of tasks will probably look something like this, from the most common to the least common:

- Look at the time.
- Perhaps look at the date.
- For an alarm clock, set the alarm time.
- Set the time (after a power outage or when Daylight Savings starts or stops).

Let's evaluate the clock interface in terms of this list. Can we look at the time? Yes, it's fairly big right on top. But the busiest part of the interface, the part that attracts our eye, is the bottom. Those four buttons, the *most* visible part of the clock with all their margins and labels, are designed to enable us to *set* the time. That is, our interface draws attention to the least common activity for the clock.

If you still have the clock code available, try running the interface again. Try clicking on the buttons. Note that it's difficult to tell when you have clicked on the buttons: They don't highlight, and there isn't any other audible or visible sign that the button has been clicked. This makes it very easy to accidentally click the hour- or minute-change buttons and simply not notice.

These observations suggest that the clock interface in Figure 6–2 is *optimized* for *user error!* The interface draws the user's attention toward the task that is least common, and any use of the interface makes invisible that the least common (and least often desired) activity—changing the time—has even occurred. We could hardly have designed a worse interface for actual use if we tried.

How could we have had a better interface for setting the time, so that it needn't have been so obvious and dangerous? You have probably seen variations of interfaces similar to these suggestions:

- Maybe there's a small button next to the clock with the label "Set". Clicking this button might bring up a dialog box for setting the time. This can work for the computer clock, but if our model were used in a wristwatch, no dialog box would be possible.
- Maybe there are up and down buttons for advancing or retreating the time. Holding them longer than a quick depress might advance or retreat the time more quickly. This works well, and is used in many alarm clocks, but it can take a while to set the time to a particular time (after, say, a power outage, or when setting the time for recording to the VCR).
- Maybe there's no way to set the time—the clock automatically sets the time to some externally accessed source. But then there's the problem of getting the right external source, moving the clock, and fixing it when you're pointing at the wrong external source.

EXERCISES: CONSIDER YOUR INTERFACES

1. Look around at the clocks that you use in your life. Which ones have interfaces that you can use easily? Why do you like them?
2. Consider a user interface that you use frequently, like your e-mail program or your Web browser. Write down a list of your most-common tasks. Now look at the user interface. Is it obvious (visible) how to perform your tasks? What tasks does your interface seem to be optimized for?
3. As a test of our Clock model, design an implementation of two of the interfaces from the earlier list (or some other interfaces that you invent). Do we have to change the Clock, or can we use the same model with multiple interfaces?

6.6 EVALUATION OF USER INTERFACES

Given a set of users' needs, you are probably a creative person who can come up with a list of possible interfaces to meet these needs. Coming up with such a list is a good idea. Expert designs actively consider many possibilities in making design decisions. But how do you decide what to implement? Or if you can implement several of them easily, how do you decide which one to actually use in the final design?

Evaluating a user interface can be done before coding or at least before involving the users with some methods, or after implementation with other methods. Evaluating a user interface means trying to measure or get some general sense of the interface's usability. The goals of an evaluation may differ dramatically between different studies. Sometimes you just want to know if a design *worked*. Other times, you may be trying to gather concrete evidence that one approach is better than another.

6.6.1 Evaluation Before User Involvement

While it sounds strange, there's a lot that can be learned about an interface design even before coding it, simply by considering a careful analysis. A *heuristic evaluation* or *guidelines review* is about carefully analyzing an interface in terms of a standard set of questions or issues. Evaluators review a user interface in terms of a set of standard heuristics (like "Is knowledge visible?") or standard user-interface guidelines (e.g., "Is the Cancel button always in the right place?"). If you really need numbers, you can even score points for each question or issue to arrive at a quantitative result.

Following are some useful heuristics:

- Can the user figure out the current state? Is everything that the user needs to know about visible on the screen?
- Is the language on the screen (in the menus, on the buttons, in labels) the language of the user, not the language of the programmer?
- Is help available?
- Are error messages adequate?

Another useful technique is a *cognitive walkthrough.* There are formal methods of cognitive walkthroughs, but an informal description is to simply imagine being the user and walking through the interface to perform a task. The goal is to figure out if the system *makes sense.*

To perform a cognitive walkthrough, you start out with a description of the system (which may be the system itself, if it's already running in some form), a description of the users' goals, and a careful process description of the how to perform a normal, useful task. The evaluator then walks through the process description, asking herself the following questions:

- Does this make sense for this user? Given what we know about users from their description, will they understand what it is that they are to do next? For example, if we're talking about a desktop-publishing system for ten-year-old students, we can't expect them to understand something about *kerning* unless we've given them lots of help first.
- Will the users be able to figure out what to do next? Again, the issue here is about visual state.
- Will the users be able to understand the feedback that they get? If everything goes well, will the user be able to tell? If something goes wrong, will the user be able to tell what went wrong—and what to do next?

6.6.2 Evaluation With Users

You want to get your interface as correct as you possibly can *before* involving your users. Most users are not computer experts who are used to software crashing. Even if your users are experts, they will be using your software to complete some *task* that they *care* about. They want your software to work. For these reasons, use all the analysis methods that you can before you involve users.

That said, you cannot really know how your software will work with users until you actually involve the users. Remember: "Know they users for they are not you." Users will almost certainly surprise you with the way that they want to use the software, or the issues that you missed in your analyses of the users and their tasks.

What you evaluate when you involve the users depends on two factors—what you want to learn, and how much effort you want to spend:

- If you just want to learn if *someone* can use your software, ask a typical user to come in and use the software while you observe her.
- If you want to show that your software is much better than a competitor's, you will want to involve enough users that you can claim statistical significance (often 25 or more per group) in two different groups—one using your software and one using your competitor's. You will want to ask each user to perform some set of standard tasks, then measure the time for completion and the accuracy.

For the user interfaces that you might create for this book, we want something that tends toward the first example. You should be able to test your designs with users, to find out if your design decisions were the right ones. You want to know if your interfaces *work,* to convince at least yourself. For that goal, a single user may not be enough, but you probably do not need a large study with careful analyses.

The first and perhaps most powerful technique to use in evaluation with users is to simply watch them. However, observation alone may not get you all the information that you want. If you see a user do something that generates an error message over and over again, you don't want to just observe—you want to know *why* the user is doing that.

There are a couple of ways of doing observations that provide more data. One technique is *think-aloud,* where you encourage your user to say out loud what she is thinking as she is working through her task. You expect to hear things like, "Okay, now I want to print the document. Where is print, anyway? Usually, it's in the File menu. There it is." A think-aloud makes clear what it is that the user is doing and *why* she is doing it. The disadvantage of a think-aloud is that it sometimes changes what the user is doing. It's particularly hard for experts to verbalize why they're doing what they're doing.

It's useful to conduct a think-aloud as explicitly occurring for the sake of improving the software, as opposed to being perceived as some test for the user. By involving the user in the evaluation process, the user feels more comfortable, and may be more likely to explore the system and provide useful insights.

You can't always use observational studies. Sometimes you simply have too many users involved, or can't afford the cost of having someone observe users, or you can't get to where the users are. For example, it's hard to use observational studies when the software is for communications that can occur day or night, even from the user's bedroom. You can request that your user use the software when you're observing, but then you're really changing the user's task to fit the evaluation, and your results may not reflect actual use.

A second possible technique is a questionnaire, perhaps followed up by an interview. In a questionnaire, you can ask the users their experiences and opinions about the software. You can get the user to answer exactly the questions that you have about the software.

However, there is no guarantee that you are asking the right questions. You may be dying to know if the users like the new WhizBang ScrollBar you invented, when the reality may be that they can't use the system because they can't figure out how to open that window. You have to phrase your questions carefully so that you get the answers you really want, but stay open to the possibility that the most important information is the piece that you do not expect.

You should have at least a few open-ended questions, to gather the information that you would not have expected. HCI researcher John Stasko advocates two questions: *What would you have me change the next time that I revise the software?* and *What should I make sure that I leave the same the next time I revise the software?* The problem with open-ended questions is that they are more difficult to analyze and summarize than closed ones.

Multiple-choice and scalar questions (e.g., "on a scale of 1 to 5, where 1 is Strongly Agree and 5 is Strongly Disagree . . .") are more useful for analysis. You can use a spreadsheet to compute the average (and even the variance) on each question. The best questionnaires explore an issue with more than one multiple-choice or scalar question. For example, if you want to know whether the user could use the WhizBang ScrollBar, you might want to ask them if they agree or disagree with the statements "I found the WhizBang ScrollBar easy to use" and, later in the questionnaire, "I was able to use the WhizBang ScrollBar to get where I wanted." If the users agree with both of these, you can be fairly confident that you have a useful widget. If the users disagree with both, or agree with only one of the two, you know that the issue isn't so clear cut.

You might want to ask for some volunteers to identify themselves as potential interviewees. In an interview, you can ask the users your favorite questions, but you can also follow up on questions you're concerned about. If the results came back from a survey mixed (e.g., users love the software, but claim that they can't always get what they want done), then it's useful to sit down with some users and find out what the response is so confusing.

If you do not have the time or budget to conduct either an observational or questionnaire, it's still possible to get feedback from the users. Provide an e-mail address, or better yet, a mailing list or newsgroup where users can provide feedback. Users' questions to one another can provie very useful insight about what's confusing about your software.

6.6.3 Evaluating Groupware

Groupware is software meant to be used by groups of people and is a class of software that is particularly hard to evaluate. Consider, for example, using a word processor that allows you to annotate versions of a draft for comments back to the author. Now the author has all these versions and annotations to deal with. Perhaps some of the comments use the annotation mechanism well, and the author can integrate the comments easily. But say that other users just INSERT THEIR COMMENTS IN ALL CAPS. Did the software just fail the author or the annotator? Maybe the software should help the author deal with all-caps annotations? Maybe the software should have made it easier for the annotator to use the supported annotation mechanism? (The answer might be *both*, but that software might get big and complicated.)

What's more, groupware is more complicated because of the design goals associated with it. The goals of usability are still there (e.g., prevent users' errors), but there is often a *social agenda* as well. For example, the annotation mechanism in the word processor is implicitly encouraging authors to collaborate with others who would comment on written work. Other agendas might be to encourage more discussion of issues, or to involve more people in a discussion. These are different goals from just usability goals.

Measuring groupware goals is more complicated, too. How do you measure whether you achieved "more discussion of issues"? Observation would not be effective, especially of any single user. Questionnaires might make sense here. You might ask users if they feel that there is more discussion with use of the software.

Another way of measuring groupware (or any interface) is to modify the interface to *record* what the users do. Typically, this is done without recording any identifying characteristics of the users, in order to protect their privacy. By recording what users do, you can answer questions that you might not otherwise be able to. For example, you can easily address the question of how many people get involved in using a groupware application. You may also be able to identify features that get used frequently—or that don't get used at all. There is a challenge to using interface recordings: You know nothing about the context of use. You don't know if a long pause indicates confusion about the interface, or a distracting phone call. You don't know why someone does something over and over again. Interface recordings are a rich source of information, but are tricky to use properly.

EXERCISES: EVALUATING INTERFACES

4. Again, pick an interface that you use. Develop a questionnaire about the interface and its usability. Ask people you know (at least three) to complete the questionnaire. Any surprises? Note differences among the three—what would account the differences? Differences in individual users, or differences in the tasks, or differences in the *strategies* for using the software?

5. Ask someone you know to let them watch you use a piece of software that you use. Does he use it differently? How? Are there features that he uses that you do not use?

REFERENCES

A recommended book that includes a lot on user-interface evaluations is

Dix, A., Finlay, J., Abowd, G., & Beale, R. (1998). *Human-Computer Interaction.* (Second ed.). London: Prentice-Hall Europe.

Tog's book is

Tognazzini, B. (1992). *Tog on Interface.* Reading, MA: Addison-Wesley.

7

Multimedia
Nuts and Bolts

It should come as no surprise that Squeak, the language for the Dynabook, should be rich in support for multimedia. Squeak already has lots of support for audio and graphics, including standard formats such as AIFF, WAV, MIDI, GIF, JPEG, VRML, MIDI, and several other acronyms. Squeak can speak, with a new plugin for text-to-speech processing. It has a terrific 3-D rendering engine (by Andreas Raab), and a powerful new scripting environment for 3-D (by Jeff Pierce). As befits an environment where the goal is to explore new kinds of media, there are some new formats that are Squeak-specific that are quite exciting.

The format for this chapter will be less tutorial than in past chapters. At this point, you have seen and worked with Squeak code, and are comfortable manipulating Morphic user interfaces. You know how to take an example and figure out how to use it in your own way. This chapter will be an overview of the various multimedia capabilities in Squeak. The presentation will point out the pieces—the "nuts and bolts"—leaving it to you to dig in for the details.

The pattern of presentation will be much the same as in previous chapters: Concrete before abstract. In each media format discussed, existing Morphic tools that support that media are presented first, then some Squeak code that provides access to the underlying functionality is described.

In general, you should be in Morphic for all of this chapter. Relatively few of the multimedia tools work well in MVC, though most of the underlying functionality will work in either. Morphic is the future of Squeak interfaces, so most new development is occurring there.

7.1 TEXT

Most people don't think about text as the very first thing to deal with when they talk about multimedia, but text is still the most important medium for communication on computer displays. Good multimedia often requires good text. Squeak's text support is very good. Besides the normal font and emphases supports, it allows linking between multiple text areas, and it has the ability to embed graphics and flow around them.

7.1.1 Exploring Squeak's Text

You should explore the Play With Me windows, which are collapsed along the side of the image when you first start Squeak. *Play With Me 5* provides an example of Squeak's ability to flow text along curves and through multiple **TextMorph** instances (Figure 7–1). If you resize the **CurveMorph** at the top to be larger (drag out on one of the yellow dots), you'll find that text flows from the bottom rectangle through the "pipe" and into the curve. Make the curve smaller, and the text flows back down.

There are actually four **TextMorph**s in this picture: One in the large **Curve-Morph**, one in the "pipe" **CurveMorph**, a third in the rectangle (an instance of **GradientMorph**), and the fourth embedded in the ellipse inside the rectangle. The first three are *linked,* in that text flows from one to the other to the other, and back again. All four text areas are embedded in their respective shapes, and they are set to *fill owner's shape* (an option in the **TextMorph**'s red-halo menu when the TextMorph is embedded in a shape).

The bottom rectangle's **TextMorph** is also set to *avoid occlusions* (another red-halo menu). When a **TextMorph** is avoiding occlusions, then text flows around a shape laid on top of it. Morphic-select the ellipse and move it around with the brown halo (which moves without pulling out of its embedded state), and you'll see the text flow around the ellipse.

You can make your own linked **TextMorph**s. Create a **TextMorph** (simply drag out "Text for Editing" from the Supplies flap or the Standard Parts Bin), and choose *Add successor* from its red-halo menu. A new, empty **TextMorph** will be attached to your cursor—just drop it somewhere. Now, start typing into your original **TextMorph**. When you stop typing, resize the **TextMorph**, and you'll see the text flow between the two.

You already saw in an earlier chapter that **TextMorph**s can change their style, font, and alignment. There are halo menus on **TextMorph**s for changing each of these. You select the text that you want to modify, then choose the appropriate menu. Changes to emphasis, font, and style always take effect on the currently selected text. There are also command keys for making text changes. Under the *Help* menu, look at *Command-key help.* On a Macintosh, command-1 will turn selected text to 10-point, command-3 will choose 18-point, and command-7 will boldface. (Repeating command-7 will toggle back to plaintext.) On Windows and UNIX, the command key is the Alt key, e.g., Alt-1 will 10-point selected text.

7.1.2 Programming Squeak's Text

As you would expect, all of the text manipulations described above are also accessible through Squeak code. The following example demonstrates several capabilities at once:

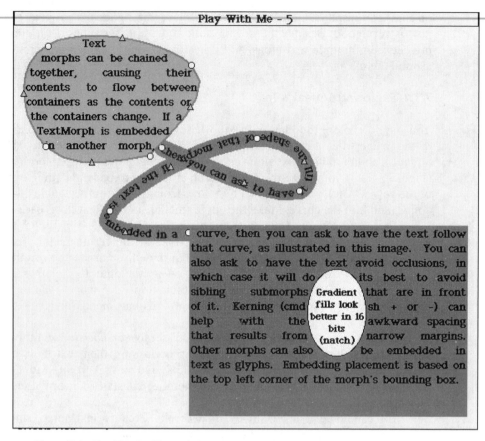

Figure 7–1   Text Flowing Through Curves

- Creating a TextMorph and embedding into an Ellipse,
- Making the TextMorph fill the Ellipse,
- Selecting text and changing its emphasis, and
- Creating a second TextMorph to fill into.

```
texta := TextMorph new openInWorld.
ellipse := EllipseMorph new openInWorld.
ellipse addMorph: texta. "Embed the text in the Ellipse"
texta fillingOnOff. "Make the text fill the Ellipse."
texta contentsWrapped: 'My first textMorph in which I explore different kinds of flowing.'.

"Demonstrating of changing emphases"
texta editor selectFrom: 1 to: 2.
texta editor setEmphasis: #bold.

"Make a second text area"
textb := TextMorph new openInWorld.

texta setSuccessor: textb. "A flows to B"
```

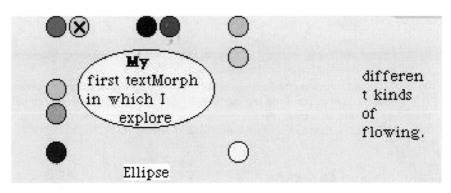

Figure 7–2   TextMorph Filling a Curve and Linking

textb *setPredecessor: texta*. "B flows back to A"
texta *recomposeChain*. "Make the flow work."

As you resize the ellipse containing the first **TextMorph** (**texta** in the example), the linked successor (**textb**) automatically takes in the overflow (Figure 7–2). You can toggle whether or not occlusions are avoided with the message **occlusionsOnOff**. (**fillingOnOff** is also a toggle—the default is to have rectangular shape.)

Notice that the **TextMorph** itself doesn't know how to change text style. The **TextMorph** uses a **ParagraphEditor** to handle those kinds of manipulation. We access the **TextMorph**'s editor with the message **editor** in the example we just saw. You can learn more about how to change alignment, emphasis, and style by looking at the **ParagraphEditor** methods for **changeAlignment**, **changeEmphasis**, and **changeStyle**.

Other kinds of fonts are possible in Squeak. The class **StrikeFont** knows how to read *BitFont* and *Strike2* formats in order to define new **TextStyle** font arrays—see **readFromStrike2:** and **readFromBitFont:** methods. The common TrueType font format is not supported for **TextMorph** instances (as of Squeak 2.7), but can be read and manipulated using the **TTFontReader** and its associated classes (such as the demonstration tool **TTSampleFontMorph**).

SIDE NOTE

Any Morph can generate Postscript for itself, including text areas. If you just ask a Morph to generate its Postscript (control-click menu or red-halo menu), it will generate EPS (Encapsulated Postscript), meant to be placed inside another document. Later, we'll introduce **BookMorphs**, which generate document Postscript. The keys to generating Postscript are the classes **EPSCanvas** and **DSCPostScript** and the method **morphAsPostScript:**, which takes a morph and returns Postscript for it.

EXERCISES WITH TEXT

1. Extend the text-style menus to support single-item selections for combinations of styles, like bold and italics, or bold and strikeout.

2. There are common font formats on the network that are not currently supported well by Squeak, such as TrueType and the MetaFont format. These are well-documented, and there is already a basic reader for TrueType fonts. Create conversion routines so that these can be read and converted into **StrikeFont** instances.

7.2 GRAPHICS AND ANIMATION

7.2.1 Simple Graphics Tools

Graphic images are easy to create or import into Squeak. From the file list, any file whose ending is *.bmp, .gif,* or *.jpeg* or *.jpg* can be directly opened as an ImageMorph (yellow-button menu, *Open image in a window*). You can also use any of these images as a background image.

To create a graphic image, choose *Make New Drawing* from the *New Morph* menu from the World Menu. An onionskin layer (partially transparent) will appear with the painting tools (Figure 7–3). The onionskin allows you to create a modification for something already on the screen, like the onionskin that animators use for drawing the next cel in a cartoon.

The painting tools allow for basic painting with a number of different sizes of brush, as well as filling (paint bucket) and erasing. The gradated colors are actually a pop-up color picker: When you mouse over that area, you are offered a wide variety of colors to choose from. You can also use the dropper tool to select a color already on the display. You can draw basic objects (lines, rectangles, etc.). To use the stamps on the bottom, click on the corresponding box, then select something already on the display. You can now stamp the object you selected. When your drawing is complete, choose *Keep,* and your drawing will be a **SketchMorph** instance.

As we've already seen, graphics are easily rotated and resized, as any morph is. The basic halos allow the rotation and resizing of any morph, **ImageMorph**s and **SketchMorph**s included. What is not immediately obvious is that any morph can also be easily animated to follow a simple path, even without use of the Viewer framework.

Every morph (even a window) has a red-halo menu item to *Draw new path.* After selecting it, the cursor changes into a square with crosshairs, and you can now drag around the screen where you want the morph to go. When a path has been defined, your red-halo menu will change with the option to follow, delete, or draw a new path. Following the path makes the morph move along the path.

7.2.2 Programming Simple Graphics

We have already seen in Chapter 3 that Squeak provides a powerful collection of image-manipulation tools in the class **Form**. **Form**s can be scaled, rotated, chopped into pieces, and manipulated in any number of ways. **Form**s can easily be used in Morphic as well.

Figure 7–3   Paint Box for Creating New Graphics

ImageMorphs and SketchMorphs are basically wrappers for Forms. You can create an ImageMorph, set its image to a form, and then tell it to openInWorld:

```
(ImageMorph new image:
     (Form fromFileNamed: 'myfile.gif')) openInWorld
(SketchMorph new form:
     (Form fromFileNamed: yourfile.gif')) openInWorld
```

Forms can be read from external format files easily. **Form fromFileNamed: 'filename.gif'** will automatically convert GIF, JPEG, BMP, and PCX file formats into a **Form**. **Form**s can also be saved out via **writeBMPfileNamed:**, using the internal format **writeOn:**, and via the **ImageReadWriter** class hierarchy that knows about several external formats (including GIF, JPEG, PCX, and XBM).

To create your own **Form**s, there are **Pen**s for drawing, and classes like **Rectangle**, **Quadrangle**, **Arc**, **Circle**, and **Spline** that know how to draw themselves onto a **Form**. Typically, the display objects and display paths like these have **drawOn:** methods that take a form as an argument. The Color class provides instances that represent various colors, including **Color transparent**.

The simple animation described earlier is built into the **Morph** class. The method **definePath** follows the **Sensor** to fill an ordered collection of points as the **Morph**'s **pathPoints** property. The method **followPath** moves the morph along the points in **pathPoints**.

More sophisticated animations can be created by digging deeper into how graphics are presented in Squeak. Animated displays are really a matter of moving bits around on the screen. The class **BitBlt** (for bit block transfer, pronounced "bit-blit") knows how to do sophisticated translations of bits where the graphics to be laid on the screen are combined in interesting ways with the bits underneath. **BitBlt** has sixteen combination rules that explain how the source and destination bits are mixed. A really compelling example is the class message **alphaBlendDemo**, which you can try with the following workspace code:

```
Display restoreAfter: [BitBlt alphaBlendDemo]
```

This demo displays several blocks of varying transparency, and then lets you "paint" (use the red button to lay-down paint), which is semi-transparent with the underlying display. However, more layers of "paint" are less transparent. This is an example of the sophisticated effects that **BitBlt** allows you to create.

BitBlt was invented by Dan Ingalls when he solved the problem of overlapping windows at Xerox PARC in 1974. The big problem with overlapping windows is saving parts of the underlying window for repainting later, updating as necessary when things move, and doing it all very quickly. **BitBlt** was made for this purpose, but is very general and enables other UI elements (pop-up menus) and animations.

For Squeak, Ingalls extended **BitBlt** for color, and then invented a successor to **BitBlt**, **WarpBlt**. **WarpBlt** takes a quadrilateral as its source pixels (not necessarily a rectangle anymore). The quadrilateral's first point is the pixel that will end up in the top left of the destination rectangle, again, combining it with the same kinds of rules that **BitBlt** had. The results are very fast rotations, reflections, and scaling. For an interesting demonstration of **WarpBlt**, try the class message **test1**:

```
Display restoreAfter: [WarpBlt test1]
```

It's **WarpBlt** that allows Squeak to easily create thumbnails of projects (and **BookMorphs**, as we'll see). It's easy to use WarpBlt to create other kinds of effects. For example, a simple modification of Project's makeThumbnail creates a method in Morph for creating a thumbnail of any Morph:

```
makeThumbnail
    | viewSize thumbnail |
```

"Make a thumbnail image of this image from the Display."

viewSize ← self extent // 8.
thumbnail ← Form extent: viewSize depth: Display depth.
(WarpBlt toForm: thumbnail)
        sourceForm: Display;
        cellSize: 2; "installs a colormap"
        combinationRule: Form over;
        copyQuad: (self bounds) innerCorners
        toRect: (0@0 extent: viewSize).
(ImageMorph new image: thumbnail) openInWorld.

7.2.3 3-D Graphics for End Users

When Andreas Raab joined the Squeak team, he built *Balloon,* a portable 3-D rendering engine. Balloon is accessed almost entirely through **B3DRenderEngine**. It's a very powerful 3-D system that supports different kinds of lights and textures, and pluggable rasterizer, shader, clipper, and transformer. The best quick example of Balloon is to create a new **B3DMorph** and play with it.

Jeff Pierce had an internship at Disney Imagineering, and he developed Wonderland in Squeak. Jeff was part of a team (led by Randy Pausch at Carnegie Mellon University) that developed a Windows-specific 3-D scripting system called *Alice.* Wonderland is essentially Alice, but on top of Andreas' Balloon.

The window *Play With Me – 7* (collapsed when you start the image) is an open Wonderland (Figure 7–4). A Wonderland has (at least) two pieces to it: A **WonderlandCameraMorph** (at left), which shows you the world, and a **WonderlandEditor** (at right), where the end user scripts the world. This Wonderland holds a **bunny**, which is added to the Wonderland by reading in a model. The Editor provides a workspace for scripting, a hierarchical view of all the objects, and buttons for manipulating the space—including an amazing ability to Undo, even to undo actions executed as scripts.

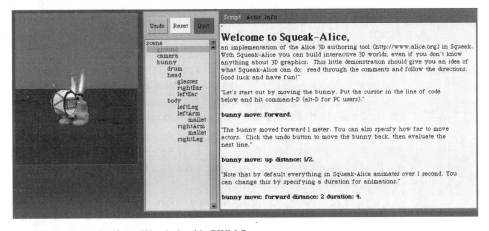

Figure 7–4 An Open Wonderland in PWM-7

To create a new Wonderland, execute **Wonderland new**. In new Wonderlands, the editor window includes a *Quick Reference* tab (like the *Script* and *Actor Info* tabs seen in Figure 7–4), which provides the basic messages that objects understand in Wonderland. There is a standard set of commands that all Wonderland objects understand with respect to motion, rotations, responding to outside actions (like mouse clicks), changing colors, and other categories.

The scripting area in the editor is a modified workspace. Like a workspace, it can have various variables predefined. **w** is predefined to represent the current Wonderland. **camera** is the current camera, and **cameraWindow** is its window. All the objects in the hierarchical list are also defined in the workspace.

Wonderland can load in *.mdl* (Alice internal format) 3-D object files, VRML files (*.vrml*), and 3-D Design Studio (*.3ds*). The Alice project (http://www.alice.org and http://www.cs.cmu.edu/~stage3) has made available a large collection of well-designed 3-D objects (copyright Carnegie-Mellon University). These are available on the CD and at ftp://st.cs.uiuc.edu/pub/Smalltalk/Squeak/alice/Objects.zip. Each of the methods to load one of these file types expects a path name to the appropriate kind of object—the following examples assume Macintosh pathnames (colon as path delimiter):

- To load a *.mdl* object (using one of provided examples, a snowman), **w make-ActorFrom: 'myDisk:Squeak:Objects:Animals:Snowman.mdl'**
- To load a *.vrml* object, **w makeActorFromVRML: 'myDisk:Squeak:VRML:OffWeb.vrml'**.
- To load a *.3ds* object, **w makeActorFrom3DS: 'myDisk:Squeak:3DS:myBox.3ds'**.

Once you have some objects to play with, scripting them is tremendous fun. There are a few really interesting insights into scripting that permeate Wonderland and help one to understand it:

- Your commands to Wonderland objects do not cause immediate jumps to the desired state. Rather, all changes *morph* between the current state and the desired state. **bunny head setColor: green** does not immediately turn from pink to green, but makes a visible transition. Morphing between states allows you to script as a series of desired states, and not worry about creating a good visual representation of the process.
- Method names are chosen so that simple actions are simple, and more selectors allow for greater specificity. **bunny turn: right** turns the bunny a bit to the right. **bunny turn: right turns: 2** does two quick rotations right. **bunny turn: right turns: 2 duration: 4** does two rotations over a space of four seconds.
- Wonderland works hard to make the language as obvious as possible. The scripting world is preloaded with symbols (like **right**), and **WonderlandActor**s get methods defined for them on the fly so that a **bunny** knows its **head** and can be accessed as **bunny head**.
- All scripts actually return an **Animation** object of some kind. The concreteness of having all scripts correspond to objects allows for a powerful Undo opera-

tion—undo can literally undo any animation operation, and, thus, any script. But even more, it allows for scripting sequences and patterns without a method ever being written. **fd←snowman move: forward** is valid, and fd points to an Animation that causes the snowman to go forward. **rt←snowman turn: right** also works, and **w doTogether: {fd . rt}** causes the snowman to walk and turn at the same time.

It's possible to construct objects even without using any external modeling program. Wonderland understands the core creation commands **makeActor** and **makeActorNamed:** The default Objects folder has lots of base shapes like spheres and squares. These can be moved around and then attached to an actor with **newObject becomeChildOf: newActor**. Objects can easily be colored.

Even more powerful, objects can easily have textures wrapped onto them. **snowman middle setTextureFromUser** will let the user select a portion of the display (a **Form**), will convert that to a texture, and will wrap it around the snowman's middle section. The method **setTexture:** will allow for setting the texture to an external file.

Most powerful is to create an active texture. An active texture means that the texture for the object comes from the appearance and size of an external Morph (Figure 7–5). To make an active texture work,

Figure 7–5 A Wonderland CameraWindow and WonderlandActor, with an ActiveTexture

- Open a Wonderland, then morphic-select the camera morph (e.g., click in the "sky" area).
- Use the red-halo menu to set *open to drag and drop*.
- Now, create an object (e.g., **w makePlaneNamed: 'myPlane'**)
- Use the red-halo menu on the object to *enable active texture* and (optionally) *auto adjust to texture*.
- Finally, take the morph (say, **BouncingAtomsMorph**) and drop it into your object.

You can do this all from the Wonderland editor, too:

```
camera getMorph openDragAndDrop "Make the camera open to morphs"
snowman middle hasActiveTexture "Checks - printIt to see if enabled"
snowman middle setProperty: #activeTexture toValue: true "Makes it enabled"
snowman middle setTexturePointer: (RectangleMorph new openInWorld) "Sets the snowman's
    middle to a rectangle"
snowman middle setProperty: #adjustToTexture toValue: true "Makes the snowman adjust the
    size to the morph's size"
snowman middle adjustToTextureIfNecessary "Causes the adjustment to happen"
```

If you do not set **adjustToTexture** to be true, then the 3-D object retains its own shape and just adjusts the texture, perhaps with borders showing. If you do **adjustToTexture**, the shape changes. Figure 7–6 is an example of mixing the adjust-

Figure 7–6   Snowman with the Middle Auto-Adjusting and the Bottom not

ing—the middle of the snowman is adjusting to its rectangle texture, while the bottom is not.

It is quite possible to embed something dynamic in the texture (e.g., the pluggable-text area from the Scamper web browser)—one can have a working browser sitting in 3-D. With an active texture, the 3-D space can use anything from the 2-D space, and complex, dynamic textures are easily applied to Wonderland actors.

7.2.3.1 Programming Wonderland without the script editor

It is possible to use Wonderland as a general world for 3-D graphics. It is less efficient this way—the underlying Balloon 3-D rendering engine is powerful and can be accessed directly, and Wonderland's morphing makes exact control of animation a bit more difficult. But since Wonderland is so wonderfully scriptable, the transition from scripting to lower-level programming is eased by continuing to use Wonderland outside of the script editor.

To create a Wonderland that is under your control without an editor, execute this code:

```
w ← Wonderland new.
w getEditor hide
```

To bring the editor back:

```
w getEditor show
```

All the basic commands to the Wonderland will still work here, as they did in the script editor, e.g., **w makeActorFrom: 'myDisk:Squeak:Objects:Animals:Snowman .mdl'** as long as **w** is set to a Wonderland correctly. Obviously, executing a command like this will not put a variable named snowman in your method, as it does automatically for you in the scripting window. However, the step is very small—simply ask the Wonderland for its namespace. (**w getNameSpace at: 'snowman'**) does actually return the **WonderlandActor** corresponding to the Snowman model, if you've already created it.

Better yet, all the other niceties of the scripting world are still available. Symbols like #right and #left are understood by WonderlandActor methods. Even more amazing, the methods that WonderlandActors understand for accessing the objects in their hierarchy still work. Thus, these messages do what you would expect:

```
(w getNamespace at: 'snowman') turn: #right
(w getNamespace at: 'shark') torso tail turn: #right
```

7.2.4 Flash Movies

Flash is a vector-based animation format that Macromedia supports with its Flash and Shockwave products (http://www.macromedia.com/). Flash animations are small and interactive, and can contain music as well as graphics. They are also well-supported by Squeak.

Flash movies (with file endings *.fla* and *.swf*) can be opened from the file list, using the yellow-button menu. A FlashPlayerMorph will open with the Flash movie embedded. All the interactive components work (e.g., clicking on Next buttons), and sounds will play as expected. Figure 7–7 is an example taken from Macromedia's Flash tutorial.

The red-halo menu on a Flash player provides some interesting capabilities. A control panel is available for stepping through and exploring a Flash movie. A thumbnail view shows an entire Flash movie at once, and through the selection of a subset of the frames, a new Flash movie can be created.

The Flash support in Squeak is very powerful in its integration with the rest of Morphic. Individual Flash characters can be dragged out of the Flash movie and laid on the desktop, to be reprogrammed or reused as desired (Figure 7–8). You can Morphic-select objects in the Flash movie, then use the pickup (black) halo to drag them out onto the desktop.

EXERCISES WITH GRAPHICS AND ANIMATION

1. Create a drawing tool, rather than a painting tool, in Squeak. Let the user draw rectangles, lines, and ellipses, with a palette for choosing colors and line thicknesses and the ability to change layering. Provide an option for allowing the user to create the drawing as individual morphs or as a composite **SketchMorph**.

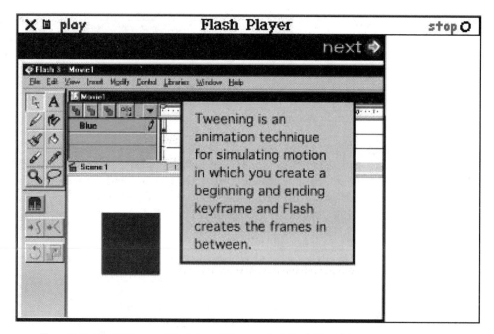

Figure 7–7   Flash Player on Movie from Macromedia's Flash Tutorial

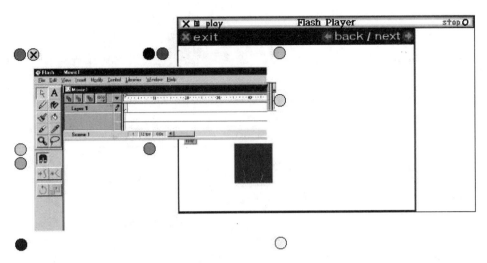

Figure 7–8   Dragging a Flash Character out of a Flash Movie

2. The painting tool currently lays down colored pixels in strips that completely overwrite the underlying background. Some painting tools today (like Dabbler and Painter) provide more complex painting, where laid paint can interact with the underlying paint (as do oils or watercolors in the real world) and can even be laid in smaller elements, as if by the individual threads in a brush. Create modified brushes in the Squeak paint tool to gain some of these effects.

3. Create a movie or play (depending on your definition) using Wonderland.

4. Build a Flash composition tool, perhaps using the built-in path animation tools to create easy Flash movies.

5. Create a video game using Wonderland. Use the reaction methods so that clicking on objects does things, perhaps changes scenes or moves objects.

6. Use Wonderland to create a metaphor for other things in your system. For example, create a 3-D file manager by mapping files in a directory to objects in 3-D that can be opened if they're moved to a certain spot, or deleted if dropped into another spot.

7.3 SOUND

Squeak's sound support is terrific. Excellent sound support helps to achieve the goal of a Dynabook. Squeak can handle sampled sound, can synthesize sound, and can handle higher-level sound formats like MIDI.

7.3.1 Recording, Viewing, and Editing Sound

The basic sound-recording capability is the **RecordingControlsMorph**, which allows the user to record and play back sound, up to available memory (Figure 7–9). (This works only on platforms whose VMs have sound-recording implemented, which are Macintosh, Windows, and Linux as of this writing.) Once a sound is recorded, it can be trimmed (to remove the lack of sound at the beginning of a recording), tiled,

Figure 7–9   Recording Controls Morph

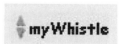

Figure 7–10   Tiled Sound

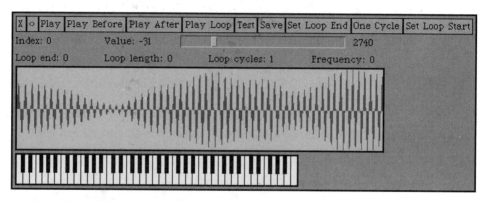

Figure 7–11   Showing a Wave Form

or shown. A tiled sound can be titled, and is then available in the Viewer framework (Figure 7–10).

Showing a sound means opening a **WaveEditor** on it (Figure 7–11). A **Wave-Editor** provides an impressive collection of tools for exploring and modifying the sound—setting a cursor, playing before or after the cursor, trimming before or after a cursor, even generating a Fast Fourier Transform (FFT) of the sound (Figure 7–12). (Roughly, an FFT is a graph of the sound, where the frequencies are on the horizontal axis and the amplitude of each frequency is the vertical axis.) There are additional editing functions available in the menu triggered by the **<>** button that are not available in the obvious buttons.

The sound tile shown in Figure 7–10 references a named sound that is stored in an internal sound library. Other sound tiles also just point to the named sound, which saves on space. However, for some applications (like embedding sound in a **BookMorph**, discussed later in this chapter), you'd like a sound tile that embeds

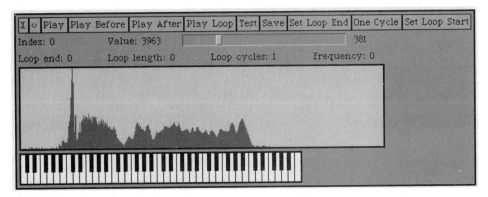

Figure 7–12   Fast Fourier Transform of the Recording

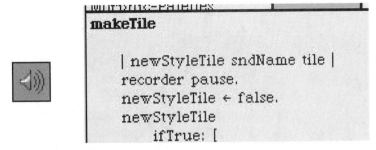

Figure 7–13   Old-style Tiled Sounds, and Where the Code is Changed

the sound in the tile itself. The original sound tile in Squeak did that, and it's possible to get it back by simply setting a boolean value to **false** in the **makeTile** method of **RecordingControlsMorph** (Figure 7–13).

There is one additional morph that is very valuable for exploring sound, and that's the **SpectrumAnalyzerMorph** (Figure 7–14). The SpectrumAnalyzerMorph can display incoming sound in three different ways: as a sonogram, as a continuous waveform, or as a continually updating FFT. You can choose between types in the *Menu* button, and pressing the *Start* button starts recording. The **SpectrumAnalyzerMorph** is an amazing tool for exploring sound—and it makes for a wonderful demonstration when someone claims that Squeak is too slow to do real-time processing!

7.3.2 Sound Classes

The heart of Squeak's sound support is the class **AbstractSound**. As the name implies, **AbstractSound** is an abstract class—it defines functionality for its subclasses, but it's not really useful to instantiate on its own. **AbstractSound** provides the default behaviors of being able to **play** a sound, to **viewSamples** (to open it up in a **Wave-Editor**), to concatenate sounds, and others.

The model of sounds used in **AbstractSound** is that all sounds consist of a set of

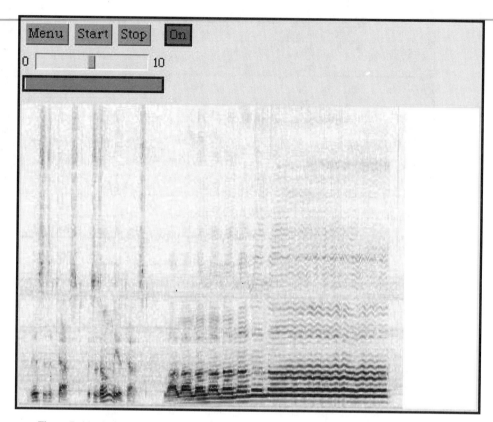

Figure 7–14   SpectrumAnalyzerMorph

samples (which are typically stored in a **SoundBuffer** instance). If you were to graph these samples, you'd get the same kind of waves that you see in the Wave Editor—periodic (at some point, they start repeating), with values alternating between positive and negative. The **samplingRate** is the number that tells you how many samples map to a second. The basic model of sound-as-samples works just as well for sounds that are *synthesized* (i.e., the samples are actually computed) as well as for those that are recorded or *sampled* (i.e., the samples are actually the input numbers from the interface to the microphone on your computer, via the **SoundRecorder**). Sound *envelopes* can be used as filters or functions that shape the samples as they're being generated to create different effects.

The method that generates the samples to be played is **mixSampleCount:into :startingAt:leftVol:rightVol:**. For objects that synthesize sounds (like **FMSound** and **PluckedSound**), this method actually figures out the sound of an instrument like an oboe or a plucked-string instrument and computes the appropriate samples on the fly. For classes that handle recorded sounds (like **SampledSound**), this method provides the right number of samples from the given recording. As you might expect from the name of the method, Squeak's sound support automatically mixes sounds played together and can handle stereo sound with different volumes for the left and right speakers. The actual production of the sound (that is, sending the samples to the sound-generation hardware) is handled by the class **SoundPlayer**.

AbstractSound is one of those classes that gives away many of its secrets when one pokes through its class methods. There are example methods there for playing scales and a Bach fugue. There are also examples of the simple class methods that provide for easily generated music, the most significant of which is **noteSequence-On:from:**. This method takes a sound and a collection of triplets in an array, and has that sound play those triplets. The triplets represent a pitch (name or frequency number), a duration, and a loudness, or **#rest** and a duration.

A collection of synthesized instruments is built into Squeak. They are available through the class message **AbstractSound soundNames**. (**FMSound**, as a subclass of **AbstractSound** that doesn't override **soundNames**, also has access to the same method.) By asking for the **soundNamed:**, you can get the sound object that synthesizes a given instrument, then use it as input to **noteSequenceOn:from:**. Sample code is as follows:

```
(AbstractSound noteSequenceOn:
      (FMSound soundNamed: 'brass1') from:
            #((c4 1.0 500) (d4 1.0 500) (e4 1.0 500)
            (c5 1.0 500) (d5 1.0 500) (e5 1.0 500))) play
"Play c, d, e in the fourth octave, then c, d, e in the fifth. 1.0 duration. 500 volume."
```

You can add to the synthesized instruments in a couple of different ways. One way is to create an instance (e.g., of **FMSound**) that will generate samples that simulate an instrument. That's how the oboe and clarinet instruments are provided in Squeak. Another way is to provide a sample (recording) of an instrument. Most commercial synthesizers use samples to generate instruments. The advantage is high quality, but the disadvantage can be very large memory costs. (A 5Mb or more sample is not uncommon.) To create a sampled instrument, you need to make one or more recordings of different notes on the same instrument, then identify *loop points*—points in the wave that can be repeated for as long as a given note needs to be sustained. The **WaveEditor** can be used for this process, as can many commercial and shareware sound-recording packages.

A second sound library is built into the **SampleSound** class, also available through **soundNames** and **soundNamed:**. These are the sounds that are available as tiles in the Viewer framework. New-style sound tiles store their samples into this library, but the sound tile only stores the name of the sound in the library.

Sounds can be compressed, decompressed, and read and stored from standard compressed-sound formats. AIFF files can be read and written (**fromAIFFfileNamed:** and **storeAIFFOnFileNamed:**) (as seen in the case studies on MAT and Audio Notes), WAV files can be read (**fromWaveFileNamed:**) and easily written, and U-Law files are easily handled (**uLawEncode:** and **uLawDecode:**). The more general compressing-decompressing (*codec*) classes are those inheriting from **SoundCodec**. **SoundCodec** is an abstract class that defines an architecture for codec classes (see **compressSound:** and **decompressSound:**). Squeak comes with codec classes for ADPCM, GSM, MuLaw, and Wavelect codecs. These can be explored with the **CodecDemoMorph**, which accepts dropped (new-style) sound tiles, then compresses them, plays them back, and finally returns them to their original state. Since some of these are "lossy" algorithms (i.e., some sound quality is lost in favor of better compression), this gives you an opportunity to explore the sound-quality tradeoffs of different algorithms.

7.3.3 MIDI Support

MIDI is the Musical Instrument Digital Interface. It is a hardware and software protocol that defines how to get different instruments to communicate with one another, so that different keyboards, MIDI guitars, drumpads, and other instruments can talk to one another and be easily controlled. MIDI files (typically ending in *.midi* or *.mid*) are found in many repositories on the Internet.

Squeak can play and manipulate MIDI files. The easiest way to open up the MIDI **ScorePlayerMorph** is by selecting a MIDI file in the FileList, then playing it as MIDI from the yellow-button menu. The ScorePlayerMorph (left side of Figure 7–15) lets you see all the tracks in the MIDI piece and the textual description of what instrument is in the track. Each track can be muted, be panned from left to right, and have its volume changed.

A Piano Roll representation of the MIDI score can be generated from the **ScorePlayerMorph**. The Piano Roll representation shows each track as a separate color, where each note is a line segment (right of Figure 7–15). The vertical position of the line segment indicates the pitch of the note, and the length indicates the duration. The vertical red line is a cursor indicating the current position in the song.

The Piano Roll notation allows for manipulation of the song and the representation. Red-button clicking in the piano roll opens up a menu that allows you to change the view (e.g., contract or expand time) or to open a keyboard (lower right of Figure 7–15) for inserting new notes into the score. Yellow-button clicking and dragging over the notes allows them to be selected, copied, and pasted.

MIDI scores can be played several different ways in Squeak. The default is to use the internal music-synthesis classes. When using the internal classes, each individual track's instrument can be changed. In Figure 7–15, they're all set to *oboe1*. Clicking on the instrument name opens a menu for changing the instrument or even editing the instrument.

When you edit the instrument, you can change its *envelopes* (Figure 7–16) or even add new envelopes. Envelopes modify the volume, pitch, or other parameters of the sound as it's being generated. For example, in Figure 7–16, the oboe1 sound increases its volume sharply as it's first being generated (note the first vertical bar,

---

HISTORICAL NOTE

The Piano Roll notation in Figure 7–15 dates back to the *Twang* music editing system built by Ted Kaehler for Smalltalk-72.

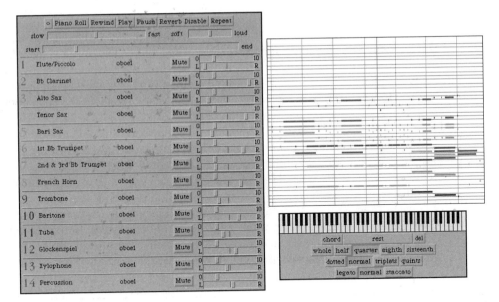

Figure 7–15   MIDI Tools in Squeak

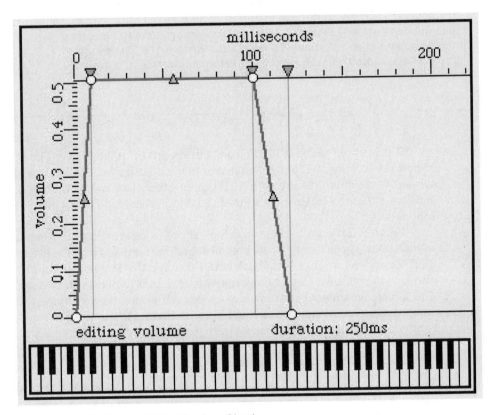

Figure 7–16   EnvelopeEditorMorph on Oboe1

which can be adjusted) called the *attack,* then held for the length of the note (*sustain*), then dropped as the note *decays.* By clicking and dragging the **Envelope-LineMorph** (a subclass of **PolygonMorph**), you can make changes like having the volume drop during the sustain for a warble effect. The editing label is actually a pop-up menu for choosing or adding a different envelope. The keyboard beneath the editor lets you test the sound as you edit it. The control-click menu on the **EnvelopeEditor-Morph** allows you save your new instrument.

The MIDI player also allows you to play the score through an external MIDI device or a platform-specific software MIDI synthesizer. (Access to the platform-specific software MIDI synthesizer is currently only available for Macintosh and Windows systems, though all the code is available to port it to other platforms.) The **<>** button on the **ScorePlayerMorph** pops up a menu for choosing what synthesizer you wish to use. If any software synthesizers are available (e.g., via Apple Quick-Time), they'll appear as an option, and the MIDI player will output through the selected one. If you choose an external MIDI synthesizer, the controls on panning, volume, and instrument selection are ineffective.

CAUTIONARY NOTE

If you tell the **ScorePlayerMorph** to output to an external MIDI synthesizer, *but you don't actually have one,* you can cause your system to hang. The timing access for an external MIDI interface is written at a low level that can't be interrupted from Squeak. If the external interface isn't available, your system will hang waiting for it.

It is possible to input MIDI from a keyboard or other device. The **MidiInput-Morph** will let you input MIDI and map it to a synthesized voice. There isn't built-in support to do anything else with MIDI input other than simply playing it, but the classes are there to create more sophisticated tools that blend MIDI input with other sound tools.

When MIDI plays back through Squeak, it's using the sounds in **AbstractSounds soundNames**. If you create a new kind of sound, you can add it to the list and have it available for use when playing back MIDI through the **ScorePlayerMorph**. You can also load in your own recorded instruments as sounds to play back through Squeak. The **SampledInstrument** class loads in *looped* AIFF files, which can then be used to create a **SampledInstrument**. See the class methods for examples on making new recorded instruments for Squeak's MIDI.

7.3.3.1 MIDI support classes

The classes to support MIDI in Squeak are rich and well designed. A **MIDIFileReader** reads a MIDI file (which must be in binary mode, as opposed to the default character mode). The **MIDIFileReader** can generate a **MIDIScore** with the **asScore** conversion message. A **ScorePlayer** can play a score on the internal MIDI synthesizer, by default. The following workspace code will play a given MIDI file (here with a Macintosh path and filename):

```
f ← FileStream fileNamed:
        'MyHardDisk:midi:candle.mid'."Open the file"
f binary.        "and make it binary."
        "Read it as MIDI and convert it to MIDIScore"
score ← (MIDIFileReader new readMIDIFrom: f) asScore.
f close. "Close the file"
        "Open a ScorePlayer"
scorePlayer ← ScorePlayer onScore: score.
scorePlayer reset.        "Reset it to start playing."
scorePlayer resumePlaying.        "And start it playing."
```

Access to external MIDI devices involves some extra classes. The **SimpleMIDI-Port** class is used as the interface to the external MIDI output devices. The class **MIDISynth** is used to handle input from external MIDI devices. The following variation of the workspace code asks the user for an external MIDI port, then plays the MIDI score through that:

```
f ← FileStream fileNamed:
        'MyHardDisk:midi:candle.mid'. "Open the file"
f binary.        "and make it binary."
        "Read it as MIDI and convert it to MIDIScore"
score ← (MIDIFileReader new readMIDIFrom: f) asScore.
f close. "Close the file"
        "Open a ScorePlayer"
scorePlayer ← ScorePlayer onScore: score.
        "Ask the user where to send the output: External vs. Platform-specific internal"
portNum ← SimpleMIDIPort outputPortNumFromUser.
        "Tell the scorePlayer to use this MIDI port."
scorePlayer openMIDIPort: portNum.
        "Reset it to initialize, then start playing."
scorePlayer reset.
scorePlayer resumePlaying.
```

CAUTIONARY NOTE

While playing around, it's possible to get your external MIDI ports into an odd state, e.g., where some are opened but you've lost an object reference to close them. **SimpleMIDIPort closeAllPorts** is usually effective for putting everything back into a usable state.

EXERCISES ON SOUND

1. Create a new kind of instrument by editing the envelopes of the oboe sound. Can you express what each of the different envelopes does to the sound?
2. Find a piece of music and transcribe it into Squeak. (This is best if you have to play multiple voices at once.) Try different orchestrations (different instruments) for the piece.
3. Use the Sonogram and see if you can figure out the wave-pattern difference between each of the vowel sounds. Is it the same for you as for someone else?
4. Use the Wave Editor and create a **SampledInstrument**. (There are directions on the Squeak Swiki.)
5. Try filling a **SoundBuffer** of your own and playing it. The contents of a **SoundBuffer** are just numbers, and by computing those numbers right, you should be able to play your own tones and even invent new instruments!

7.3.4 Speech in Squeak

The *Klatt* file in your distribution of Squeak is what enables the text-to-speech translation capabilities. Start your exploration from the **Speaker** class and the various class methods there:

Speaker child say: 'Hello. I am a child speaking.'
Speaker creaky say: 'This is my creaky voice with high jitter and shimmer.'
Speaker woman say: 'Do you hear? I am a woman speaking.'

To understand how it is implemented, start at **KlattVoice**. The model of voice implemented here (by Luciano Notarfrancesco) is based on the MITTalk model, which later grew into the popular, commercial DecTalk. The model is quite rich, capable of generating many different kinds of voices and even singing!

Figure 7–17 Gestural voices singing a "Silent Night" duet

Luciano's exploration of text-to-speech includes **GesturalVoices**—voices which have faces that move their lips along with the music. Try **DECTalkReader silentNight-DuetExample4** for an amazing rendition of *Silent Night* with lip-synching animated characters. See Figure 7–17.

7.4 NEW MEDIA IN SQUEAK

Squeak is also being used to invent new media forms unique to Squeak. These media are being invented as stepping-stones toward the Dynabook vision of personal dynamic media. Two of these media, SqueakMovies and BookMorphs, are presented in this section. Both are fairly new and are still in development, but they point toward exciting new areas for inventing media in Squeak.

7.4.1 SqueakMovies

SqueakMovies are not as sophisticated as MPEG or QuickTime movies (though they may be in their final form). But they do allow you to easily capture activity in Squeak. Used in combination with things like Wonderland, they form a fascinating way of exploring animated movies—using Wonderland to script, and SqueakMovies to capture and deliver the final presentation.

To create a movie from Wonderland, first create one with **Wonderland new**, and then load up an actor.

```
w makeActorFrom: 'MyHardDisk:Squeak:Objects:Animals:Snowman.mdl'
```

The code that follows (to be executed in a Wonderland script editor) creates a movie named *snowman.movie,* in which the snowman wanders around in a circle. There was an important problem that had to be solved to make this code work. Wonderland creates intermediate steps in an animation, and schedules them over some period of time to create a pleasing effect. But to capture the Wonderland script to movie, it was important to get the animation to occur immediately, in order to capture the movie. The tricks were (a) to tell Wonderland that the duration was **right-Now** and (b) to get the Morphic **World** to update the Wonderland by forcing it to **doOneCycle**. Here is the code:

```
| frame1 |
out ← FileStream newFileNamed: 'snowman.movie'.
out binary.
"Create a header"
frame1 ← (Form fromDisplay: (cameraWindow bounds)).
out nextInt32Put: 22. "Treat as Magic number for now"
out nextInt32Put: (frame1 extent x).
out nextInt32Put: (frame1 extent y).
out nextInt32Put: (frame1 depth).
out nextInt32Put: 44. "frames"
out nextInt32Put: 100000. "Time in microseconds between frames"
```

```
                    (7 to: 32)          "Padding"
                       do: [:i | out nextInt32Put: i].
```

"Now, do the walking and turning, and create frames.
Each frame is a Form snapped from the Display within the
cameraWindow's bounds. Forms understand writeToMovie:"

```
    1 to: 22 do: [:count |
            snowman move: forward distance: 0.3
                    duration: rightNow.
            World doOneCycle.
            (Form fromDisplay: (cameraWindow bounds))
                    writeOnMovie: out.
            snowman turn: right turns: 0.3
                    duration: rightNow.
            World doOneCycle.
            (Form fromDisplay: (cameraWindow bounds))
                    writeOnMovie: out.
    ].
    out close. "End the movie"
```

To view the movie, find it in a file list and use the yellow-button menu to open
it as a movie (Figure 7–18). (Click on the rightside hollow circle to get all the con-

Figure 7–18 Squeak Movie Player

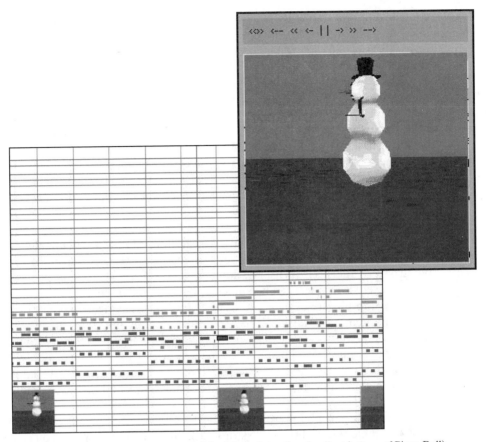

Figure 7–19   Synchronizing MIDI with a Movie (note thumbnails at bottom of Piano Roll)

troller buttons seen in Figure 7–18.) The movie player can be used to add a sound-track to a movie. Choose *Add soundtrack* from the menu button (**<<>>**). A list of WAV and AIFF files in your current directory will pop-up. Pick one, and when you play the movie, the sound will be played at the same time.

You can synchronize a movie with MIDI in an even more interesting manner. The thumbnails that you can generate from a movie frame are actually synchroniza-tion tools. If you open a Piano Roll for drag-and-drop (from its red-halo menu), you can drop the thumbnails at key points in the music. When the MIDI score is played, the movie will make sure that the right frame is showing at the right point in the score (Figure 7–19).

7.4.2 BookMorphs

Apple's HyperCard was a really powerful tool, in that it allowed anyone to easily cre-ate small applications. These applications could contain text, buttons, and links to other kinds of media. In that way, HyperCard took a step closer to a Dynabook.

The basic metaphor of HyperCard was a *stack* of *pages*. Each page could contain different elements, and a basic structure for a set of pages could be defined in a shared *background*. Users could use HyperCard stacks as notebooks or as libraries (storing things on different pages with a common structure in the background), as slide shows (with transitions and sounds between pages), or even as more complex applications by *scripting* (programming in a simple language) the stack.

The HyperCard stack maps to Squeak through the **BookMorph** (Figure 7–20). Like HyperCard stacks, BookMorphs consist of pages—**PasteUpMorph**s. Like HyperCard, basic structures can be stored on the book prototype (any page can be made the prototype by clicking on the solid-circle menu button) and are then available on every new page. Like HyperCard, transitions and sounds can be defined between pages. (BookMorphs also offer a PowerPoint-like page sorter, which is available from the same solid-circle menu button.)

Unlike HyperCard, a **BookMorph** can hold *any* morph, so it can be dynamic and well-structured. Embedded in a **BookMorph**, **ClockMorph**s update, **BouncingAtomMorph**s bounce, and live graphs can change in response to updates in Web-based data or queries from users. Simulations, construction kits, and even whole programming environments can be embedded inside a **BookMorph**.

BookMorphs are designed to be easily saved and loaded from disk or network. The menu item *Send all pages to server* from the circle-button menu will let you save your book. Choose *Use page numbers* when prompted, and then provide a URL for the book. **BookMorph**s know how to deal with ftp:// and file:// URLs for both reading and writing, and with http:// URLs for reading a book. Your book will be saved with a filename ending in *.bo* for the book index and *.sp1, .sp2,* and so on for the pages.

You can open a book from a FileList by using the yellow-button menu with the book index file selected (from disk or FTP). Or, from a workspace, you can execute **BookMorph grabURL: 'file://My Hard Disk/mybook.bo'** with any URL. The **BookMorph** is smart about managing memory and pages. No page is loaded until it is needed, and older pages are purged as they are no longer needed.

A **BookMorph** becomes a powerful mechanism for creating multimedia documents in Squeak and sharing them with others. Ted Kaehler, who worked on HyperCard and built most of the **BookMorph**s, talks about using them to write *active essays*—documents that have text and graphics, but in which some illustrations are active, dynamic explorations of the concepts in the book. In this way, the **BookMorph** becomes an exploration space for Dynabook ideas.

BookMorphs generate Postscript in a document, rather than EPS, format. We can do it from the workspace, too, using code like this:

```
b := BookMorph new openInWorld. "Books generate .ps"
b currentPage addMorph: ellipse. "Put the ellipse in the book"
ellipse topLeft: (b currentPage topLeft). "Position it properly"
f := FileStream fileNamed: 'book.ps'. "Pick file"
f open.
f nextPutAll: (DSCPostscriptCanvas morphAsPostscript: b rotated: true).
f close.
```

Figure 7–20   A Simple BookMorph

7.5 MAKING THE DYNABOOK IN SQUEAK

Despite the rapid pace of this chapter and the many forms of media supported in Squeak, there is much more in Squeak than is discussed here that moves it toward being a Dynabook—and even more that needs to be built and explored yet. Some of the additional features of Squeak 2.7 that we're not discussing, but that are relevant include the following:

- Support for high-resolution tablets, as in the original Flex. (See class methods in **Pen** for these.)
- Digital signatures
- Support for writing recognition (see class **CharRecog**).
- Support for language understanding (see class **WordNet**).
- Support for exceptions in order to create more robust systems (see class **Exception**).
- Support for extending the VM and creating low-level primitives through Squeak. (See the class category *Squeak-Plugins* for information on this.)

Even then, there's much more to be done before a Dynabook is realized, and many questions to be answered. While the basic functionality for a Dynabook is emerging in Squeak, it's not all in a form that any user can use. Reading and writing are skills that most people learn, and pen and paper can be used by just about everyone. A Dynabook should enable people to read and write personal dynamic media, and the creation tools should be as easy (and omnipresent) as pen and paper.

But even once all that functionality is available, there is a question of what's possible and how it will be used. In books, we have standard features like page numbers and tables of contents. What will the equivalent standard practices be in computer-based media? Web pages are slowly developing standards (e.g., the common navigation links across the left-hand side or the top of a page), but the Web is not nearly as dynamic as the Dynabook may become.

It's commonly stated that Thomas Edison invented the motion picture but D.W. Griffith invented films. The distinction highlights the difference between the technology and its use. Edison created the tools with which Griffith created editing and filming techniques that are in common use today in everything we see on television or in the movies. This chapter highlights some of the technologies that can lead to the creation of a Dynabook, but these only suggest the potential available in its use. How a Dynabook is used and what can be done with it are important questions in the consideration of what the impact of personal computers can be.

PART 2
Case Studies

The second part of the book provides some case studies of using Squeak to create multimedia applications. Each case study provides a different kind of example and a different kind of perspective: On object evaluation, on design, on multimedia.

An important goal in these is to provide examples of evaluation, both of design and of user interface. Evaluation is an important part of good design, and an important part of learning—you may not know what you don't understand until you face an evaluation that shows it.

8

Case Study: Audio Notes

Audio Notes is a small Morphic application that saves and plays back audio recordings. The design is not very good (it suffers the common object-oriented design problem of everything in one class), but is interesting to improve. The user evaluation described here is a heuristic evaluation. While the interface seems obvious and good, there are some subtle errors that a careful consideration of heuristics points out—even before a user tries the system.

8.1 MOTIVATION FOR AUDIO NOTES

Jeff was a new Ph.D. student looking for an interesting but small (only three-week) project to do in Squeak for a class that he had. I proposed an application I had wanted: a tool for keeping a diary or journal with audio notes. I had found that writing or even typing a journal was more time than I was willing to spend, but I wished that I'd recorded some of the stories that I used to remember (e.g., of my children when they were toddlers). I wanted a way to record a 30-second story at the end of the day, on my desktop computer. I requested some way to associate keywords with it, and to be able to later search for keywords to recover stories.

For Jeff, this was his first audio project in Squeak, and one of his first object-oriented programs ever. He was able to get a good bit of Morphic and audio working in Squeak, and he successfully met most of the requirements of the project. However, this project was an example of good functionality, but in a weak design that would be difficult to extend, with an interface that could still use work.

8.2 USING AUDIO NOTES

FileIn the code, then do **AudioNotes openAsMorph** to create the application. The application shows the recorded audio notes' names in a scrolling list on the left (Figure 8–1).

To record a new note, press the *record* button, speak your note, then press the *stop* button. Enter the name for the note in the text field in the upper right (above the *record* and *stop* buttons). When you press the *save* button, the note is saved to disk (as an AIFF file), and the name of the note appears in the list on the left.

To hear a note, click on its name in the list on the left, then press *play*.

8.3 DETAILS ON USE

In order to be able to conduct a heuristic evaluation, we need more detail than the simple description just given.

The details of recording are as follows:

- The user presses the *record* button and the button highlights (becomes darker).
- The user speaks the note.
- The user clicks on *stop* and the record button becomes lighter (unhighlights).
- The user types a name into the text field.
- The user clicks *save*. The *save* button highlights during the save, then returns to normal. The note's name appears in the text field on the left.

To play back a recording, the details are as follows:

- The user clicks on the name of the sound in the list on the left.
- The name appears in the textbox on the right.
- Click *play* to hear the note play. The *play* button stays highlighted during the play. If you click on *stop* during the play, *stop* highlights for a moment, but it doesn't actually impact playing—the stop button only impacts recording.
- When playback stops, the *play* button becomes unhighlighted.

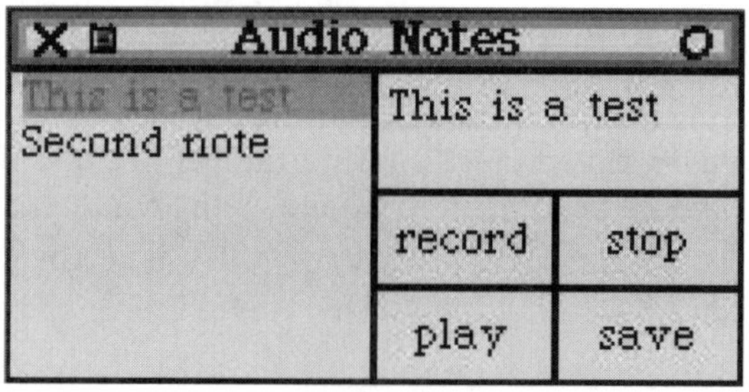

Figure 8–1   Audio Notes

It may not be obvious, but you can also rename sounds in the Audio Notes tool. Click on a name in the list, so that the name appears in the textbox. Now, type a new name and click the *save* button. The new name replaces the old name on the list.

You can also delete notes. Click on the name in the list, then use the yellow-button menu to choose *delete*.

8.4 OBJECT-ORIENTED DESIGN AND PROGRAMMING OF AUDIO NOTES

Since we're looking at Audio Notes after its development, CRC cards are lost to us. However, we can build a class diagram from the code (Figure 8–2).

The very first thing that should occur to you is, "Wow! There's an awful lot in the **AudioNotes** class!" And there is, and it probably shouldn't be like that. As we walk through the code, we'll see that the application was designed to make the initial implementation as easy as possible—all audio, all interface, all names for notes, and so on, are handled from a single class. However, it doesn't make for clear and easy-to-read methods, nor for an easy-to-enhance system.

We'll discuss most of these pieces in context, later.

8.4.1 Building the User Interface

The user interface of Audio Notes was constructed using the pluggable components of Morphic. The most important method to study, then, is the **openAsMorph** method, which assembles all the pluggable components:

```
openAsMorph
"Class method of AudioNotes"
I window instance aColor nameText recordButton stopButton playButton saveButton I
"Instance of Audio Notes"
instance := self new.
```

Consider what's going on here. **openAsMorph** is a class method that creates an instance of itself and then uses it to set up the interface. An alternative design makes an instance of **self**, then delegates **openAsMorph** to it. This way, the same class method **openAsMorph** would continue to work for subclasses of **AudioNotes** that want to override the original interface.

The lines that follow create the **SystemWindow** for the Audio Notes application and then load it with the notes list (**PluggableListMorph**), the name-text area (**PluggableTextMorph**), and each of the buttons (**PluggableButtonMorph**). Note that the position of each of these is set up using **addMorph:frame:** into the window, as opposed to using **AlignmentMorph**s. You might also note that some of the optional behaviors are being turned off here: **autoDeselect** on the list, **askBeforeDiscardingEdits** on the name-text area, the **askBeforeChanging** (highlighting) on the buttons. These enable additional selectors to move between the view and the model, letting the model control more of the view. That's how highlighting can be more tightly con-

Figure 8–2 Class diagram of Audio Notes

trolled to serve as feedback on the record and playback processes, for example. Here is the code:

```
"Display Morph"
window := (SystemWindow labelled: 'Audio Notes') model: instance.
"Notes List"
window addMorph:
    ((PluggableListMorph on: instance list: #notesList
        selected: #notesListIndex
        changeSelected: #notesListIndex:
```

```
                menu: #notesMenu:)
        autoDeselect: false)
        frame: (0@0 corner: 0.5@1.0).
"Name Text"
nameText := PluggableTextMorph on: instance text: #name accept: #nameText:.
nameText askBeforeDiscardingEdits: false.
window addMorph: nameText frame: (0.5@0 corner: 1.0@0.4).
"Buttons"
aColor := Color colorFrom: instance defaultBackgroundColor.
"Record Button"
recordButton := PluggableButtonMorph on: instance getState: #isRecording action: #record.
recordButton label: 'record'; askBeforeChanging: true.
recordButton color: aColor; onColor: aColor darker offColor: aColor.
window addMorph: recordButton frame: (0.5@0.4 corner: 0.75@0.7).
"Stop Button"
stopButton := PluggableButtonMorph on: instance getState: #isStopped action: #stop.
stopButton label: 'stop'; askBeforeChanging: true.
stopButton color: aColor; onColor: aColor darker offColor: aColor.
window addMorph: stopButton frame: (0.75@0.4 corner: 1.0@0.7).
"Play Button"
playButton := PluggableButtonMorph on: instance getState: #isPlaying action: #play.
playButton label: 'play'; askBeforeChanging: true.
playButton color: aColor; onColor: aColor darker offColor: aColor.
window addMorph: playButton frame: (0.5@0.7 corner: 0.75@1.0).
"Save Button"
saveButton := PluggableButtonMorph on: instance getState: #isSaving action: #save.
saveButton label: 'save'; askBeforeChanging: true.
saveButton color: aColor; onColor: aColor darker offColor: aColor.
window addMorph: saveButton frame: (0.75@0.7 corner: 1.0@1.0).
"Add to World"
window openInWorld.
```

Accessors in the Audio Notes application are pretty much as you'd expect. For example, here are the accessors for getting and setting the name (note the call to **changed:** when the name is set):

```
name
        name ifNil: [name := ''].
        ^name
name: aString
        name := aString.
        self changed: #name.
```

There is one accessor that is significantly different and deserves some discussion. Normal **PluggableTextMorph**s don't send the changed text from the view to the model until the model is accepted. Jeff didn't want users to have to type Alt/Cmd-S to set the name of the text, so he provided a dummy accessor, in case the user happened to *Accept* the text:

nameText: aText
>"Empty. Just to satisfy Morphic interface."
>^self

But if the view never sends the input text to the model, how does the model ever get the input text when it's needed? There are several ways to make it happen. One is to retain a pointer to the text area (in an instance variable) and then query it for its **contents**. Jeff was still new to Morphic when he built this, and he figured it out using mostly the Object Explorer and Inspectors. So, he got the text the same way he found it using these tools. (Note that the comment is Jeff's.) He figures out where the view is in the model's **dependents** list (thus breaking one of the rules of MVC, that the model remain blissfully ignorant of its dependent views), then walks the submorphs list until he finds the text morph, and finally asks for its **contents** as a string:

textMorphString
>"I wonder if there's a better way."
>^(((self dependents at: 3) submorphs at: 1) submorphs at: 1) contents string

8.4.2 Handling the Notes List

The storage of notes in Audio Notes is another oddity of implementation. Each of the instance variables **notes** and **names** is just an **OrderedCollection**. The association between a note and its name is the index of the two collections, e.g., the name at **names at: 1** is the note at **notes at: 1**. A structure like that is a clear clue that an *object* should have been created that represents a note and its name.

Notes are stored on disk as numbered AIFF and name (text) files in an *audio* directory under the directory where the Squeak image was read (**FileDirectory default**). AIFF is a sound-file format very similar to WAV files—in fact, they're nearly identical except for some header information. Each note is stored in same-number but different-suffix filenames, e.g., the second note is stored in *2.aiff* and *2.name*. To load the files into the notes structure, the **loadNotes** message is sent to the **Audio-Notes** instance. Note that the "notes" loaded into the **notes OrderedCollection** is simply the name of the AIFF file. The code is as follows:

loadNotes
```
="Load notes from the files"
| dir |
names := OrderedCollection new.
notes := OrderedCollection new.
(FileDirectory default directoryExists: 'audio')
        ifFalse: [FileDirectory default createDirectory: 'audio'].
dir := FileDirectory default directoryNamed: 'audio'.
dir fileNames do: [:fname |
        (fname endsWith: '.name') ifTrue: [
                names add: ((dir fileNamed: fname) contentsOfEntireFile).
                notes add: (fname copyFrom: 1 to: (fname size - 4))]].
```

8.4.3 Implementing the List UI

The notes list expects a series of accessors, none of which is very complicated. The first one sets up an array of note names, since that's what the **PluggableListMorph** wants for its contents:

notesList
```
    | return |
    return := Array new: (names size).
    (names size = 0) ifTrue: [^return].
    1 to: names size do: [:i | return at: i put: (names at: i)].
    ^return
```

If the list is not going to track when things are deselected, the model must keep track of the current list index. Here is the getter and setter for the notes-list index:

notesListIndex
```
        notesIndex ifNil: [notesIndex := 0].
        ^notesIndex
```
notesListIndex: index
```
        (index = notesIndex)
                ifTrue: [notesIndex := 0]
                ifFalse: [notesIndex := index].
        self name: (self notesList at: notesIndex ifAbsent: [""]).
        self changed: #notesListIndex.
```

8.4.4 Setting UI Options

Setting the color of a window and an initial size often confuses newcomers to Morphic. Jeff figured out how to handle these:

defaultBackgroundColor
```
        "In a better design, this would be handled by preferences."
        ^Color r: 1.0 g: 0.7 b: 0.8
```
initialExtent
```
        "Nice and small--that was the idea.
        It shouldn't take up much screen real estate."
        ^200@10
```

8.4.5 Recording and Playing Sound

One of the most intriguing aspects of the Audio Notes application is the recording and playback of sound, which works well cross-platform! For the most part, it's quite easy to do—you simply delegate most of the work to **SoundRecorder** and **AIFFFile-Reader**! The **recorder** gets set up in **initialize**, and the **record** method shows how to make a recording:

```
initialize
        self loadNotes.
        notesIndex := 0.
        recorder := SoundRecorder new.
record
        self isRecording: true.
        (notesIndex = 0) ifFalse: [self notesListIndex: 0].
        sound := nil.
        recorder clearRecordedSound.
        recorder resumeRecording.
```

The **recorder** stores the sound itself until the sound is written to disk. To play the sound, there are two cases: The **recorder** currently is holding the sound, so have it play it; or we have to read it from disk, so we ask **AIFFFileReader** to do it. The **isPlaying:** method is used to set whether or not the play button should be highlighted. Playback from a file is done asynchronously (with a separate process), and the last thing the new process does is set the **isPlaying:** flag to false. The following is the code:

```
play
        self isPlaying: true.
        (notesIndex = 0) "Is nothing currently selected?"
                ifTrue: [recorder pause. "If so, play what's in the recorder"
                        recorder playback.
                        self isPlaying: false]
                "Otherwise, play the sound from the file."
                ifFalse: [sound := (AIFFFileReader new readFromFile:
                ((FileDirectory default pathName),
                        (FileDirectory pathNameDelimiter asString), 'audio',
                                (FileDirectory pathNameDelimiter asString), (notes at: notesIndex), 'aiff'))
                sound.
                        [sound playAndWaitUntilDone.
                        self isPlaying: false] fork]
```

Stopping the recording impacts the **isRecording:** flag. We can look at the getters and setters of that flag, which are similar to the **isPlaying:** and **isSaving:** flags:

```
stop
        recorder pause.
        self isRecording: false
isRecording
        isRecording ifNil: [isRecording := false].
        ^isRecording
isRecording: aBoolean
        (isRecording = aBoolean) ifFalse: [
                isRecording := aBoolean.
                self changed: #isRecording]
```

Saving of sounds shows where the barnacles are in having notes stored as elements in two separate collections. The code that follows is the method for saving sound notes to files. The first part of it gets the sound from the recorder and sets the **isSaving:** flag, which seems reasonable to do here. But the rest of the method involves creating the *.name* file, and the *.aiff* file, and then updating the **notes** and **names** collections. Finally, the recorder is reset and the **isSaving:** flag is set to false. That middle part (manipulating files and sound formats) should probably be simply a message to a hypothetical **AudioNote** object to save itself to a file, making the addition of the note to the file a simple, single **add:**. Here is the code:

```
saveSound
        "Move the sound from the recorder to the files."
        | fname file |
        (recorder recordedSound) ifNotNil: [
                self isSaving: true.
                fname := self getNextName.
                "Create .name file"
                file := (FileDirectory default directoryNamed: 'audio') newFileNamed: (fname, 'name').
                file nextPutAll: (self textMorphString).
                file close.
                "Create .aiff file"
                file := ((FileDirectory default directoryNamed: 'audio') newFileNamed: (fname, 'aiff')) binary.
                self storeAIFFOnFile: file.
                file close.
                "Add to names and notes"
                names add: self textMorphString.
                notes add: fname.
                self changed: #notesList.
                self notesListIndex: (notes size).
                "Clear Recorder"
                recorder := SoundRecorder new.
                "Stop Button"
                self isSaving: false]
```

Deleting sounds is similarly complex, but could similarly have been easily cleaned up with a real **AudioNote** object:

```
deleteSelection
        "Delete the selection in the list"
        | dir |
        (notesIndex > 0) ifTrue: [
                dir := FileDirectory default directoryNamed: 'audio'.
                dir deleteFileNamed: ((notes at: notesIndex), 'name') ifAbsent: [].
                dir deleteFileNamed: ((notes at: notesIndex), 'aiff') ifAbsent: [].
                names removeAt: notesIndex.
                notes removeAt: notesIndex.
                self notesListIndex: 0.
                self changed: #notesList.
                self changed: #name].
```

The actual saving of the sound in AIFF format is handled by the **AudioNotes**

object itself. There *is* code in **AbstractSound** to store AIFF to a file. However, **Abstract-Sound**'s **storeAIFFOnFileNamed:** understands how to write only a single **SoundBuffer** to an AIFF file. For long recordings, the **SoundRecorder** can return a sound composed of multiple buffers. So, Jeff wrote his own AIFF storage routine.
There are two problems with this, though:

- First, the right thing to do would be to fix **AbstractSound**'s AIFF functionality, not add it to **AudioNotes**. The responsibility for writing AIFF files remains with the sound. Adding it to **AudioNotes** simply spreads the AIFF code across yet another class.
- The problem of multiple sound buffers was known and solved. **SoundRecorder** understands **condensedSamples**, which returns a sound with only a single buffer, so the sound could be asked to write itself out to AIFF.

Jeff may not have known about **condensedSamples**—it's not obvious that it's there. This is one of the problems of working in a large system like Squeak: finding all the relevant methods. Nonetheless, here's Jeff's version, which does work:

```
storeAIFFOnFile: file
        "In a better design, this would be handled by SequentialSound, but I figure you will need a new
            primitive anyway, so it can be implemented at that time."
        I sampleCount s I
        sampleCount := 0.
        (recorder recordedSound sounds) do: [:rsound I sampleCount _ sampleCount + (rsound samples
            monoSampleCount)].
        file nextPutAll: 'FORM' asByteArray.
        file nextInt32Put: (2 * sampleCount) + 46.
        file nextPutAll: 'AIFF' asByteArray.
        file nextPutAll: 'COMM' asByteArray.
        file nextInt32Put: 18.
        file nextNumber: 2 put: 1. "channels"
        file nextInt32Put: sampleCount.
        file nextNumber: 2 put: 16. "bits/sample"
        (AbstractSound new) storeExtendedFloat: (recorder samplingRate) on: file.
        file nextPutAll: 'SSND' asByteArray.
        file nextInt32Put: (2 * sampleCount) + 8.
        file nextInt32Put: 0.
        file nextInt32Put: 0.
        (recorder recordedSound sounds) do: [:rsound I
                1 to: (rsound samples monoSampleCount) do: [:i I
                        s := rsound samples at: i.
                        file nextPut: ((s bitShift: -8) bitAnd: 16rFF).
                        file nextPut: (s bitAnd: 16rFF)]].
```

8.5 EVALUATING THE DESIGN AND INTERFACE

As can be seen from the previous section, the Audio Notes design is fairly complex—more so than it really needs to be. What went wrong?

- A big problem is a monolithic class design. Jeff created a "God object" that held all data and took care of all responsibilities itself. A few additional classes (with an obvious one being an **AudioNote**) would dramatically simplify some of these overly-long methods.

- A second problem that is much harder to solve is not enough reuse. There were solutions to some of the things that Jeff implemented as hacks or workarounds (e.g., referencing the string in the text morph, writing the sound out as AIFF). Part of the problem here is lack of experience, and the lesson is this: If you're facing a problem, look around carefully first. Someone else may have faced the problem, and that older solution may already be in the image.

While these problems make the current implementation complex, the real problem of a weak design comes later, when we try to enhance the system. My original request to Jeff included a search function. I did try to add a search function to Jeff's code, and a sorting option, too, so that I could sort by name or even by the date of entry (which is an instance variable I wanted to add to notes). These additions were really hard to add!

- Sorting is very hard, because the notes and names are connected only by index! They must be sorted together to keep the index the same. How much easier it would be to simply toss a bunch of **AudioNotes** into a **SortedCollection** and set the **sortBlock** to **[:a :b | a name < b name]**.

- Adding a date requires a serious change to the structure, because a whole new **OrderedCollection** (**dates**) needs to be added, which must be updated in common with the **notes** and **names** lists to keep everything synched up.

- Searching over names is easy. The tough part is figuring out how to return the result: You want to return a name and note *together* . . . which, again, calls out for an **AudioNote** object.

8.5.1 Heuristic UI Evaluation

While I *was* actually the user for this application, let's not consider my use for evaluating the interface. Rather, let's try a heuristic evaluation of it. We'll use a set of heuristics and apply them to the detailed descriptions of the UI given earlier in this chapter.

Let's consider the interface of Audio Notes from just a single heuristic: *Make knowledge of the world visible.* Can the user always figure out his state in the system by looking at the screen?

Let's walk through the recording process again, as an example. Here's the detailed list of steps again (in italics) with comments next to them:

- *The user presses the record button and the button highlights (becomes darker).* The *record* button's highlight is a sign that the user is currently in a state of "recording." It's not a very visible sign, but it meets the letter of the rule.

- *The user speaks the note.* In some recording software, a timer shows how much time has been spent in the recording, or how much more memory is available. Both of these would provide *more* visible state to the user.

- *The user clicks on stop and the record button becomes lighter (unhighlights).* And now what? How does the user know that a sound has been recorded and is ready to save? How does the user know what to do next?
- *The user types a name into the text field.* How can you tell the difference between a name that has just been entered (thus needing saving yet), and one that has just been clicked on from the notes list (already saved)? You can't.
- *The user clicks save. The save button highlights during the save and then returns to normal. The note's name appears in the text field on the left.* Do you know what happens if you click *save* before you type a text entry? You get a blank-named note. You can actually select it, but you can't see it in the list.

Thus, we can identify several states that are not visible to the user: A note recorded but not named, a note named but not saved, and a note named with nothing. The state of currently-recording is visible, but not with all the state that the user might want.

How about during playback?

- The user clicks on the name of the sound in the list on the left. It's fairly obvious that a list of names is for clicking.
- The name appears in the textbox on the right. And the appearance of the name in the textbox suggests that something got selected.
- Click play to hear the note play. The play button stays highlighted during the play. If you click on stop during the play, stop highlights for a moment, but it doesn't actually impact playing—the stop button only impacts recording. The fact that the stop button doesn't work for playing is odd—it's not obvious that the state of playing can't be manipulated.
- When playback stops, the play button becomes unhighlighted.

Playback works better than recording. Most of the state is visible, though there is less state here to worry about.

There are other weaknesses in the interface design. For example, it was a surprise to me that typing a new name and save would *rename* the note. I was expecting a duplicate note. That violates the heuristic of not surprising the user—if the *save* button saves a new note with the given name, I expect it to always do that, even if the note is already saved. It's also not obvious how to *delete* notes. That's an example of not making all the user's options obvious. But just the single heuristic, applied carefully, successfully highlights weaknesses in the interface design.

None of this means that Audio Notes is a "bad" application. Rather, it's an application with almost all of the desired functionality, but with an internal object design and interface design that could be improved. It's certainly an impressive achievement for a novice Squeaker, and it certainly points out the weaknesses that can be in your first programs.

EXERCISES

1. Add an **AudioNote** object to the tool and make the system work with your new object.
2. Add facilities to search and sort the Audio Notes.
3. Move the *delete* option out to the buttons to make it more visible.
4. Make a running "recording state" interface widget that shows something useful about the incoming recording (size, gain, amount of space left in the image, etc.)

REFERENCES

There are many good references for the kind of "discount usability" approach used in this chapter. Jakob Nielsen's website, http://www.useit.com often has useful tips on this kind of usability testing. A useful book is

RUBIN, JEFFREY. (1994) *Handbook of Usability Testing* John Wiley & Sons.

9

Case Study: Pluggable Web Server and Swiki

Squeak's networking support is quite rich; it includes web browsing and serving, e-mail, and IRC. Squeak's web server, Pluggable Web Server (PWS), was built originally as part of our research at Georgia Tech into computer-supported collaborative learning. One of the PWS applications we have been exploring is *Swiki* (also called *CoWeb* for Collaborative Website).

This case study starts out with a review of the networking support in Squeak, and then presents the PWS and Swiki. The object design of Swiki is presented and critiqued, and then the usability by students is considered. In general, Swiki has good usability in terms of users being able to make use of the functionality. However, it doesn't always fit well with users' tasks, which can lead to less use than one might expect.

9.1 NETWORKING SUPPORT IN SQUEAK

Squeak has been enhanced since the original Smalltalk-80 with good support for networking. Since the advent of the Web, a lot of multimedia work has focused on making things available on the Internet and using material that is out there. Thus, good networking support becomes an important part of a multimedia toolbox. FTP, HTTP, mail protocols (SMTP and POP), and IRC are all supported. User interface tools exist for all of these in Squeak.

9.1.1 User Interfaces for Networking

Scamper is Squeak's web browser (Figure 9–1). You open it from the *Open...* menu and choose *Web browser*. It can handle basic HTML, forms, and images (in GIF,

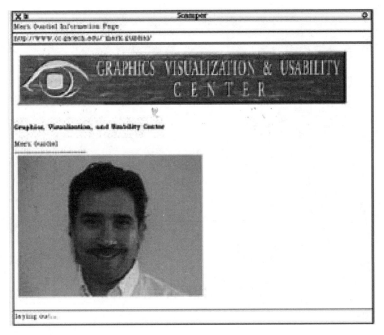

Figure 9–1   Scamper Web Browser

JPEG, and BMP formats). It has no support for Java or JavaScript. As of Squeak 2.7, there is no support for tables nor frames.

The basic FileList is also an FTP client (Figure 9–2). If you click all the way up to the top level of the directory tree, you see not only your mounted disks, but also known FTP servers (preceded by "↑" in the directory-contents pane). You can add servers by choosing *Add server...* from the yellow-button menu in the directory pane (the one containing **[]**).

Celeste is Squeak's e-mail client (Figure 9–3). Celeste speaks POP and SMTP mail protocols. It can filter messages automatically into mailboxes based on subject, sender, or custom queries. It can import or export mailboxes from Eudora or UNIX formats.

9.1.2 Programming Network Access

Squeak's networking support provides low-level and high-level access. At the low level is the basic **Socket** class. **Socket**s are a standard mechanism for creating Internet connections across many platforms. Squeak's sockets can support TCP/IP and UDP access.

Subclasses of **Socket** provide more conceptually high-level access for different protocols. **SimpleClientSocket** provides the basic mechanism for accessing a variety of protocols. **POPSocket** and **SMTPSocket** provide class methods that read and write e-mail.

FTPSocket provides access to FTP servers, though it's typically used through

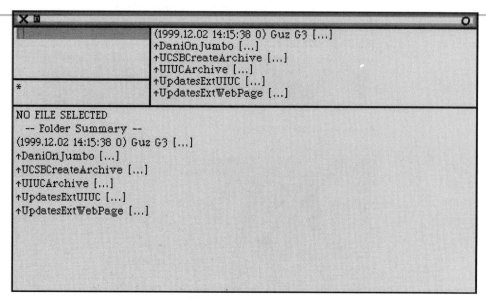

Figure 9–2   FTP Servers in FileList

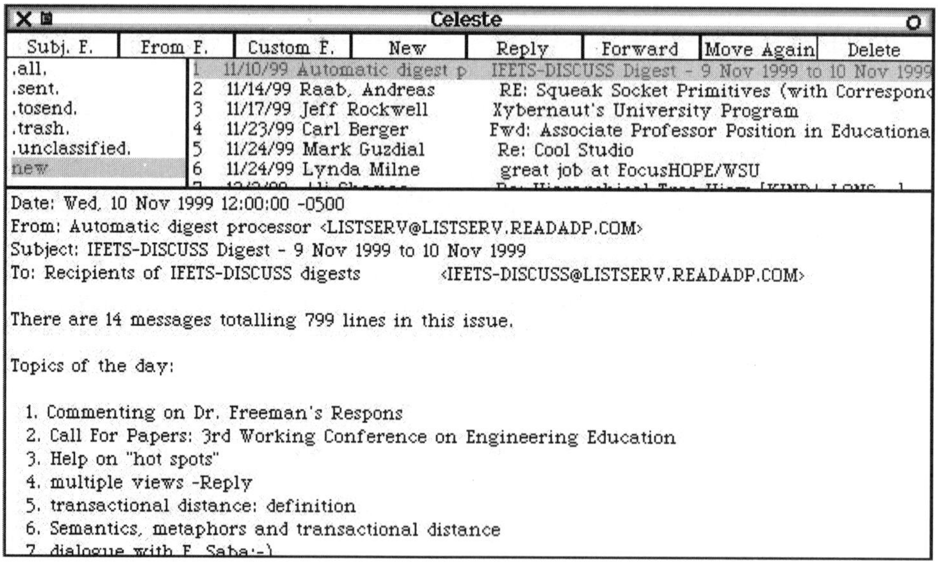

Figure 9–3   Celeste the E-mail Client

ServerDirectory which provides an abstraction for dealing with internal files, FTP, and HTTP access in a similar way. Workspace code that stores and retrieves from an FTP server follows:

```
ftp ← ServerDirectory new.
ftp server: 'cleon.cc.gatech.edu'. "host"
ftp user: 'guzdial'.
ftp password: 'fredflintstone'.
ftp directory: '/net/faculty/guzdial'.
ftp openFTP.
ftp putFile: (FileStream fileNamed: 'myfile') named: 'remotefile'.
ftp getFileNamed: 'remotefile' into: (FileStream fileNamed: 'myfile-downloaded') open.
ftp quit.
```

HTTPSocket provides several class methods for directly accessing material on web servers. The most general access method is with the class method **httpGet:**, which takes a URL as a string. What it returns is a **RWBinaryOrTextStream**, a very general stream that can be interpreted as text or binary (e.g., for images) as you choose. See the class methods **httpShowPage:** to see how to grab the text out of the returned stream, and **httpGif:** and **httpJpeg:** to see how to grab a GIF or JPEG image out of the returned stream.

Scamper has many supporting classes that enable it to interpret the network intelligently. **HTMLParser** has a class method **parse:**, which accepts an HTML document and returns an **HTMLDocument**. **HTMLDocument**, in turn, can answer conceptual entities of itself, such as **head** and **body**. The class **Url** and its subclasses (e.g., **BrowserUrl**) know how to parse themselves and retrieve their contents. The class **MIMEDocument** knows about MIME types, and can store a document and its type. These classes are designed to be reused in new network applications.

CAUTIONARY NOTE

While working with networking, some tools may assume that a network connection already exists. If one hasn't been set up, use of the tool may generate an error. To initialize the network, simply do **Socket initializeNetwork**.

9.1.3 Web Serving with PWS

Squeak also comes complete with a web server, the Pluggable WebServer (PWS). The class **PWS** serves two different roles between its class- and instance-method sides (which isn't a particularly good object-oriented design). On the class-methods side, it implements a web server. On the instance method side, it represents a specific request to the web server. The **PWS** was originally written by the author, based heavily on a Squeak-based web server by Georg Gollman.

PWS can work simply as a basic web server. You must modify the class method **serverDirectory** in the class **ServerAction** so that it returns the path to the directory in which you will serve files. (Be sure that the last character of the path is your platform's path-separator character.) You can then execute the following code:

```
"Make the default server action be serving a file."
PWS link: 'default' to: ServerAction new.
    "Start serving"
PWS serveOnPort: 8080 loggingTo: 'log.txt'.
```

To stop the server, execute **PWS stopServer**.

With the server running, any HTML, GIF, or other files stored in your server directory are available on the Web (assuming that your computer is on the Internet). That is, if you create an HTML file named *myfile.html* and place it in the directory that you specified in **serverDirectory**, any browser in the world can access that file via http://your-machines-address:8080 /myfile.html. For the author, this might be http://guzdial.cc.gatech.edu:8080/myfile.html (You can get your machine's address through PrintIt on **NetNameResolver nameForAddress: (NetNameResolver localHostAddress) timeout: 30**). The *8080* indicates the *port* number of the Web server. Most web servers serve from port 80, but many systems (notably Windows NT and UNIX systems) require the user to be an administrator to create a web server on port 80. Any user can use ports above 1024 on just about any system.

If **PWS** could only serve files, it would be only mildly interesting, but it's more powerful than that. You can also generate information dynamically and serve it via **PWS**, the way that you can with *CGI scripts* on other webservers. There is a collection of examples of PWS interactive web pages, including a couple of different collaboration tools examples (one of which is the Swiki, discussed later this chapter), at http://guzdial.cc.gatech.edu/st/server.tar (also available on the book's CD).

To use these tools, unpack the archive and move all the files into your server directory (e.g., the folder *swiki* should be within your server directory). You can use **PWS initializeAll** to install all the examples.

Several of the examples have to do with supporting different forms of collaboration on the Web. One of the examples is a simple chat page. Go to the address http://your-machines-address:8080/chat.html to conduct a chat in HTML. The page refreshes itself every so often, so other visitors to the same page will see your comments and their own. Another one is a more structured comment space: Try http://your-machines-address:8080/comment.Squeak.

9.1.3.1 Programming the PWS

The purpose for the **PWS** was to provide a simple mechanism for building new kinds of interactive Web applications. **PWS** makes it simple by providing some pieces for making Web applications simple and by supporting embedded Squeak. This section introduces both of these.

You write a **PWS** application by defining an object that responds to the message **process:** with an argument of a **PWS** instance (that is, a request to your webserver).

Let's say that you define a class named **SimpleExampleAction** (with no instance variables, and it can just be a subclass of **Object**) and gave it an instance method like this:

```
process: aRequest
        "Return a code indicating success"
        aRequest reply: PWS success.
        "Now, tell the browser that we're giving it HTML."
        aRequest reply: PWS contentHTML, PWS crlf.
        "Send it the HTML. Note the commas concatenating generated stuff from literal text"
        aRequest reply: '<html>
<head><title>A Simple Example</title></head>
<body>The time is: ',(Time now printString),'
<p>The date is: ',(Date today printString),'
<p>The URL you used to get here was: ',(aRequest message printString),'
</body></html>'
```

This method does the following things:

- Tells the connecting browser that the connection was successful. The request object knows how to reply to the browser, and **PWS success** is the appropriate code. (As opposed to **PWS notFound**, which tells the browser that it has a bad URL.)
- Tells the browser that what's being returned is HTML (**PWS contentHTML**) and returns a final carriage-return-line-feed (**PWS crlf**) to end the header.
- Returns the HTML to the browser. The HTML above happens to generate some elements on the fly, like the time, the date, and the URL used to reach this method (**message**). The PWS request instance also responds to the message **fields**, which returns a dictionary of all the HTML form elements that may have been posted to the URL, already all parsed out into easily accessible elements. This makes creation of interactive Web applications easy.

To install this application as a URL, we have to link it to PWS with a *keyword*. The keyword is the first token (basically, any alphanumeric delimited by punctuation) in the URL after the site name. The keyword is used to match the URL to a given action object, and the corresponding action object is what will be asked to **process:** the input request. **PWS link: 'example' to: (SimpleExampleAction new)** would work for this example, so that http://your-machines-address:8080/example would trigger the earlier method (Figure 9–4). All the PWS linkages are stored in its **actions Dictionary**.

Your "*Bad design!*" flag may have been raised at the admission a few paragraphs back that the **request** object passed into the **process:** method is an instance of **PWS**. Yes, it's true—**PWS** on the class side is an implementation of a web server, and on the instance side, it's an HTTP (Web) request. It's a bad decision, but it wasn't clearly bad at the time of the original design. The original thinking was that one would never have more than one web server in an image, and that PWS was essentially a *request* and the class methods of PWS were *producing* those requests. How-

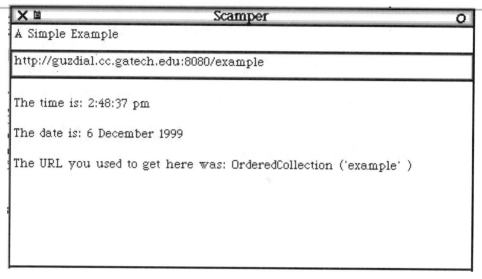

Figure 9–4   Scamper view of SimpleExampleAction

ever, in actual practice, people do sometimes want to have multiple web servers in one image (e.g., one serving risky stuff whose access you wish to be more obscure, and another expected to serve more static content and be more stable), and serving really is a different responsibility from just producing request objects. It's a case of actual practice being different from expectations at the time of original design.

The class that implements basic file serving in PWS is **ServerAction**. It is designed to be easily overriden by subclasses to implement specific serving features. One of these subclasses is **EmbeddedServerAction**. Before returning files referenced through instances of this class, the action first asks **HTMLformatter** to evaluate embedded Squeak in the file. Anything enclosed in the made-up tags <? and ?> is treated as Squeak code and evaluated, and the returned result is included in the returned file. This simple model of embedded language elements in an HTML file appears in many servers with many different languages, and it allows for flexible and easy-to-generate dynamic Web pages.

The **SimpleExampleAction** can be done with embedded Squeak like the following (this example is included in the examples and is available at http://your-machines-address:8080/embedded/Sample.html:

```
<html><title>Sample Embedded Page</title>
<body> <h2>Welcome</h2>
<p>Today is <?Date today printString?>
<p>Now is <?Time now printString?>
</body> </html>
```

Using embedded Squeak and accessing forms input via the **fields** message, it's easy to create a one-file interactive application. The variable **request** can be accessed from within embedded Squeak to get the actual **PWS** instance. The file at http://your-machines-address:8080/embedded/Factorial.html prompts the user for a number and then returns the factorial of that number. Note that **fields** returns **nil** if no form data is available (like when you first visit this page), and returns a string for everything else (which is why **asNumber** is needed before computing the factorial). Specifying the same file as the *action* for the *POST* means that this same file will be served again when the *submit* button is pressed. The code is as follows:

```
<html><title>Factorial Calculator</title>
<body>
<form method="POST" action="factorial.html">
<p><b>Number to compute:</b>
<input type=text name="number"
        value="<?request fields notNil
                ifTrue: [request fields at: 'number' ifAbsent: ['0']]
                ifFalse: ['0']?>"
        size=10 maxlength=10>
<p><input type=submit name="action" value="Compute Factorial"> <hr>
<p><b>Factorial</b>
<p> <?request fields notNil
        ifTrue: [(request fields at: 'number' ifAbsent: ['0'])
                asNumber factorial]
        ifFalse: ['nothing yet']?>
</form> </body> </html>
```

9.2 SWIKI AS A PWS APPLICATION

The most powerful of the example PWS applications is the *Swiki*. Ward Cunningham (who invented CRC cards with Kent Beck) invented a kind of website called the *WikiWikiWeb*. WikiWiki is Hawaiian creole for "quick." The quickest way in the world to create a website is to invite everyone on the Internet to edit and create pages on your website. The original WikiWikiWeb is available at http://c2.com/cgi/wiki?WelcomeVisitors. Swiki is a Squeak interpretation of Ward's idea, thus, a Squeak Wiki or *Swiki*. The Squeak Swiki is at http://minnow.cc.gatech.edu/squeak and the Swiki about Swikis is at http://pbl.cc.gatech.edu/myswiki. The term Swiki is vaguely confusing to our non-technical users, so a graduate student, Ben Hall, started referring to it as a CoWeb (Collaborative Website), and the name stuck among students. So, both names are used for the same thing.

When you visit a Swiki, it looks like a normal website (left of Figure 9–5) containing text, figures, and other Web page elements. The look of the page (e.g., background color, frames or not, etc.) can be different for different Swikis. (Pages are served through templates containing embedded Squeak, like in the Factorial Calculator above, and that's where the look of the page is determined.) But every page contains an *Edit this Page* link. When you click on the Edit link, you get the source of the page in a text area that you can edit (right of Figure 9–5). Any user can thus edit or add to the page, and the view of the page will update after saving. HTML can be used within the page, but simply typing text like in an e-mail (e.g., hitting Return

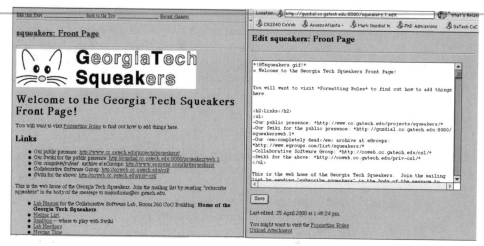

Figure 9–5 A Swiki page (on the left), and what you see when you "Edit this Page" (right)

twice between paragraphs) will create reasonable text. (The text will be formatted into HTML by the Swiki.) By inserting text with the name of a page between asterisks (e.g., "*My New Page*"), a link to the page with that name is created, and if the page didn't exist previously, it will be created.

There are a number of facilities built into the Swiki that help make it useful for hosting collaborative websites. A *Recent Changes* page lists all the pages in the Swiki, by name and date of last change in reverse chronological order, so that the most recently changed pages always appear at the top of the page. A *Search* mechanism is also provided for finding information in the Swiki.

To create a Swiki (assuming that the *server.tar* files are downloaded and installed), you start by creating a folder in your server directory. You should make the folder's name a single word (no spaces) to make it easier to access, like *myswiki*. Now, set up the Swiki with **SwikiAction setUp: 'myswiki'** (replacing *myswiki* with the name of your folder). Just before you start up your server, you execute **SwikiAction new restore: 'myswiki'** (to read in the pages saved on disk into objects in your image). When you start your server, your Swiki will be available at http://your-machines-address:8080/myswiki.1.

9.2.1.1 Uses of the Swiki

We started using the Swiki in classes at Georgia Tech in January 1998. The range of uses that teachers and students have developed for it over the last two years has been amazing. While the basic structure and interface of the Swiki is pretty simple, and even primitive (e.g., no nice drawing tools, no nice WYSIWYG interface), it's been enough to inspire some fascinating new kinds of classroom activities:

- Some students do their collaborative writing in the Swiki. Group members edit the shared group pages, and the *Recent Changes* page lets members know when someone else edited the group pages.

- In other classes, students post their work (e.g., architectural drawings and photographs of models) and external experts visit to review and critique their work.
- Extra credit is sometimes offered to students who write tutorials or post their homework with explanations for future students. When the same Swiki is used in the class again, the next group of students have tutorials and annotated examples to get them started.

9.2.2 Object Design of Swiki

The Swiki has worked well for literally thousands of users, yet it is not particularly well designed. It works, and the design has been good enough to be adapted for many different kinds of Swikis. But it has not had enough flexibility to support all the user tasks that we've been interested in supporting, so a successor system has been implemented in Squeak, the Comanche webserver by Bolot Kerimbaev and Commanche's Swiki by Jochen Rick. However, PWS Swiki is simpler, it's what you have in your hands with Squeak 2.7, and it's a usable product worth taking apart and figuring out—and perhaps reassembling in an entirely new form.

A UML class diagram of the Swiki classes appears in Figure 9–6. The next subsection describes the responsibilities of each class and how it all fits together. In general, a request comes in at **SwikiAction** and flows through **URLmap**, which knows all the individual **SwikiPage**s. The **HTMLformatter** defines how text is translated from what the user enters into what the browser expects (HTML), and that set of formatting rules is uniform for a given Swiki.

9.2.2.1 Responsibilities of Swiki classes

SwikiAction implements **process:**. An instance of **SwikiAction** is what gets entered into the **PWS actions** table. Its job is to figure out what the user wants from the format of the URL—in some sense, it could also be named a **SwikiURLParser**.

Swiki URLs have one of two formats:

- http://yourserver/SwikiName.[PageRef].[edit|versions]. The Swiki name always has to be there to map to a SwikiAction. A URL like http://yourserver/SwikiName.1 would be a request for the first page in the Swiki. A URL like http://yourserver/SwikiName.5.edit would be a request to edit page 5.
- http://yourserver/SwikiName.[searchResult|recent]. A search result or the *Recent Changes* page spans multiple pages, so a specific page isn't mentioned in the URL.

The **SwikiAction process:** method parses out these requests, and sends itself messages like **browse:** page **from:** requestor's machine name or **edit:** page **from:** requestor. That is, the SwikiAction translates from the URL requests into Squeak messages. These messages can be overriden by subclasses. For example, **AuthorizedSwikiAction** overrides these messages by challenging the user for a username and password before serving the pages.

The **SwikiAction** provides the **formatter** (an instance of **HTMLformatter**) for

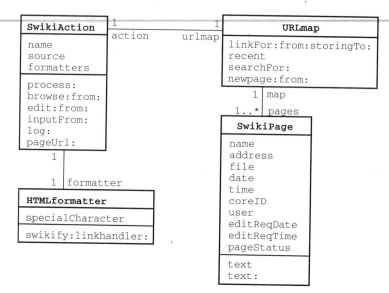

Figure 9–6 Swiki Class Diagram

translating users' text into HTML, but also the **formatters** for serving pages. A Swiki serves a handful of different *kinds* of pages: normal page views, edit views, Recent Changes pages, etc. Each of these pages is served through a *page template,* which is an HTML file containing embedded Squeak. A requested page is passed to the embedded code as a **request** variable. For example, the template for serving a page from the basic server files looks like the following (message-sends like **request name** insert the name of the page into the title, and expressions like **request url,'.edit'** assemble a URL to the edit view for this page):

```
<!DOCTYPE HTML PUBLIC "-//IETF//DTD HTML 3.0//EN">
<HTML>
<HEAD>
<TITLE><?request name?></TITLE>
</HEAD>

<BODY>
<font size=-1>
<a href="<?request url,'.edit'?>">Edit this Page</a> _____
<a href="<?request map action name,'.1'?>">Back to the Top</a>
</font>
<HR><p><p>
<h2><a href="<?request url,'.searchresult'?>"><?request name?></a></h2>
<p>
<HR>
<?request formatted?>
<hr>
<font size=-1>
```

```
<a href="<?request url,'.edit'?>">Edit this Page</a>
  <br><a href="<?request url,'.searchresult'?>">Search for References to this Page</a>.
  <FORM ACTION="<?request map action name,'.'?>searchresult" METHOD=POST>
  Search for text in all pages:
  <INPUT TYPE="text" NAME="searchFor"> <INPUT TYPE="submit" VALUE="Start Search">
  </FORM>
  <a href="<?request url,'.all'?>">Display this Page and all its References</a></font>
  </BODY>
  </HTML>
```

The **SwikiAction** keeps track of its page templates through its **source** instance variable. To give a specific Swiki its own templates (for a unique look and feel), the **source** need only be changed to a directory containing the new templates to be used. The templates are read into the **formatters** instance variable when the Swiki is restored from disk.

The **HTMLformatter** class provides the basic processing of embedded Squeak (for the **formatters**) and also the generation of HTML from user input on the edit view of a page. The message for creating the HTML representation is **swikify:linkhandler:**. The block provided as a link handler is for processing links (*Some page*) found during page formatting. Typically, this is a call to **URLmap**, which knows how to convert names to URLs, but it can be used for other purposes, such as tracing all the links on a given page.

The **URLmap** is the connection between the world of the URL and the world of the Swiki. The **URLmap** provides both matching facilities (e.g., when a named link is found and a URL is needed in order to generate HTML) and facilities that traverse all the pages. URLmap handles searching and generating Recent Changes page. It also handles creation of new pages (as part of its processing of name->URL requests from **HTMLformatter**).

The **SwikiPage** is the basic page. It knows its name, the time and date of its last edit (and also the time and date of the last edit *request,* so it can detect if someone tries to save a page after someone else starts a new edit), the IP address of the last updater, etc. **SwikiPage**s handle saving themselves to disk and retrieving themselves from disk. The **text** and **text:** methods are fairly complicated because **SwikiPage**s actually maintain *all* versions of a page in the file, too, so that any accidental or malicious damage to the file can be recovered from.

9.2.2.2 Critiquing Swiki's object design

The most significant flaw of Swiki's object design is probably the over-emphasis on class methods. The basic PWS webserver is implemented entirely in class methods, and the original **HTMLformatter** was implemented entirely in class methods. In both cases, a basic design assumption suggested that only one instance of each would ever be needed (e.g., only one set of text-to-HTML rules would ever be desired in the **HTMLformatter**), but actual use by real users led to requests for different rules and different web servers in the same image.

A flaw that has limited some exploration of different kinds of Swikis was a bad assignment of responsibilities with respect to **URLmap** and **SwikiPage**. It's the **URLmap** that creates instances of **SwikiPage** and initializes it. The problem is that **URLmap** and **SwikiPage** became tightly coupled. One can't create new kinds of **SwikiPages** without creating new kinds of **URLmaps**, too. Thus **PSwikiPages** that allow for protected pages have to be used with **PURLmaps**. In the current version of PWS, the problem has been worked around by having **URLmaps** send a message to themselves regarding the kind of class to use when creating new pages. In this way, it's possible to tune **URLmaps** to create different kinds of pages, but it's still a workaround.

9.2.2.3 Evaluating Swiki's usability

Swiki has been used by scores of classes in two years. Evaluation of its usability has been based mostly on questionnaires, with some interviews to follow up. For example, on a recent survey across three classes (in biology, chemical engineering, and computer science), 93 students rated the Swiki's usability (Table 1). The responses suggest that students found the CoWeb quite easy to use to read, edit, and create pages, and that the students used it often.

Even though it's *usable*, the actual *usefulness* of the Swiki in some classes has been in question. For example, during one term, a 150-person architecture class started using the Swiki at the same time as a 30-person chemical engineering class. Ten weeks into the term, the architecture class had created over 1500 pages, while the chemical engineering students had yet to create a single page!

Several hypotheses explain why the engineering students were not using the Swiki much:

- Part of the problem may be perceived benefit. You don't download every piece of software that might run on your computer—you only use software that you think might be useful to you. If students do not see the usefulness of the Swiki (in terms of grades or learning), they have little motivation to use it.
- It could be a problem of medium. Engineering classes often involve discussion of equations or graphs. Neither is easy to create or use on Web pages. If the medium (the Web) makes natural communication (e.g., equations and graphs) too complicated, then natural communication will not take place.
- Finally, the most common response we've heard in interviews with students is, "Oh, it's *editable?*" If the students' *tasks* don't require them to create or edit Swiki pages, then students will simply ignore the *Edit this Page* link—in much the same way that most of us ignore some features of our word processors and spreadsheet programs if we simply don't need those features. The challenge to teachers is to invent activities that are *useful* (for grades and learning) and that encourage collaboration in the Swiki.

It's interesting how the different issues of object design and interface design interact in the case study of the Swiki. The Swiki was designed to be modifiable into new forms of Swiki, but the object design only achieved that goal to a limited extent. The basic usability of the Swiki is quite good, but the usefulness differs in different classes based on the kinds of activities in those classes. Thus, there's a real need for different kinds of Swikis to meet the needs of different kinds of users in different

Table 1   Swiki Usability Questionnaire Results

Question	Average Response across all classes (standard deviation)
How long did it take you to learn to read pages in the CoWeb? 1 = Immediately obvious 3 = 5 Minutes 5 = A Day of Use	1.58 (1.06)
How long did it take you to learn to edit pages in the CoWeb? 1 = Immediately obvious 3 = 5 Minutes 5 = A Day of Use	1.93 (1.08)
How long did it take you to learn to create pages in the CoWeb? 1 = Immediately obvious 3 = 5 Minutes 5 = A Day of Use	2.18 (1.25)
How often did you check your class CoWeb? 1 = Several times a day, 2 = Daily, 3 = Weekly, 4 = Every couple of weeks, 5 = Never	2.6 (1.0)

kinds of classes. Having code *work* is simply not enough to meet the needs of users over time. Maintainability and reusability are actually quite related to usability.

EXERCISES

1. Modify Scamper so that each visit to a page generates a thumbnail of the page *so that* clicking on the thumbnail opens the same Web page. This creates a new kind of web history.

2. Use the networking primitives to create MIDI-at-a-distance. Input MIDI from a keyboard, send it across the network to a client, and play the sound on the client's computer.

3. Use the Web access methods in **HTTPSocket** and the **TextMorph**s seen earlier to create a personal newspaper. Generate a well-formatted newspaper of your users' favorite websites, with multiple columns and images.

4. Create a kind of Swiki that allows you to enter in musical notes in some kind of simple notation (e.g., "c#q de ee" might mean C-sharp quarter note, D for an eighth, E for an eighth), and return an AIFF file of those notes being played when the page is served as HTML.

REFERENCES

The Swiki on Swikis is at http://pbl.cc.gatech.edu/myswiki.

Comanche Swiki is available at http://seaweed.cc.gatech.edu/docs/.

We are continuing to explore how users use the Swiki. A couple of recent papers on this research are:

Abowd, G., Pimentel, M. d. G., Kerimbaev, B., Ishiguro, Y., & Guzdial, M. (1999). Anchoring discussions in lecture: An approach to collaboratively extending classroom digital media, *Proceedings of Computer Supported Collaborative Learning'99* (pp. 11–19). Stanford, CA. http://kn.cilt.org/cscl99/A01/A01.HTM.

GUZDIAL, M., REALFF, M., LUDOVICE, P., MORLEY, T., KERCE, C., LYONS, E., & SUKEL, K. (1999). Using a CSCL-driven shift in agency to undertake educational reform, *Proceedings of Computer-Supported Collaborative Learning'99* (pp. 211–217). Palo Alto, CA. http://kn.cilt .org/cscl99/A25/A25.HTM.

CRAIG, D., UL-HAQ, S., KHAN, S., ZIMRING, C., KEHOE, C., RICK, J., & GUZDIAL, M. (2000,). *Using an unstructured collaboration tool to support peer interaction in large college classes.* Paper presented at the International Conference of the Learning Sciences 2000, Ann Arbor, MI. http://www.umich.edu/~icls/proceedings/abstracts/ab178.html.

10

Case Study: MAT (Multimedia Authoring Tool)

MAT (Multimedia Authoring Tool) was a project by Aibek Musaev to develop a WYSIWYG (What You See Is What You Get) editor for HTML. MAT is an interesting project because of its simplicity, power, and reuse:

- There are only two classes in MAT, and less than 10 methods.
- Yet it can handle things like audio clips that most HTML editors don't.
- The reason that MAT is both so small and so powerful is because it leverages off existing code. It's mostly an example of reuse.

That isn't to say that MAT's design couldn't be improved. MAT makes changes only to one existing class in the base Squeak image. The design for MAT might be better if it touched *several* base classes.

We tested MAT as a text-annotation tool for a graphical collaboration tool called *MuSwiki* by Lex Spoon. We used a questionnaire to get students' opinions on the usability of MAT. The results are mixed. In part, the task didn't leave much opportunity to try out all the power of MAT, but some of the concerns about MAT's usability are due to the negatives of reuse. When MAT just builds on all the power already in Morphic, all the weaknesses of Morphic also become MAT's weaknesses.

10.1 MOTIVATION FOR AND USE OF MAT

The Web is a fairly powerful multimedia platform, with evidence offered of all the websites providing graphics, recorded sound, MIDI, Flash, streaming video and audio, and more. But it's fairly complicated to build multimedia components for the Web. Director and Flash are fairly hard to use, and while tools like FrontPage are easy to learn, they can't do much. Aibek and I discussed this problem as one he'd attack for an undergraduate research project by creating a FrontPage-like editor, by leveraging Morphic. He decided that he'd support text, graphics, and recorded sound, too, with a goal of creating a structure that could be easily extended for additional media later. Aibek tackled this project with only a little prior Squeak experience, so his success and ability to learn a great many classes in Squeak is impressive.

MAT is simply a subclass of **PluggableTextMorph**. This means that Aibek's code can be used literally anywhere you'd use a normal pluggable-text component. The ability to generate an HTML representation comes for free. The reverse implication is that all the Squeak facilities for manipulating text styles, sizes, and colors are inherited by MAT.

To open **MAT** as a standalone editor, you do **MAT new openInWorld**. From there, you can type in text and use the various command keys to change text style, size, and colors. Graphics can be created using the *New Morph...* and then *make new drawing* menus, and then inserted into the MAT by simply dragging and dropping the graphic onto the **MAT** instance. **MAT** accepts a **SketchMorph** and displays it wherever the cursor last was. You can use a similar method to combine different text areas into **MAT** — it accepts other **TextMorph**s and inserts them at the cursor point.

Sounds are only slightly more complicated. You can record a sound using the **RecordingControlsMorph**. You create a **SoundTile** for it by clicking on the *Tile* button (Figure 10–1). When a sound is tiled, it's stored by name in a library stored in a class variable of **SampledSound**. The **SoundTile** object is actually a tool for walking through all the different sounds in the library by using up and down arrows on the tile. Aibek needed to have a single sound be inserted into **MAT**, but he didn't want to invent a new single-sound **SoundTile**. So, **SoundTile**s can be dropped into **MAT**, and they'll "appear" at the cursor point like text or graphics, but as a text notation (Figure 10–2).

To generate HTML, you use the red-halo menu to *Save as HTML*. Figure 10–3 shows an example **MAT** instance with colored, resized, and mixed-style text, a graphic, and a sound. When the user chooses *Save as HTML,* she is prompted for the name of the HTML file to save to, and then the name of the GIF and AIFF files to generate for each **SketchMorph** and sound notation in the editor.

The MAT in Figure 10–3 generates a GIF file (*mat2.gif*), an AIFF file (*sound2.aif*), and the following HTML code:

```
<!DOCTYPE HTML PUBLIC "-//W3C//DTD HTML 3.2//EN">
<HTML>
<HEAD>
<TITLE>Page created in MAT</TITLE>
<BODY>
<PRE><I><FONT SIZE="7"><FONT COLOR="#FF0000">This</I></FONT></FONT><FONT
    SIZE="3"> </FONT><FONT SIZE="7">is</FONT><FONT SIZE="3"> </FONT><FONT
    SIZE="3"><B>a</FONT></B><FONT SIZE="3"> </FONT><FONT SIZE="5">test</FONT><FONT
    SIZE="3">

</FONT><FONT SIZE="3"><IMG SRC="mat2.gif"> </FONT><FONT SIZE="3">

<A HREF="sound2.aif">sound2.aif</A></FONT></PRE></BODY>
</HTML>
```

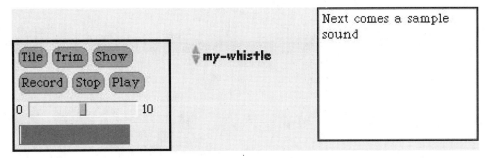

Figure 10-1   Preparing a sound for dropping into MAT

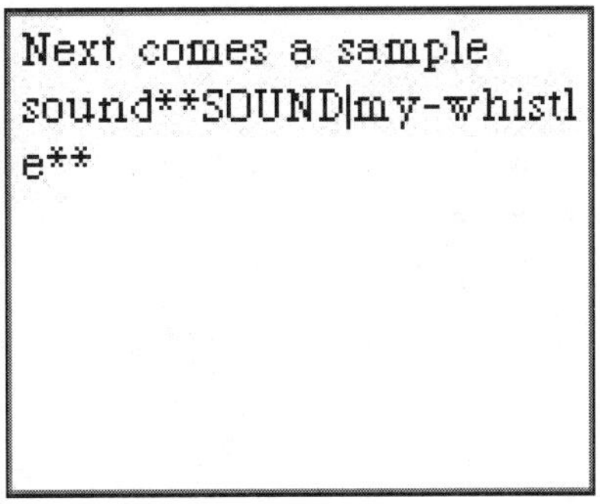

Figure 10-2   MAT after accepting the "my-whistle" sound

Figure 10-3   An example of MAT in Squeak

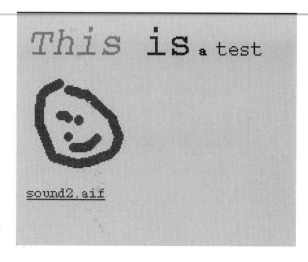

Figure 10-4 The MAT-generated file opened in Netscape

When this file is opened in Netscape, the result looks surprisingly like the original MAT representation in Squeak (Figure 10-4).

10.2 OBJECT DESIGN AND PROGRAMMING IN MAT

As mentioned, **MAT**'s object design is quite simple. The class diagram appears in Figure 10-5. In reality, Aibek only designed and implemented *one* class, **MAT**. **ParagraphEditor** is already part of the system. Implementing the whole toolkit didn't involve even a single new instance variable!

Basically, the class **MAT** provides the user interface to the user, leaving the actual computation involved in text editing to **ParagraphEditor**. It supports drag-and-drop of morphs, and it modifies the red-halo menu to insert the *Save as HTML* option in Squeak. But even the **saveAsHTML** method (as we'll see) simply delegates to the **ParagraphEditor**. It's the **ParagraphEditor** that actually provides all the functionality for saving as HTML.

Then why not simply provide all of the behavior in a single class, **MAT**? Why involve the **ParagraphEditor** at all? It has to do with how responsibilities are handled in the existing text-support classes in Squeak. **MAT** is implemented as a subclass of **PluggableTextMorph**, as mentioned earlier. **PluggableTextMorph** is actually a subclass of **ScrollPane**. What the **PluggableTextMorph**'s hierarchy is really about is how the text is *presented,* not how it's *edited.* **PluggableTextMorph** contains a **textMorph** explicitly for editing (a **TextMorphForEditView**) which in turn has an **editor** (an instance of **ParagraphEditor**). Most of **PluggableTextMorph**'s menu items for supporting text editing simply delegate to its **ParagraphEditor**. For example, the method for **cut** simply passes the request to the **editor** through a special **handleEdit:** method, which passes on the request and then updates the view to deal with any changes (e.g., in what is currently selected):

cut
```
self handleEdit: [textMorph editor cut]
```

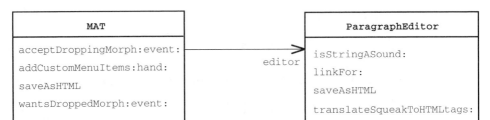

Figure 10–5 MAT's classes

Aibek may have wanted to contain all of the code in **MAT**, but because he was trying to reuse as much as possible, he tried to follow the patterns already in use in Morphic. **MAT** could be the user's interface, but actual text manipulation belonged in **ParagraphEditor**, because that's where that kind of responsibility lay in the existing system. It made sense for him to create **MAT** and change **ParagraphEditor**.

The second possibility to consider is to *subclass* **ParagraphEditor** (e.g., **MAT-ParagraphEditor**) instead of modifying the existing **ParagraphEditor**. That's a more complex decision. One reason for *not* subclassing is that, in the end, Aibek only *added* functionality to **ParagraphEditor**. That's a fairly safe thing to do to an existing class, so he was unlikely to break anything by making those changes.

The more significant reason for not subclassing **ParagraphEditor** is the complexity of *doing* it! **PluggableTextMorph** does not directly reference **ParagraphEditor**, so it's not easy to simply add a method in MAT to override the method in **Pluggable-TextMorph** so that the new **MATParagraphEditor** might be installed in **MAT**. Tracing back to where **ParagraphEditor** gets referenced directly and how it ends up appearing in a **PluggableTextMorph** is fairly complicated. The text-editing classes in Squeak are designed such that each class just has a single responsibility—as they should be designed. But since a text editor involves many kinds of responsibilities (e.g., scrolling, text-editing operations, display of text, management of styles and fonts), there are lots of classes involved. We could create **MAT** versions of every class between **PluggableTextMorph** and **ParagraphEditor**, but that seems like overkill when we're only talking about adding a mere handful of methods to **ParagraphEditor**. Aibek's decision *not* to subclass **ParagraphEditor** seems like the right one.

There is another critique of **MAT**'s design that is probably more correct: It doesn't change *enough* classes. As we'll see, **MAT**'s implementation frequently asks an object what kind of object it is and then takes action on the basis of the response. Whenever you see a query to an object about whether it's a **kindOf** some class, you should think "But couldn't you just ask the object for whatever you want, and let *it* take the responsibility for handling the query?" **MAT** actually interacts with a lot of different classes: **SoundTile**, **TextMorph**, **SketchMorph**, and several **TextAttribute** sub-classes, as well as **HTMLformatter**. Many of the tests (and thus, the overall size of the methods in **MAT**) could be reduced by providing methods in each of these classes for some **MAT**-specific queries.

10.2.1 Implementing MAT

The implementation of MAT (as mentioned) is quite small. An argument can be made that it should be a bit bigger, and perhaps involve some more classes in order to reduce the complexity of some classes. But overall, it's an easy-to-understand implementation.

Recall that **MAT** is a subclass of **PluggableTextMorph**. It adds no instance variables to its superclass' definition. Since **MAT** is the easier class to understand, we'll present **MAT** first, and then describe the classes added to **PlugglableTextMorph** to enable writing to HTML (and other formats).

10.2.1.1 Drag-and-drop into MAT

Dragging and dropping into **MAT** is actually amazingly simple. It involves (a) telling Morphic when it *wants* a drop event and (b) actually accepting the dropped Morphic. To *want* a drop event is to return **true** when the object being dropped is of the type that the target (**MAT**) wants. That's pretty simple, because **MAT** accepts text, sound, or image morphs:

```
wantsDroppedMorph: aMorph event: evt
    " allow only SketchMorph, SoundTile, and TextMorph to be dropped "

    ^ (aMorph isKindOf: SketchMorph) |
    (aMorph isKindOf: SoundTile) |
    (aMorph isKindOf: TextMorph)
```

Once the target reports that it wants the drop, it has to *accept* it. It's during the acceptance that the target has to do whatever it wants with the dropped morph. In **MAT**'s case, there are three different kinds of media to deal with, and three different procedures. It's actually implemented as one big method, with **ifTrue:** tests to figure out which procedure to follow. It's definitely not the cleanest implementation, but it's still fairly simple to understand.

In every case, the morph that is dropped gets deleted, to encourage the illusion that the morph has been dropped *into* **MAT**. Also, in every case, the object is inserted by asking the **ParagraphEditor** (**editor**) to replace the current selection with the appropriate representation of the dropped morph (using **zapSelectionWith:**). The creation of that representation differs for each object. A better design might have been to send a message like **asMATobject** to the dropped morph, then insert the response into the text—a design that would have necessitated changing several morphs (**SketchMorph**, **TextMorph**, **SoundTile**, and probably a default representation in **Morph**):

- If the dropped morph is an image (a **SketchMorph**), the **Form** of the image is retrieved. Text in Squeak can have an associated attribute, a **TextAttribute**. A subclass of **TextAttribute**, **TextAnchor**, is a particular kind of attribute designed for placing images in text. An image is inserted into the text by creating and inserting something (even just a single character) whose attribute is the **TextAnchor** bound to the desired **Form** instance.

- If the dropped morph is a sound (a **SoundTile**), a string is created that represents the sound (by name) and that gets inserted into the editor.
- If the dropped morph is another text, the text is retrieved (by sending the morph **contents**) and then inserted into the editor.

```
acceptDroppingMorph: aMorph event: evt
I contents form soundName txt attrib I
(aMorph isKindOf: SketchMorph) ifTrue: [
        form ← aMorph form copy. "Get the morph's form and make a copy"
        aMorph delete. "Get rid of the dropped morph"
        attrib ← TextAnchor new anchoredMorph: form. "Make a text 'attribute' out of the Form"
        txt ← ' ' asText. "Just some blank space"
        txt addAttribute: attrib from: 2 to: 2. "Make the Form the attribute of the blank space"
        self handleEdit: [textMorph editor zapSelectionWith: txt]. "Ask the editor to insert it" ].
(aMorph isKindOf: SoundTile) ifTrue: [
        " generate corresponding link "
        soundName ← aMorph literal copy. "Make a copy of the sound NAME"
        aMorph delete. "Dump the dropped Morph"
        self handleEdit: [textMorph editor zapSelectionWith: '**SOUNDI',soundName,'**']. "Insert" ].
(aMorph isKindOf: TextMorph) ifTrue: [
        contents ← aMorph contents copy. "Make a copy of the text"
        aMorph delete. "Dump the dropped Morph"
        self handleEdit: [textMorph editor zapSelectionWith: contents]. "Insert the text" ].
```

10.2.1.2 Handling the menu in MAT

MAT adds a single menu item to its red-halo menu—a *save as HTML* item. Adding it to the menu is simple:

```
addCustomMenuItems: aCustomMenu hand: aHandMorph
        super addCustomMenuItems: aCustomMenu hand: aHandMorph.
        aCustomMenu addLine.
        aCustomMenu add: 'save as HTML' action: #saveAsHTML.
```

The method **saveAsHTML** simply delegates the actual processing to the **ParagraphEditor**:

```
saveAsHTML
        self handleEdit: [textMorph editor saveAsHTML]
```

10.2.1.3 Generating HTML in the ParagraphEditor

The **saveAsHTML** method in **ParagraphEditor** looks pretty forbidding because of its length, but it's not all that complicated. It asks the user for a filename for storing the HTML and then opens up the file for text. The method **translateSqueakToHTMLtags:** actually does the processing of images, size, style, and color. The rest of the method figures out where the sound links are by carefully looking for the special character (it's '*' but is set up so that it could be something different) and then strips out the words between the double asterisks. The **linkFor:** message converts the specially tagged string into whatever it needs to be—in this case, an AIFF sound, but Aibek designed it to be flexible enough to support other kinds of media, too. The code for **saveAsHTML** is as follows:

```
saveAsHTML
I sourceStream targetStream aLine start end specialCharacter text htmlFileName file link I

" ask the user for a name to create a new file "
htmlFileName ← FillInTheBlank request: 'Save as HTML' initialAnswer: 'mat.htm'.
htmlFileName isEmpty ifTrue: [^nil].
file ← FileStream newFileNamed: htmlFileName.
file text. "it'll be text, not binary"

specialCharacter ← $*. "Special character for Sound (and possibly future) tags"
" translate Squeak-rendered text to HTML tags "
text ← self text.
text ← self translateSqueakToHTMLtags: text. "Handle size, style, and color"

sourceStream ← ReadStream on: text.
targetStream ← WriteStream on: ".
[sourceStream atEnd] whileFalse: [
aLine ← sourceStream upTo: (Character cr).
 " Now, look for links "
 start ← 1.
 [(start ← aLine indexOfSubCollection: (specialCharacter asString)
   startingAt: start ifAbsent: [0]) ~= 0
  and: [start < aLine size]] "If there's a specialCharacter there..."
 whileTrue: ["extract **LINK** combination"
 (aLine at: start+1) = specialCharacter
 ifFalse: [start ( start + 1]
 ifTrue: [
  (end ← aLine indexOfSubCollection: (specialCharacter asString)
   startingAt: (start+2) ifAbsent: [0]) ~= 0
 ifFalse: [start ← start + 2 "Eat up the second specialCharacter"]
 ifTrue: [
  (aLine at: end+1) = specialCharacter
  ifFalse: [start ( end+1]
  ifTrue: [
   "Grab the link string from aLine, convert via linkFor:"
   link ← self linkFor: (aLine copyFrom: start+2 to: end-1).
   "Now insert the link into the output line"
   link isNil ifFalse: [
   aLine ← aLine copyReplaceFrom: start to: end+1 with: link asString.
   ].
   start ← end + 2.
  ].
 ].
 ].
]. " whileTrue: "
targetStream nextPutAll: aLine. "Put aLine into the output HTML file"
targetStream cr.
```

]. " whileFalse: "

" put HTML data into file "
file nextPutAll: targetStream contents.
file close.

We'll look into how the images and other text attributes are converted to HTML in just a moment, but let's first finish up the processing of the sound. The **linkFor:** message is what does the actual conversion of the **SampledSound** into AIFF *and* returning of the appropriate HTML for that AIFF file. **linkFor:** is written to be able to handle more diverse media than just sounds—note that the first thing it does is check if this is a sound string. Other kinds of MAT-tagged strings could be easily added.

Recall that a tiled sound is stored into a **SampledSound** library under a name that is what appears inside the asterisk-tag in **MAT**. The linkFor: method grabs the entry from the library, pulls out the actual **samples** (the digital representation of the sound) and **samplingRate** (the number of times per second that the recorded sound was tested to create the digital representation), and converts the sound to AIFF. The AIFF conversion could have been simpler, it seems, since **AbstractSound** is already a superclass of **SampledSound**. In the end, the HTML tag for referencing the new AIFF file is returned (for insertion into the target HTML file by **saveAsHTML**). Following is the **linkFor:** code:

linkFor: aString
| fileName returnStr soundName entry samples samplingRate f |

```
(soundName _ self isStringASound: aString) ifNotNil: [
 "SOUND link is encountered"
 fileName ← FillInTheBlank request: 'Save as AIFF' initialAnswer: soundName,'.aif'.
 fileName isEmpty ifTrue: [^nil].
 " retrieve samples and sampling rate info "
 entry ← SampledSound soundLibrary
  at: soundName asString
  ifAbsent:
  [self inform: soundName asString, ' not found in the Sound Library'.
   ^ nil].
 "Convert the SampledSound representation into AIFF"
 entry ifNil: [^ nil].
 samples ← entry at: 1. "Get the actual samples"
 samples class isBytes ifTrue: [samples ← SampledSound convert8bitSignedTo16Bit: samples]. "Is this needed?"
 samplingRate ← (entry at: 2) asInteger. "Get the sample rate"
 f ← (FileStream fileNamed: fileName) binary.
 AbstractSound new storeAIFFSamples: samples samplingRate: samplingRate on: f.
 f close.
 returnStr ← '<A HREF="',fileName,'">',fileName,'</A>'.
 ^returnStr.
 ].

 " don't know what to do, return nil "
 ^nil.
```

At the beginning of **linkFor:** is the test to see whether the tag pulled out of **MAT** is a string. That's a fairly simple method:

```
isStringASound: aString
    "check the string to see if it is a SOUND link"
    "basic error checking"
    (aString isNil) ifTrue: [^nil].
    "if sound, extract sound"
    (aString beginsWith: 'SOUND!')
    ifTrue: [^(aString copyFrom: 7 to: aString size)]
    ifFalse: [^nil].
```

The most complex method of the bunch is **translateSqueakToHTMLtags:**, and it's really doing something quite interesting. Aibek tried to handle the general case of text attributes in Squeak and convert them to HTML tags. He handles several subclasses of **TextAttribute**, including **TextEmphasis** (e.g., italics), **TextURL** (a URL attached to text), **TextColor**, and **TextFontChange** (for size).

Text instances in Squeak use an instance of **RunArray** to track the *runs* (a starting index in the text and a length) of a given set of attributes. A **RunArray** is a "space-efficient storage of data which tends to be constant over long runs of the possible indices. Essentially repeated values are stored singly and then associated with a *run* length that denotes the number of consecutive occurrences of the value" (quoted from the **RunArray** class comment). The value associated with a run is a collection of attributes. Multiple attributes can be associated with a run of text at once.

translateSqueakToHTMLtags: also uses **HTMLformatter** (see the PWS chapter). Besides handling Swiki processing and embedded-Squeak processing, **HTMLformatter** contains several class methods for generating different kinds of HTML. **translateSqueakToHTMLtags:** uses **HTMLformatter** for creating the HTML associated with the start and end of an HTML document.

The basic structure of the method for **translateSqueakToHTMLtags:** is to walk through all of the runs in the text and figure out what kind they are. If it's a style, color, or size change, it outputs the start tag in HTML. If it's an image or URL, it outputs the corresponding tag (and, in the case of an image, generates the GIF of the **Form** as well). Then it outputs the string inside the run. Then it checks the run array again, figuring out what kind of thing it just saw and sending out the appropriate end tag to the target file. The code is as follows:

```
translateSqueakToHTMLtags: aText
" translate Squeak-rendered text to HTML tags.
TextAttribute's considered: TextEmphasis, TextURL, TextColor, TextFontChange "
| runArray runs value values readStream targetStream rgbColor fontSize fileName |
readStream ← ReadStream on: (aText string). "For reading the actual text"
targetStream ← WriteStream on: ''. "For writing the actual text"

"Store a default page header and default title into the target"
targetStream nextPutAll: (HTMLformatter startPage: 'Page created in MAT').
targetStream nextPutAll: '<PRE>'. "All text should be considered pre-formatted"
```

"The 'runs' are where the text attributes apply"
runArray ← aText runs. "Returns a RunArray"
runs ← runArray runs.
values ← runArray values. "Gets the attributes"
1 to: (runs size) do: [:index |
value ← values at: index. "Get the attributes associated with this run"
value do: [:attr |
 (attr isKindOf: TextEmphasis) ifTrue: [
  (attr = TextEmphasis bold) ifTrue: [targetStream nextPutAll: '<B>'].
  (attr = TextEmphasis italic) ifTrue: [targetStream nextPutAll: '<I>'].
  (attr = TextEmphasis underlined) ifTrue: [targetStream nextPutAll: '<U>'].
 ].
 (attr isKindOf: TextColor) ifTrue: [
  rgbColor ← MAT generateHTMLRGBfromColor: (attr color).
  targetStream nextPutAll: '<FONT COLOR="',rgbColor,'">'.
 ].
 (attr isKindOf: TextFontChange) ifTrue: [
  fontSize ← attr fontNumber + 2.
  targetStream nextPutAll: '<FONT SIZE="',fontSize asString,'">'.
 ].
 (attr isKindOf: TextURL) ifTrue: [
  targetStream nextPutAll: '<A HREF="',attr info,'">'.
 ].
 (attr isKindOf: TextAnchor) ifTrue: [
  fileName ← FillInTheBlank request: 'Save as GIF' initialAnswer: 'mat.gif'.
  fileName isEmpty
  ifFalse: [
   GIFReadWriter putForm: attr anchoredMorph onFileNamed: fileName.
   targetStream nextPutAll: '<IMG SRC="',fileName,'">'.
  ].
  " skip ' ' part "
 ].
].
"Put the actual string out onto the target"
targetStream nextPutAll: (readStream next: (runs at: index)).
"Did the run just end? Put in the ending tag!"
value do: [:attr |
 (attr isKindOf: TextEmphasis) ifTrue: [
  (attr = TextEmphasis bold) ifTrue: [targetStream nextPutAll: '</B>'].
  (attr = TextEmphasis italic) ifTrue: [targetStream nextPutAll: '</I>'].
  (attr = TextEmphasis underlined) ifTrue: [targetStream nextPutAll: '</U>'].
 ].
 (attr isKindOf: TextColor) ifTrue: [targetStream nextPutAll: '</FONT>'].
 (attr isKindOf: TextFontChange) ifTrue: [targetStream nextPutAll: '</FONT>'].
 (attr isKindOf: TextURL) ifTrue: [targetStream nextPutAll: '</A>'].
 ].
].

targetStream nextPutAll: '</PRE>'.
targetStream nextPutAll: (HTMLformatter endPage).
^targetStream contents.

There is one helper message in there. MAT knows a class message for converting from Squeak's internal color into an HTML format color specification. It isn't too complicated, but could be made even simpler by using the ability of **Number** to generate numbers in any radix:

```
generateHTMLRGBfromColor: aColor
 "MAT generateHTMLRGBfromColor: Color black"
 | r g b |
 (aColor isKindOf: Color) ifFalse: [^nil].
 r ← (aColor red * 255) asInteger.
 (r < 16)
 ifTrue: [r ← '0', r asHexDigit asString]
 ifFalse: [r ← r hex copyFrom: 4 to: 5].

 g ← (aColor green * 255) asInteger.
 (g < 16)
 ifTrue: [g ← '0', g asHexDigit asString]
 ifFalse: [g ← g hex copyFrom: 4 to: 5].

 b ← (aColor blue * 255) asInteger.
 (b < 16)
 ifTrue: [b ← '0', b asHexDigit asString]
 ifFalse: [b ← b hex copyFrom: 4 to: 5].

 ^'#',r,g,b.
```

Aibek has produced a much more advanced form of MAT that improves on both the design and the user interface of MAT. The new MAT allows the user to specify a title, and provides a much clearer interface. We're looking at this version because it has a simple (if slightly-flawed) design and, more importantly, because we actually tested this version of MAT with real users. Aibek improved the usability of MAT in response to these results.

10.3 USER EVALUATION OF MAT

We evaluated MAT as part of an effort to evaluate another project: A collaboration tool by Lex Spoon called *MuSwiki*. The name MuSwiki is a combination of the word *Mu* meaning "Neither yes nor no" and *Swiki* (from Chapter 9) —MuSwiki is both like and unlike Swiki. MuSwiki is like Swiki in that it allows any user to visit *pages* and edit them (as well as create new pages). MuSwiki is unlike Swiki in that it has nothing to do with the Web. Instead, MuSwiki uses **PasteUpMorph**s for collecting any morph that a user might want to drop into a MuSwiki page. The MuSwiki then saves the page and all its submorphs onto a server, creating shared Swiki-like pages that can hold any kind of morph at all. MuSwiki uses its own browser, but still includes the Swiki-like *Edit* button (Figure 10–6). (The code for MuSwiki is also available on the CD and on the Web.)

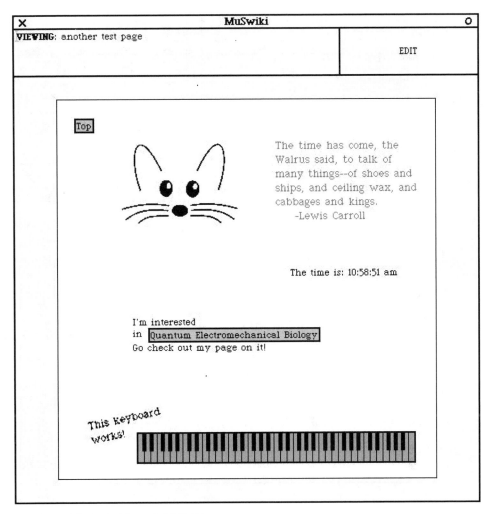

Figure 10–6   An Example MuSwiki

To evaluate MuSwiki, we asked students to collaboratively develop CRC-Card analyses of a design situation, and to then use MAT as an annotation tool (Figure 10–7). Students were instructed on how to use MAT and to manipulate text attributes in MAT (such as the color change seen in one note in Figure 10–7). They were asked to comment on at least two other groups' designs.

Set up like this, MAT was not being evaluated as an HTML editor at all! It was simply a kind of Post-it® note, with interesting abilities to hold different kinds of media (i.e., graphics) and text attributes. On the other hand, if it didn't work out well for this task, there were flaws to address before we could have users generate HTML, AIFF, and GIF files with it.

We surveyed students after completion of the CRC Card and critique tasks. Students were asked to agree or disagree with each statement on a scale of 1 (strongly

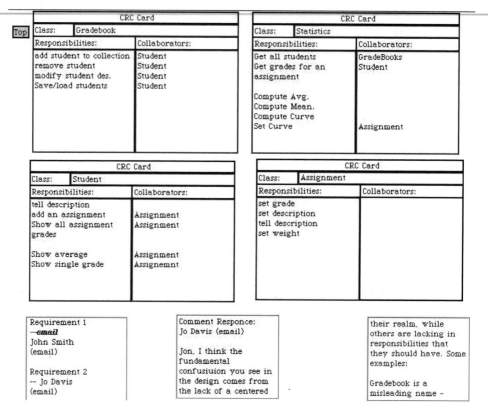

Figure 10–7 Student CRC Cards in MuSwiki with MAT annotations

disagree) to 5 (strongly agree). Most of the questions were about MuSwiki, but several explicitly asked about MAT (Table 1). Among the results were the following:

Table 1 MAT usability responses

Statement	Average (standard deviation)
It is easy to add text to a MuSwiki page using a MAT.	3.2 (1.2)
It is easy to modify text that is in a MAT	3.6 (1.1)
It is easy to change the color of text in a MAT	3.3 (1.0)
It is easy to resize a MAT window	2.0 (0.9)

- Users generally agreed that it was easy to add text and modify text in a MAT. The just-over-neutral responses indicate that users weren't overwhelmingly positive about it. Also, note the low standard deviation: Users generally agreed with one another on these points.

- Users definitely agreed (with very low standard deviation) that it was *not* easy to resize a MAT window.

Basically, resizing a MAT is the same process as resizing any other morph—which isn't a particularly user-friendly process. Resizing a morph involves knowing how to select a morphic and figure out which of the several halos is the right one to use for resizing. It's more complex when the morph might be a part of another morph, or have submorphs itself.

Aibek's later version of MAT uses a **SystemWindow** to provide clear boundaries, to make it easier to select, and to make it easier to resize. Once it's a **SystemWindow**, it can no longer be swapped for **PluggableTextMorph**. But on the other hand, the usability for Aibek's original goal of a FrontPage-like editor with richer support for multimedia is probably better met with his later interface.

EXERCISES

1. Make **TextAttributes** and morphs respond to **MAT**'s queries for (a) a text-embeddable representation and (b) an HTML representation of themselves. Change **MAT** to use these new messages.
2. Improve the sound code in **MAT** so that it doesn't have to create an **AbstractSound** to convert to AIFF.
3. Add to the media supported by **MAT**. For example, add the ability to drop in a Flash movie.
4. Create a single-sound version of **SoundTile**, and use that to provide a sound representation in **MAT** other than the embedded '**' tags.
5. Add the ability to pull media back out of **MAT**. Let users select and drag out graphics or sounds.

REFERENCES

Lex Spoon wrote a paper about his experiences with MuSwiki and MAT:

SPOON, STEVEN "LEX", & GUZDIAL, M. (1999). MuSwiki: A graphical collaboration tool, *Proceedings of Computer Supported Collaborative Learning'99* (pp. 590–599): Stanford, CA. http://sll.stanford.edu/CSCL99/papers/wednesday/Lex_Spoon_590.pdf.

11

Case Study: Prototyping a Play-Writing Workbench

Many of the developers of Squeak are using it to explore multimedia applications for students, especially children. For example, Kim Rose and B.J. Allen-Conn have been using Squeak in the LA Open Charter School during the last year. Squeak's Viewer framework is especially designed to allow children to build programs. The key word here is *exploration:* Developers are using Squeak to *explore* ideas, to try things out with students, and *not* to design and code a solution for a well-understood model.

The process for exploring software for students is a somewhat different process with somewhat different goals from those of the process described in the first part of this book. It's not *completely* different. For example, the design process is still about creating reusable, maintainable code. The user evaluation should still aim to avoid user error:

- The goal for the design is a *prototype* that one can iteratively develop based on available development time and on feedback from users. These are related. You don't want to pour lots of development effort into a design that you haven't done any testing on, so you want to develop a little, test a little, and iterate to improve the prototype based on testing.
- The goal for the interface is somewhat different as well. The kind of user-interface design we described in Chapter 6 is called *user-centered design:* Put the user first in the design of the interface. *Learner-centered design* is about recognizing the special needs of your user as a *learner.* Learners know less about their tasks than users who do the same task day after day, they're less motivated than adult users, and they have more diverse interests than adult users with similar jobs. Thus, software for learners needs to be supportive and engaging, *as well as* easy to use, not prone to fostering errors, and satisfying all the needs of user-centered design.

In this case study, I present a prototype that I built for my eight-year-old son: A workbench for writing plays or skits. I describe my design and implementation process for the prototype, and then evaluate it (a) by asking experts in learning software to comment upon it and (b) by watching a typical user try to use the software.

11.1 MOTIVATION AND SETTING THE GOAL

My eight-year-old son is interested in plays and skits. He's a frequent actor in school plays, and he and his friends invent skits for talent shows. Recently, he became enamored with a toddler's toy that played music using human voices as instruments. That gave me an idea: Squeak can do text-to-speech in different voices. I could build him a "workbench" where he could type in his plays and try them out with speaking "actors." I liked the idea of giving him the opportunity to do more reading and writing, while encouraging his growing interest in theater.

I started out by making a sketch of what I wanted for the software (Figure 11–1). In developing a real application, I wouldn't presume to start out by sketching the interface—I'd first try to understand the problem and the user more. But here, I'm thinking about building just a prototype (so I *expect* that I'll have to change it), for a

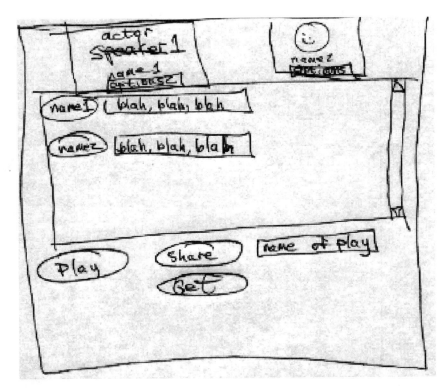

Figure 11–1 Sketch of the Prototype Workbench

task that doesn't exist yet, for a user who doesn't know yet that I'm inventing a task for him! I might as well start thinking about what I want and how it might look:

- I'd want to have *actors* appear (at the top of the workbench) with their names and perhaps faces (using the **GesturalVoice**s of the text-to-speech system). I thought about thinking of them as "speakers," but felt that "actors" fit better for a play workbench. Names of the actors should be modifiable from the display. There should be some way to set options on the voice (e.g., male or female, younger or older) and on the face (e.g., hair color and style).
- The main place for assembling the script should allow the user to specify actor names and their lines in some order. I drew in a scrolling list to suggest that there should be any number of lines for actors. My initial idea is some kind of drag-and-drop of actors and creation of lines by simply clicking in the work area.
- A *Play* button is needed to ask the actors to read their lines. It occurred to me that it would be neat to be able to share the scripts with others, perhaps through a Swiki. I imagine the user typing a name of a play and then clicking *Share*, or typing the name of a collaborative play and clicking *Get*.

11.2 OBJECT ANALYSIS OF THE WORKBENCH

At this point, I had a rough idea of where I wanted to go, but I had only started thinking about components. Rather than define the interface in terms of specific UI components in Squeak, I wanted to think through an object model in terms of components that made sense in my sketch of the workbench. CRC cards seemed like the right kind of approach for continuing to flesh out the design.

I had basically two scenarios I wanted to support at the start:

- The user should be able to define his play. He should be able to specify the appearance of an actor and edit the voice characteristics. He should be able to define a script in terms of actor names and their lines.
- The user should be able to play the script, which means that each actor should speak its lines.

I thought of the whole workbench as a kind of **ScriptingBench** (Figure 11–2). It might have been a **Stage**, but I wanted to emphasize the workbench as a kind of rehearsal or creation space. A real **Stage** would have to have props and other attributes that I didn't want to deal with at this point. A **ScriptingBench** would need to collaborate with **Actor**s (at least for setting them up), a **Script**, and some kind of controls (**BenchControls**). A **SwikiAction** would be a collaborator to implement the *Share/Get* functionality.

After filling out the **ScriptingBench** card, I had a lead on other objects I'd need. The CRC card for the **Actor** object was straightforward (Figure 11–3). The **Actor** would collaborate with the face morph (which I didn't know the name of, so I just filled in **SpeakerMorph**) for specification of appearance, and use the **Speaker** object for changing voice characteristics and speaking lines.

The Script seemed to really be two kinds of objects. There would be a **Script**,

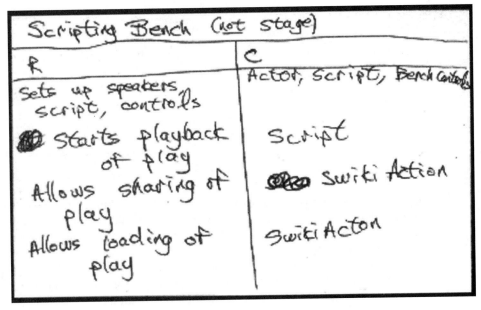

Figure 11–2   CRC Card for ScriptingBench

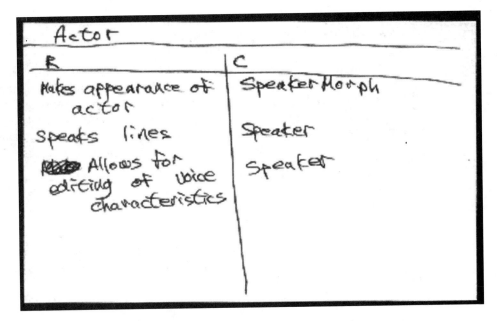

Figure 11–3   Actor CRC Card

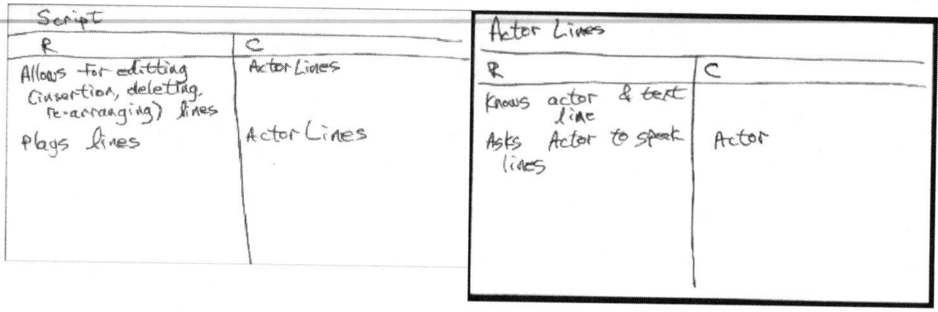

Figure 11–4 Script and ActorLines CRC Cards

but it would be composed of **ActorLines**. The **Script** would be some kind of container for **ActorLines**, and it would be the **ActorLines** that would actually talk to the Actor. The **ScriptingBench** would still ask the **Script** to *Play,* but it would delegate the task to the **ActorLines**. See Figure 11–4.

At this point, I could start doing an object design with a UML class diagram. I decided not to. I did not know the technology that I was going to be working with. I had never built anything with the **Speaker** class. It's not uncommon, even for expert programmers, to do some coding *before* design to get an understanding of the design issues of the actual implementation. I decided to use the basic definition of objects that I had developed with the CRC cards to start implementation.

11.3 IMPLEMENTATION OF THE PLAY WORKBENCH

I started the implementation with the main workbench class. I decided to rename it **PlayBench**. I knew that it would have to know the **actors** (some kind of collection) and the actual **script**, as well as whatever object implemented the **scriptBench** area. When a Morphic object is going to contain other morphs in a structured way, it's often easiest to subclass **AlignmentMorph** (see **Tetris** and **SameGame** as two other examples):

```
AlignmentMorph subclass: #PlayBench
        instanceVariableNames: 'script scriptBench actors '
        classVariableNames: "
        poolDictionaries: "
        category: 'PlaySpace'
```

I started from the creation of a PlayBench. I wanted the pieces within to line up vertically, so I used the definition of the class method newColumn in Alignment-Morph to define how to create the PlayBench:

```
new
        | me |
        me ← super new "Accept submorphs vertically"
                orientation: #vertical;
                hResizing: #spaceFill;
                vResizing: #spaceFill.
        ^me setUp "Set up the pieces"
```

Setting up the **PlayBench** with the submorphs was straightforward from the CRC-card analysis:

```
setUp
        "Add in the pieces"
        self addMorph: (self addScriptingControls).
        self addMorph: (self addScriptingBench).
        self addMorph: (self addActors).
        ^self
```

11.3.1 Prototype ScriptingBench and ScriptingControls

The key development tradeoff of a prototype is "How much do I implement now according to the requirements (when I'm not sure whether the goal is right), and how much do I put together more simply?" The answer to the question depends on what the main functionality is: What is absolutely necessary to implement in order to demonstrate the main functionality or purpose of the prototype? I decided that the **ScriptingBench** and **ScriptingControls** would be simplified at this point. Having a drag-and-drop **ScriptingBench** was nice, but simply typing would work for defining a script. Having sharing of the scripts on the Swiki would be neat, but it wouldn't be necessary for playing a script.

The **ScriptingBench** would become a **PluggableTextMorph** with accessors for setting and getting the **script**. (Note that the setter must return **true** in order to tell Morphic that the accept was successful.) The getter for the **script** checks whether the **script** is defined, and if it's not, a default script is provided.

The **scriptBench** is not just inserted into the overall **PlayBench**. First, its **extent** is multiplied by two. That doubles the size of the text area. I didn't have that at first, so the **scriptBench** appeared the same size as the text areas for the actors' names, which didn't look at all like the original sketch. I placed the **scriptBench** inside an **AlignmentMorph** before returning it for insertion into the **PlayBench**. My thought was for future versions, where I may want more than just a text area as the script area, but it's really not necessary here. The code is as follows:

```
addScriptingBench
        "To start, the scriptingBench is just a simple PluggableTextMorph"
        scriptBench ← PluggableTextMorph on: self text: #script accept: #script:.
        scriptBench extent: (scriptBench extent * 2.0). "Make it larger"
        ^(AlignmentMorph newColumn addMorph: scriptBench)
script: someText
        script ← someText.
        ^ true "To accept the accept"
script
        script ifNil: [ script ←
'Bert: Hi, Ernie!
Ernie: Hello, Bert. How are you?
Bert: Oh, I"m fine, Ernie. Where are you going?
Ernie: Where else? I am going to Sesame Street!'].
        ^script
```

Note that the default script defines the syntax for the script, by example. Each line begins with an actor's name, followed by a colon, and ends with the line for the actor to say. This is certainly more error-prone and even less attractive than drag-and-drop actor names as graphical objects, with lines appearing as blocks after the name, as originally suggested in the prototype sketch. Nonetheless, this meets the requirement of being enough to demonstrate the key idea.

ScriptingControls becomes even simpler—just a single **PluggableButtonMorph** for playing the script:

```
addScriptingControls
        "For now, just a play button"
        ^PluggableButtonMorph on: self getState: nil action: #play label: #playLabel.
playLabel
        ^'Play'
```

We'll define **play** after we define the actors.

11.3.2 Implementing the Actors

The **PlayBench** creates the **PlayActor**s and assigns them their voices. I randomly decided to pick the predefined voices for **man** and **child** as being distinct and interesting. They are stored in an **OrderedCollection** named **actors** (as opposed to instance variables **actor1** and **actor2**) for flexibility in having more actors later. An **Alignment-Morph** is used to collect the morph representations of each **PlayActor** and return it for addition into the **PlayBench**. Following is the code:

```
addActors
        | actorRow |
        actorRow ← AlignmentMorph newRow.

        "Let's start with just two actors"
        actors ← OrderedCollection new.
        actors add: (PlayActor named: 'Bert').
        actors first voice: (Speaker man).
        actors add: (PlayActor named: 'Ernie').
        actors last voice: (Speaker child).

        "Ask each actor for its morphic representation, and store in the row"
        actors do: [:a | actorRow addMorph: (a morph)].
        ^actorRow
```

A **PlayActor** has a **name**, a **face** (the Morphic representation), a **voice**, and a **nameSlot** (the representation of the name in the **PlayBench**). You may be wondering, "Why does the actor need to know its **nameSlot**?" and that would be a good question. We'll see why later, when it comes to playing the script. The code is

```
Object subclass: #PlayActor
        instanceVariableNames: 'name voice face nameSlot '
```

```
classVariableNames: "
poolDictionaries: "
category: 'PlaySpace'
```

The access methods for **PlayActor** are fairly straightforward. For example, the class method **named:** simply creates the instance and sets the name:

```
named: someActorName
        | me |
        me ← super new.
        me name: someActorName.
        ^me
name: someName
        name ← someName asString.
        self changed: #name.
        ^true
```

Implementing the **morph** method involves making a choice: What will be the initial visual representation of the **PlayActor**? The original sketch identified a face, a name, and an *options* button for changing the characteristics of the voice and the face. The suggested question to ask is "What is absolutely necessary to implement in order to demonstrate the main functionality or purpose of the prototype?" For a first round, the actor need have only a name, so we'll simply use a **TextMorph** with the name as the representation of the actor:

```
morph
        "Start out with just a textMorph for name"
        nameSlot ← PluggableTextMorph on: self text: #name accept: #name:.
        ^nameSlot
```

When you're prototyping, one of the realities that you have to face is that you're going to generate a *lot* of bugs. It's a natural consequence: You're prototyping because you don't know the application or kind of technology well, and because you don't know the application or technology well, you're going to make mistakes. Thus, it's useful to make debugging as easy as possible. One of the things that we can do to make things easier in Squeak is to make the **printString** of an object meaningful, by including key data in the output string. **printString** gets its string by sending **printOn:** to the object. By overriding **printOn:**, you can get a more meaningful string representation. I provided a **printOn:** for **PlayActor** so that I could see the name of the actor during debugging:

```
printOn: aStream
        aStream nextPutAll: 'a PlayActor named: ',name.
```

11.3.3 Implementing Playing the Script

Let's get back to the **PlayBench** to trace through how playing the script is implemented. Recall that the **PlayBench** has two **PluggableTextMorphs** in it for the actors' names and a **PluggableTextMorph** for the script. Recall, also, that the way that entered text gets into the underlying model is by *accepting* the text. Now, I didn't want an eight-year-old to type Alt/Command-S or bring up a menu just to rename an actor. I figured that the user would be able to figure out (with a little tutoring) to type the actor's name in, but I also figured that I'd have to take care of accepting the text for him. That's why the **actors** know their **nameSlot**, and why the beginning of **play** tells all the **textMorph**s to **accept**. I didn't have this part in play at first, but when I started walking through the interface and thinking about what I really expected the user to do, it became clear that I had to take care of accepting for him:

play

```
"Play each of the lines in the scriptingBench"
| scriptStream scriptLine actor line thisActor |
"Make sure that we have the script, and that it's a string"
scriptBench accept.
script ← scriptBench getText asString. "Get the script"
"Make sure all the names are saved"
actors do: [:a | a nameSlot accept].

scriptStream ← ReadStream on: script.
[scriptStream atEnd] whileFalse:
        [scriptLine ← scriptStream nextLine.
        actor ← (scriptLine copyUpTo: $:) copyWithout: (Character space). "Get the actor name"
        line ← scriptLine copyFrom: (scriptLine findString: ':')+1 to: (scriptLine size).
        Transcript show: actor,' is going to say "',line,'"'; cr.
        thisActor ← (actors detect: [:a | a name = actor]).
        thisActor say: line.
        SoundPlayer waitUntilDonePlaying].
```

The rest of the method involves walking the script, parsing out each line and actor's name, and then asking the actor with that name to say the line. The **script** string is used as the source for a **ReadStream**, which gets read a line at a time (**nextLine**). We copy the **scriptLine** up to the ':' for the actor's name, but remove any spaces first. Like accepting for the user, this is an example of trying to avoid potential error—I wanted "Ernie:" and "Ernie :" both to be acceptable. I copy the **scriptLine** from one character past the colon to the end of the **scriptLine** into the **line** for the actor to say. To help with debugging, I then **show:** this to the **Transcript**. I find **thisActor** (the one with the right **name**) by using **detect:** over the collection of **actors**, then ask **thisActor** to **say:** the **line**.

To actually say the line was simple—just a delegation to the **Speaker** instance stored in the actor's **voice**:

say: something
```
voice say: something.
```

In the original version of the **play** method, there was no **SoundPlayer waitUntil-DonePlaying**. And the **PlayBench** *did* work without it—but the actors did not wait until the other was done before saying their lines. That was a pretty hard problem to solve. I hunted through the **Speaker** code, but I didn't see any easy way to figure out when a **Speaker** was finished. I knew that sounds were played through the **SoundPlayer** in Squeak, so I looked into that. There I found a method for checking for a specific sound, **waitUntilDonePlaying: aSound**. But I didn't have the sound object being passed to the **SoundPlayer** from **Speaker**. (I wasn't even sure that it was a single sound object, as opposed to a series of them sent one after the other.) I noticed that **waitUntil-DonePlay:** searched for the sound in a class variable named **ActiveSounds**. I added a new class method to **SoundPlayer** to access the **ActiveSounds**:

```
activeSounds
    ^ ActiveSounds
```

Fortunately for me, I found that the **ActiveSounds** was empty when all the sounds were done, so it was an easy method to write to check that all sounds were done:

```
waitUntilDonePlaying
    "Wait until any sound is no longer playing."
    [PlayerSemaphore critical: [ActiveSounds isEmpty not]]
        whileTrue: [(Delay forMilliseconds: 100) wait].
```

And with that, I was able to execute **PlayBench new openInWorld** and play my sample script (Figure 11–5).

11.4 ITERATING ON THE PLAYBENCH

At this point, I was ready to test—or to develop a little more. I had something working, but I started to rethink whether just the name was compelling enough a representation for the actor. The **HeadMorph**s were really cute—adding them might make the overall **PlayBench** much more motivating, which would be more in line with learner-centered design.

Not sure if this would work, I decided not to touch the morph method that returned just the **nameSlot** for the actor, and instead to add a **morphWithFace** method. I changed **addActors** in **PlayBench** to add **morphWithFace** instead of morph into the actor's row across the top:

```
"Ask each actor for its morphic representation, and store in the row"
actors do: [:a | actorRow addMorph: (a morphWithFace)].
^actorRow
```

morphWithFace was tricky to write. I knew that it was possible to get a Speaker to have a face. The **Speaker** class method **manWithHead** did what I wanted. But **manWithHead** created a head using **newHead**, which both created a head and opened it in the Morphic world. I wanted to actually have the **HeadMorph** that I could use for inserting into the **PlayBench**. I had to trace through how **manWithHead** worked (to figure out how to add a **GesturalVoice** to a **Speaker**, which was necessary for getting the head to "lip synch" the words) and how **newHead** worked (to figure out how to get the new **HeadMorph**).

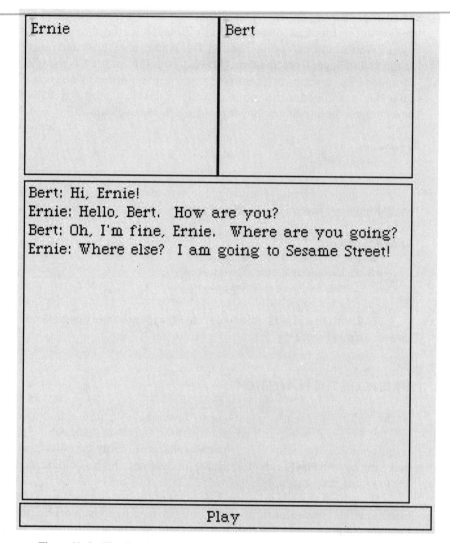

Figure 11–5 The First Iteration Working PlayBench

Because **morphWithFace** had to make the **voice** gestural, it needed to have the voice set already. In my current code, that would be okay, but I wanted to be safe, so I tested **voice** and put up a relevant error message if it wasn't set. I then used the code that I had found in **Speaker** to set up the face, and used the old **morph** code to create a **nameSlot**. The whole thing got put into an **AlignmentMorph** for insertion into the **PlayBench**. (There's a good argument to be made that I probably should have modified **Speaker** to do the gestural-and-face stuff, rather than replicate the code and move the responsibility over to **PlayActor**.) Following is the code:

morphWithFace

```
| faceColumn |
faceColumn ← AlignmentMorph newColumn.
```

```
"Assume that the voice has been set with a Speaker by this point"
voice isNil ifTrue: [^self error: 'Must set voice first'].
voice makeGestural.
face ← HeadMorph new. "Generates a random head"
(voice findAVoice: GesturalVoice) head: face. "Connect voice to head "
faceColumn addMorph: face.
"Start out with just a textMorph for name"
nameSlot ← PluggableTextMorph on: self text: #name accept: #name:.
faceColumn addMorph: nameSlot.
^faceColumn
```

This worked! By writing this one method (and making a modification to another method), I gave my actors faces (Figure 11–6).

But the great lip-synching was broken. The voices spoke, but the mouths in the faces didn't move. It took me a moment to realize what was happening. My **waitUntilDonePlaying** was keeping the faces from updating. I wasn't sure how they were updating: via a background process or via a **step** method. But I rewrote **waitUntilDonePlaying** to give both a chance to execute:

```
waitUntilDonePlaying
    "Wait until any sound is no longer playing."
    [PlayerSemaphore critical: [ActiveSounds isEmpty not]]
        whileTrue: [(Delay forMilliseconds: 100) wait.
            Processor yield. World doOneCycle].
```

With that, the **PlayBench** was ready for testing. While some of the steps might have been slightly "tricky," the whole process took me less than two hours to get working to this point. The advantages of some powerful objects and powerful development tools were clear in this exercise.

11.5 EVALUATING THE PLAYBENCH: EXPERT EVALUATION AND OBSERVATION

I did two kinds of evaluation of the **PlayBench**. The first was what's called an *expert evaluation*. An expert evaluation is a good way to get a fresh eye looking at your software. While not as thorough or careful as a heuristic evaluation or cognitive walkthrough, an expert evaluation can sometimes point out things to look into that you might not have realized.

I know several people who build software for children of this age range. I asked a couple of them to look at the **PlayBench** and give me their comments. The experts thought it was "cute" but had several concerns:

- The first concern was the clarity of the voice. Would kids be able to make out the words? One expert commented that they sounded like the voices were "echoing."
- The second issue was the faces. Sometimes the randomly-generated skin tone was too dark to see the mouth. One expert asked if the mouth movement was

Figure 11-6   PlayBench with Actors' Faces

"random" because he simply couldn't see the mouth clearly enough to tell that it was synched to the voice.

The experts pointed out a couple of things for me to look for when I did my second evaluation: Observation of a real user. I asked my son to try out the software.

I started out the observation session by demonstrating the software. I opened a **PlayBench**, used the *Play* button, then changed the names and wrote a little script, and finally played the new script. "Cool! It's *so* awesome!" he said. Then he started to use it:

- The very first thing he did was to change an actor's name, and the very first name he typed in was two words, e.g., *John Doe.* I thought, "No big deal—it'll work." But when he hit *Play* and an error box came up, I realized what the problem was. When I parsed out the name of the actor *I stripped out all spaces!* So, the **PlayBench** was looking for "JohnDoe" while the actor's name was "John Doe". Clearly, support of multiple-word names would be something I'd have to have.
- "Can I change how they look?" That was certainly in my overall plans, but wasn't in the prototype. I generated a few new **PlayBench**es until one came up with two faces he wanted to play with.
- "Can you write that down for me? Just the way I wrote it!" My son quickly grew tired of typing in the actor names over-and-over. The drag-and-drop of actor names from the original goal is clearly a better way to go.
- He had a hard time figuring out how to get *another* line—he didn't know to hit Return! It hadn't occurred to me that he didn't know that part of text editing.
- "You can't make his voice sound very good." There were several things my son did which led to that comment. For one, the default text-to-speech wasn't quite right. Simple words that he wanted to use were mispronounced, e.g., "Hi" was pronounced "Hey," and "Oh" was pronounced "Ah." More unusual words (like "Woof", in Figure 11–7) had really strange pronunciations. Another problem was that there was an echoing, like what the experts noted. I later realized that the **SoundPlayer**'s reverb was on, which improves music sound, but made the voices less clear. (**SoundPlayer stopReverb** fixed that.) In general, his comment suggests that the goal of being able to change the voices might be something that kids would like to do.
- "There's something bad. If I type an exclamation point, it should be fast and loud." My son wanted the text to follow more of the rules he knew for reading text. It seemed to handle question marks well, but didn't do any interpretation of exclamation points.
- The faces weren't the problems that the experts predicted. It may be that the colors that came up just worked, but my son pointed at the mouths and laughed as the actors spoke their lines.

Figure 11–7   The PlayBench produced in the Observation Evaluation

11.5.1.1 Summarizing the evaluation

The observation and expert evaluation were useful in pointing out some strengths and weaknesses of the design:

- Several comments suggested that the additional features that I put into my sketch would be important. Kids probably would want to change the face and voice, and would like to have some drag-and-drop alternatives to traditional typing. The latter was somewhat surprising to me, that plain text editing would be hard, but that's why you do observational studies.
- I hadn't realized that multiple-word names were going to be an issue.
- Finally, there were several flaws in the text-to-speech area, but none of them was hard to fix. The mapping to phonemes in Squeak's text-to-speech is a rule-based system that can be tweaked to improve it, including handling exclamation points.

EXERCISES

1. Try improving the text-to-speech translation in Squeak to handle simple words like "Hi" and "Oh." See the class **PhoneticRule** and its class methods for examples of rules.
2. Add an *Options* menu with submenus for changing voice characteristics (first cut: Just offer the pre-defined voices in the **Speaker** class methods) and face characteristics (see **HeadMorph** and its related classes).
3. **EyeMorph** and **LipsMorph** actually understand a bunch of messages, like showing dilation and showing horror. One could imagine defining some directions to the actors in the script (e.g., **[Bert dilate]**). Try adding that to the script processing.
4. Rather than controlling the **HeadMorph**, try controlling characters in Alice. Open a **Wonderland**, and insert a **WonderlandCameraMorph** in your **PlayBench**. Now the directions (from previous exercise) might include telling the actors to walk around and use their 3-D bodies in the play.

REFERENCES

A nice book on how to design software for children is

DRUIN, ALLISON (Ed). (1998) *The Design of Children's Technology.* Morgan Kaufmann Publishers.

The concept and methodologies of learner-centered design are still being developed. Some of the papers on the subject are as follows:

SOLOWAY, E., GUZDIAL, M., & HAY, K. E. (1994). Learner-centered design: The challenge for HCI in the 21st century. *Interactions, 1*(2), 36–48.

QUINTANA, C., ABOTEL, K., & SOLOWAY, E. (1996). *NoRis: Supporting computational science activities through learner-centered design.* Paper presented at the International Conference on the Learning Sciences, Northwestern University.

SOLOWAY, E., JACKSON, S. L., KLEIN, J., QUINTANA, C., REED, J., SPITULNIK, J., STRATFORD, S. J., STUDER, S., ENG, J., & SCALA, N. (1996). Learning theory in practice: Case studies of learner-centered design. In M. J. Trauber (Ed.), *CHI96 Conference Proceedings* (pp. 189–196). Vancouver, British Columbia, Canada.

GUZDIAL, M. (1999). Supporting Learners as Users. *The Journal of Computer Documentation, 23*(2), 3–13.

Appendix:

A Quick-Start Guide of Squeak Examples

The examples that follow are a collection of real Squeak expressions, tested in Squeak 2.7, to serve as a kind of quick-start guide to the key classes and messages. Most of these expressions are followed by a comment showing the result of the expression when printed, and some explanatory text. The content of this appendix is based on the excellent *Squeak Smalltalk: A Quick Reference* by Andrew Greenberg at http://www.mucow.com/squeak-qref.html.

1 CONSTANTS

```
#(1 2 3) "This is the literal array filled with the SmallIntegers 1, 2, and 3"
8r177 "127 - the decimal value of the octal number"
16rFE "254 - the decimal value of the hexadecimal number"
3.14e-10 class "Float - floats understand exponential notation"
$3 class "Character - $ defines a Character"
#alpha class "Symbol - # defines a Symbol"
'123' class "String - single quotes defines a String"
#(1 2 3 ( 4 5)) last "(4 5 ) - parentheses within a literal array defines a nested array"
#(1 + 2) size "3 - the three elements are 1, 2, and #+"
{1. 2} "(1 2 )"
a := 1. {a} "(1 ) - a way of creating a non-literal array"
```

2 CONTROL STRUCTURE EXPRESSIONS INVOLVING BLOCKS

```
[3 + 4] value "7"
[:a | a + 4] value: 3 "7"
[:a :b | a + b] valueWithArguments: #(3 4) "7"
```

3 < 4 ifTrue: [Smalltalk beep] "Smalltalk (the SystemDictionary is returned - A beep is heard"
3 < 4 ifFalse: [Smalltalk beep] "silence..."
3 ifNil: [Smalltalk beep] "silence..."
nil ifNotNil: [Smalltalk beep] "silence..."
a := 1. "Evaluated before each of the following..."
[a := a + 1. Smalltalk beep. a < 5] whileTrue. "4 beeps"
[a < 5] whileTrue: [a := a + 1. Smalltalk beep] "ditto -- whileFalse and whileFalse: also exist"
3 timesRepeat: [Smalltalk beep] "3 beeps"
1 to: 3 do: [:index | a := a + index]. a "7 - a := 1, then + 1 + 2 + 3, so PrintIt returns 7"
1 to: 4 by: 2 do: [:i | Smalltalk beep] "2 beeps"
#(1 2 3) do: [:number | Transcript show: number printString] "Puts 123 on Transcript"
#b caseOf: {[#a]->[1+1].
          ['b' asSymbol]->[2+2].
          [#c]->[3+3]}. "4 - because #b matched ['b' as Symbol]"

3 TESTING OBJECTS

a := 'abc'. b := a copy. c := a. d := 'duck'. "For all of the below..."
a = b "true - they have the same values"
a == b "false - they are not the same object"
a == c "true - they are the same object"
a < d "true - alphabetically"
a hash "4757 - a hash value is representative of the value of the object"
d hash "4903"
a isNil "false"

4 BASIC OBJECT BEHAVIOR

Smalltalk perform: #beep "beeps once"
1 perform: #+ with: 2 "3"
123 printString "'123' - the String"
w := WriteStream on: (String new). 123 printOn: w. w "a WriteStream - whose contents are '123'"
123 class "SmallInteger"
123 isKindOf: Number "true"
123 isMemberOf: Number "false"
123 respondsTo: #* "true - yes, SmallIntegers understand multiplication"
123 error: 'You are wrong!' "Opens an error notifier with this message"

5 BOOLEAN OPERATIONS

true & true "true - it's And"
true & false "false"
true | false "true - it's Or"
true and: [false] "false - the keyword and: can short-circuit (block isn't evaluated if receiver is false)"
true or: [false] "true - the or: keyword can also short-circuit"

true xor: [false] "true - Exclusive Or"
true not "false - negation"

6   MAGNITUDE AND NUMBER OPERATIONS

3 < 4 "true"
3 >= 4 "false"
3 between: 1 and: 4 "true"
3 min: 2 "2"
3 max: 5 "5"
13 // 4 "3 - quotient, also quo:"
13 \\ 4 "1 - remainder, also rem:"
-4 abs "4 - absolute value"
4 reciprocal "(1/4)"
4 reciprocal asFloat "0.25"
4 negated "-4"
5 exp "148.4131591025766 - e ^ 5"
2 raisedTo: 10 "1024 - 2^10"
10 log: 3 "2.095903274289385"
4 even "true"
4 odd "false"
2 positive "true"
3.2 ceiling "4 - round up"
3.2 floor "3 - round down"
Float pi "3.141592653589793"
(Float pi / 2) sin "1.0 - sine of Pi/2 radians"
90 degreeSin "1.0 - sine of 90 degrees"
1024 isPowerOfTwo "true"
25 factorial "15511210043330985984000000 - gotta love that precision! :-)"
12 gcd: 9 "3 - Greatest Common Divisor"
3 lcm: 4 "12 - Least Common Multiple"
4 take: 2 "6 - number of combinations of four items possible taking two at a time"
1 bitShift: 3 "8"
7 bitAnd: 2 "2 - only two's bit in common"

7   CHARACTER OPERATIONS

$a asciiValue "97 - ASCII of lowercase a"
$1 asciiValue "49"
$1 digitValue "1 - the SmallInteger"
$a isNumber "false"
$a asUppercase "$A"
$a isVowel "true"
$A asLowercase "$a"

8 COLLECTION OPERATIONS

```
a := #(31 32 33). "An array used below"
a at: 2 "32 at second element"
a at: 2 put: 42. a "(31 42 33) - the array with changed value"
a at: 1 modify: [:x | x * 2]. a "(62 42 33 ) - note that the first element has been doubled"
'alpha' first "$a"
'alpha' last "$a"
'alpha' middle "$p"
'alpha' allButFirst "'lpha'"
#(1 2 3) allButLast "(1 2 )"
'alpha' indexOf: $p "3 - where the first $p is"
'alpha' indexOfSubCollection: 'ph' startingAt: 1 "3 - where the first 'ph' starts"
'alpha' replaceFrom: 2 to: 3 with: 'gh' "'aghha' - replaces with 1-to-1 mapping"
'alpha' copyReplaceFrom: 2 to: 3 with: 'blah' "'ablahha' - can shrink or expand original"
'alpha' shuffled "'lhaap' - random shuffle"
#(1 2 3) reversed "(3 2 1 )"
Array with: 32 with: $a "(32 $a )"
OrderedCollection withAll: #('a' $b 32 14.566) "OrderedCollection ('a' $b 32 14.566 ) - makes an
OrderedCollection from the input array"
'abc' anyOne "$a - picks one at random"
#() isEmpty "true"
'alpha' , 'beta' "'alphabeta' - concatenation"
#(1 2 3) , #(4 5 6) "(1 2 3 4 5 6 ) - concatenation of Arrays, too"
'alpha' occurrencesOf: $a "2 - two $a's in 'alpha'"
'alpha' anySatisfy: [:x | x isVowel] "true - yes, there's a vowel in there"
'beta' includes: $b "true"
'beta' includesAllOf: 'te' "true - yes, both $t and $e are in there"
'beta' includesAnyOf: 'ge' "true - yes, at least one of $g and $e is in 'beta'"

b := (OrderedCollection new). "For next few examples"
b add: 19. b "OrderedCollection (19 )"
b remove: 19. b "OrderedCollection ()"
c := (OrderedCollection withAll: 'alpha').
c removeAllSuchThat: [:letter | letter isVowel]. c "OrderedCollection ($l $p $h ) - that's what's
left"
String withAll: c "'lph' - convert back"

c := 'alpha'. "For next few examples"
c reject: [:l | l isVowel] " 'lph' - removes the vowels, returns a String. Non-destructive to c"
c collect: [:c | c asUppercase] "'ALPHA' - uppercases each letter"
c count: [:c | c isVowel] "2 - vowels in ALPHA"
c select: [:l | l isVowel not] "'lph' - selects only those non-vowels"
c detect: [:l | l isVowel not] "$l - stops at the first match"
#(1 2 3) inject: 0 into: [:subTotal :next | subTotal + next] "6 - adds 'em up"

d := Dictionary new. "For next few examples"
d at: 'fred' put: 'wilma'.
d at: 'barney' put: 'betty'.
d keys "Set ('fred' 'barney' ) - the two keys"
```

d values "('wilma' 'betty') - the two values"
d at: 'fred' "'wilma' - the match"
d includesKey: 'barney' "true - checks for the key"
d includes: 'wilma' "true - checks for the value"

o := OrderedCollection withAll: #(1 2 $b 'abc' (4 5)). "For next few examples"
o size "5 - 1, 2, character b, 'abc', and a subArray"
o last "(4 5)"
o add: $c before: 'abc'. o "OrderedCollection (1 2 $b $c 'abc' (4 5))"
o addLast: 'def'. o "OrderedCollection (1 2 $b $c 'abc' (4 5) 'def')"
o removeAt: 6. o. "OrderedCollection (1 2 $b $c 'abc' 'def')"

9   STRING OPERATIONS

s := 'This is a test string'. "For next few examples"
s findTokens: (Character space asString) "OrderedCollection ('This' 'is' 'a' 'test' 'string')"
s findString: 'test' "11 - starts at character 11"
s indexOf: $s "4 - first 's' is at 4"
'apple' compare: 'bear' "1 - 1 reciever before arg, 2 equal, 3 receiver after"
'a*' match: 'apple' "true - apple starts with an 'a' and has anything after"
'apple#' match: 'apples' "true - apples has one 'anything' character after 'apple'"
s beginsWith: 'Th' "true"
s endsWith: '.' "false"
s asUppercase "'THIS IS A TEST STRING'"
'ta dah' capitalized "'Ta dah'"

Index

YOU SHOULD CAREFULLY READ THE FOLLOWING TERMS AND CONDITIONS BEFORE OPENING THIS CD PACKAGE. OPENING THIS CD PACKAGE INDICATES YOUR ACCEPTANCE OF THESE TERMS AND CONDITIONS. IF YOU DO NOT AGREE WITH THEM, YOU SHOULD PROMPTLY RETURN THE PACKAGE UNOPENED, AND YOUR MONEY WILL BE REFUNDED.

IT IS A VIOLATION OF COPYRIGHT LAWS TO MAKE A COPY OF THE ACCOMPANYING SOFTWARE EXCEPT FOR BACKUP PURPOSES TO GUARD AGAINST ACCIDENTAL LOSS OR DAMAGE.

Prentice-Hall, Inc. provides this program and licenses its use. You assume responsibility for the selection of the program to achieve your intended results, and for the installation, use, and results obtained from the program. This license extends only to use of the program in the United States or countries in which the program is marketed by duly authorized distributors.

LICENSE

You may:

a. use the program;
b. copy the program into any machine-readable form without limit;
c. modify the program and/or merge it into another program in support of your use of the program.

LIMITED WARRANTY

THE PROGRAM IS PROVIDED "AS IS" WITHOUT WARRANTY OF ANY KIND, EITHER EXPRESSED OR IMPLIED, INCLUDING, BUT NOT LIMITED TO, THE IMPLIED WARRANTIES OF MERCHANTABILITY AND FITNESS FOR A PARTICULAR PURPOSE. THE ENTIRE RISK AS TO THE QUALITY AND PERFORMANCE OF THE PROGRAM IS WITH YOU. SHOULD THE PROGRAM PROVE DEFECTIVE, YOU (AND NOT PRENTICE-HALL, INC. OR ANY AUTHORIZED DISTRIBUTOR) ASSUME THE ENTIRE COST OF ALL NECESSARY SERVICING, REPAIR, OR CORRECTION.

SOME STATES DO NOT ALLOW THE EXCLUSION OF IMPLIED WARRANTIES, SO THE ABOVE EXCLUSION MAY NOT APPLY TO YOU. THIS WARRANTY GIVES YOU SPECIFIC LEGAL RIGHTS AND YOU MAY ALSO HAVE OTHER RIGHTS THAT VARY FROM STATE TO STATE.

Prentice-Hall, Inc. does not warrant that the functions contained in the program will meet your requirements or that the operation of the program will be uninterrupted or error free.

However, Prentice-Hall, Inc., warrants the cd(s) on which the program is furnished to be free from defects in materials and workmanship under normal use for a period of ninety (90) days from the date of delivery to you as evidenced by a copy of your receipt.

LIMITATIONS OF REMEDIES

Prentice-Hall's entire liability and your exclusive remedy shall be:

1. the replacement of any cd not meeting Prentice-Hall's "Limited Warranty" and that is returned to Prentice-Hall with a copy of your purchase order, or
2. if Prentice-Hall is unable to deliver a replacement diskette or cassette that is free of defects in materials

or workmanship, you may terminate this Agreement by returning the program, and your money will be refunded.

IN NO EVENT WILL PRENTICE-HALL BE LIABLE TO YOU FOR ANY DAMAGES, INCLUDING ANY LOST PROFITS, LOST SAVINGS, OR OTHER INCIDENTAL OR CONSEQUENTIAL DAMAGES ARISING OUT OF THE USE OR INABILITY TO USE SUCH PROGRAM EVEN IF PRENTICE-HALL, OR AN AUTHORIZED DISTRIBUTOR HAS BEEN ADVISED OF THE POSSIBILITY OF SUCH DAMAGES, OR FOR ANY CLAIM BY ANY OTHER PARTY.

SOME STATES DO NOT ALLOW THE LIMITATION OR EXCLUSION OF LIABILITY FOR INCIDENTAL OR CONSEQUENTIAL DAMAGES, SO THE ABOVE LIMITATION OR EXCLUSION MAY NOT APPLY TO YOU.

GENERAL

You may not sublicense, assign, or transfer the license or the program except as expressly provided in this Agreement. Any attempt otherwise to sublicense, assign, or transfer any of the rights, duties, or obligations hereunder is void.

This Agreement will be governed by the laws of the State of New York.

Should you have any questions concerning this Agreement, you may contact Prentice-Hall, Inc., by writing to:

> Prentice Hall
> College Division
> Upper Saddle River, NJ 07458

Should you have any questions concerning technical support you may write to:

YOU ACKNOWLEDGE THAT YOU HAVE READ THIS AGREEMENT, UNDERSTAND IT, AND AGREE TO BE BOUND BY ITS TERMS AND CONDITIONS. YOU FURTHER AGREE THAT IT IS THE COMPLETE AND EXCLUSIVE STATEMENT OF THE AGREEMENT BETWEEN US THAT SUPERSEDES ANY PROPOSAL OR PRIOR AGREEMENT, ORAL OR WRITTEN, AND ANY OTHER COMMUNICATIONS BETWEEN US RELATING TO THE SUBJECT MATTER OF THIS AGREEMENT.

ISBN:0-13-028028-3